BLOOD FEUD

BLOOD FEUD

DETROIT RED WINGS
COLORADO V AVALANCHE

THE INSIDE STORY OF PRO SPORTS' NASTIEST AND BEST RIVALRY OF ITS ERA

ADRIAN DATER

TAYLOR TRADE PUBLISHING
Lanham • New York • Boulder • Toronto • Plymouth, UK

Copyright © 2007 by Adrian Dater
First Taylor Trade Publishing edition 2007

This Taylor Trade Publishing paperback edition of *Detroit Red Wings v. Colorado Avalanche* is an original publication. It is published by arrangement with the author.

Published by Taylor Trade Publishing
An imprint of The Rowman & Littlefield Publishing Group, Inc.
4501 Forbes Boulevard, Suite 200, Lanham, Maryland 20706

Estover Road
Plymouth PL6 7PY
United Kingdom

Distributed by NATIONAL BOOK NETWORK

Library of Congress Cataloging-in-Publication Data

Dater, Adrian.
  Blood feud : Detroit Red Wings v. Colorado Avalanche, the inside story of pro sports' nastiest and best rivalry of its era / Adrian Dater.—1st Taylor Trade Publishing ed.
    p. cm.
  Includes index.
  ISBN-13: 978-1-58979-319-4 (pbk. : alk. paper)
  ISBN-10: 1-58979-319-6 (pbk. : alk. paper)
    1. Colorado Avalanche (Hockey team)—History. 2. Detroit Red Wings (Hockey team)—History. 3. Stanley Cup (Hockey) 4. Sports rivalries—United States—History. I. Title.
  GV848.C65D378 2007
  796.962'640977434—dc22
                                        2006008931

∞ ™ The paper used in this publication meets the minimum requirements of American National Standard for Information Sciences—Permanence of Paper for Printed Library Materials, ANSI/NISO Z39.48-1992.

Manufactured in the United States of America.

CONTENTS

Contents

FOREWORD

A drian Dater has captured the drama of a hockey rivalry that matches the best of sports rivalries, and he has gone to great lengths to capture the feelings of the legendary players involved with this special rivalry—Hall of Famers from each team like Ray Bourque, Larry Murphy, Paul Coffey, Patrick Roy, and future Hall of Famers like Peter Forsberg, Joe Sakic, Steve Yzerman, Nick Lidstrom, Chris Chelios, and Brett Hull, along with many others.

In the seven playoff seasons from 1996 to 2002, the Colorado Avalanche and the Detroit Red Wings battled each other five times to compete for hockey's greatest prize, the Stanley Cup. The two teams' regular-season games were epic struggles that drew the highest television ratings, and when the NHL had a national TV broadcast, their games were always first choice on the requests.

Dater delves into the controversy of the Avalanche's illegal visitors' bench, as well as the Claude Lemieux–Kris Draper incident, and the goaltender battles between Patrick Roy and Mike Vernon, Chris Osgood, and Dominik Hasek. These incidents and many others resulted in heated exchanges between Avalanche coach Marc Crawford and me. In all my 30-plus years in the NHL, I had never before witnessed media battles like those that resulted from this on-ice rivalry.

The action on the ice was second to none, and while both teams enjoyed sold-out arenas for all of their games, the games between each other caused a ticket frenzy never before seen. I think what made the rivalry so special was that the comparative strength of each franchise was so similar and the prize to the winner was so special. Any sport would dream of a rivalry so bitter, yet for the most part healthy, and this book captures all the exciting battles both on and off the ice. It is a must-read for all hockey followers.

Scotty Bowman

ACKNOWLEDGMENTS

A book such as this one wouldn't be possible without the generous time and insight of the people and players who actually made this great rivalry.

So I've got a lot of people to thank. First, an extra-special thank you to Scotty Bowman for writing the foreword to this book and for the extensive interviews he granted. To think that, in my opinion, the greatest coach in sports history introduced a book by me is overwhelming and humbling.

Another big thanks to Claude Lemieux for several hours of insightful interviews on some occasionally tough subjects.

Thank you to the following players, coaches, reporters, public relations people and others who were interviewed for this book: Darren McCarty, Kris Draper, Dave Lewis, Pierre Lacroix, Mike Kuta, Curtis Leschyshyn, Mike Vernon, Brendan Shanahan, Bob Wojnowski, Joel Quenneville, Mike Keane, Aaron Ward, Jimmy Devellano, Stan Bowman, Brian Hayward, Pierre McGuire, Jean Martineau, Mike Haynes, John Kelly, Norm Jones, Damon Zier, Charlie Lyons, Brent Severyn, Pat Karns, Jason La Canfora, Joe Sakic, Adam Foote, Chris Osgood, Paul Devorski, Sylvain Lefebvre, Red Fisher, Randy Sportak, Jerry Green, Chuck Carlton, John Niyo, Lucien DeBlois, Warren Rychel, Troy Murray, Shjon Podein, Bob Hartley, Chris Chelios, Bill Ranford, Michael Farber, Ken Holland, Dave Reid, Terry Frei, Patrice Brisebois, Bob Gainey, Ralph Backstrom, Adam Deadmarsh, Mike Ricci, and Chris Drury.

Thank you to former *Denver Post* columnist Woody Paige for the many contributions to this book through his work over the years, and also to Mark Kiszla of the *Post*. Both men were mentors and friends through the years. Thank you to Neil Devlin for giving me my big break in the newspaper business. Thanks to *Post* colleague Terry Frei for his tutelage and friendship over the years.

Thanks to several people for various research help or other tidbits, including Kristy Fogler, Mike Schanno, John Hahn, Peter Hanlon, Hayne Ellis, Brendan McNicholas, Dan Hinote, Rob Blake, Peter McNab, Dave Wright, Sandy Clough, and Jacquie Brown. Thanks to the helpful staff at the Henry Ford Library in Dearborn, Michigan, and the library staff of the *Denver Post*.

Thanks to *Denver Post* editor Greg Moore, managing editor Gary Clark, and sports editor Kevin Dale for graciously allowing me to write this book.

A major thank you to Rick Rinehart and the staff of Taylor Trade for agreeing to publish this book.

Thanks to my mother, Martha; stepfather, Michael; father, Alan; and his significant other, Lisa, for all their love and support over the years.

Lastly, thanks to my great wife, Heidi, for putting up with me all these years and for giving me a beautiful son, Thomas Alan Michael.

"A Car Crash in Slow Motion"

As a boy growing up in Toronto, Kris Draper loved those distortion mirrors, the kind at amusement parks and circuses.

A husky kid with red hair and freckles, Draper liked how the fun mirrors made him look a little slimmer. A tilt of the head, a step to the side, and he went from short and squat to tall and athletic looking.

On May 29, 1996, Draper looked into a mirror inside the visitors' dressing room of Denver's McNichols Sports Arena—and gasped. Please let this be another distortion mirror, Draper thought. No way—*no way*—could this be his real face.

His right cheek looked like it was stuffed with 10 cans of Skoal. His right eye, rapidly swelling shut, had as many colors as a Jackson Pollock painting. His nose looked like a piece of wadded-up newspaper, his jaw like somebody had moved it a couple inches to the left. I've turned into Frankenstein, Draper thought.

A defensive-oriented center in his third season with the Detroit Red Wings, Draper had no idea who had done this to him. Playing a loose puck along the boards by the Red Wings' bench,

Draper had his head down, a no-no in the sport of hockey. But Draper knew he needed to use all of his body for better positioning to get control of the puck.

Getting control of that puck, he knew, could make the difference in getting his team a victory it had to have. Despite setting a National Hockey League record with 62 victories in the 1995–96 regular season, despite entering the playoffs as prohibitive favorites to win their first Stanley Cup since 1955, the Red Wings entered Game 6 of the 1996 Western Conference finals down three games to two to the Colorado Avalanche.

A franchise that had been known as the Quebec Nordiques for the previous 23 seasons, first in the old World Hockey Association and then in the NHL, the Avalanche played in a city scorned by Original Six hockey markets such as Detroit: scorned for losing its first NHL team, the Colorado Rockies, which left town to become the New Jersey Devils in 1982.

Those same Devils had beaten the Red Wings for the Stanley Cup the year before, sweeping them in four humiliating games. A trash-talking right wing named Claude Lemieux was the hero for New Jersey, winning the Conn Smythe Trophy as the playoffs' most valuable player.

A contract dispute with the Devils led to Lemieux's trade to the Avalanche on October 3, 1995, and here he was again leading his team to an upset series win over Detroit.

Not if Draper could help it—which is why he was determined to get that puck for his team, trailing 1-0 with time running out in the first period. Get the puck to a teammate, get a quick goal, and she's all tied up. Go on to get the win, and it's back to friendly Joe Louis Arena for Game 7, where it would be advantage, Red Wings. That was the plan, anyway.

But then, with 5:53 showing on the clock, a deep, sickly thud sounded on the ice. As he was skating backward slightly to make his way to the bench, the 185-pound Draper's head was driven into the top edge of the boards, face first, by a 220-pound man skating at roughly 25 mph from behind. The man was Lemieux.

Sitting right in front of Draper was close friend and teammate Darren McCarty, a third-year forward known for his toughness and occasional scoring touch.

"I mean, it was right in front of me," McCarty recalled, "and all I can remember was thinking I'm about to watch a car crash in slow motion, and I can't believe it's happening. I could see Lemieux coming from 20 feet away, and I kept waiting for him to slow up. I kept thinking, 'He's going to stop, right?'"

Wrong.

"Heyyyyy!" McCarty yelled.

McCarty was immediately sickened by what he saw of Draper's face. "You could see it cave inward," he said.

By then, Lemieux had already turned and skated away. Referee Bill McCreary, respected by players as probably the NHL's best, whistled to halt play.

Players from both benches leaned over to see the ice rapidly turning the color of Draper's uniform. Lying facedown, gripping his face with his gloves, Draper was conscious but knew he was in big trouble. He could taste his own blood. It felt like his neck might have snapped in two. He couldn't move his jaw to talk.

"I remember trying to get up. And I knew things didn't feel right," Draper recalled nearly 10 years later.

Red Wings trainer John Wharton immediately jumped the boards to aid Draper. Wharton was often teased by opponents for his many trips onto the ice—more TV time was what he wanted, the kidding went—but there was no laughing this time. The partisan Avalanche crowd was silent.

Able to stand after a few minutes, Draper was led off the ice with Wharton pressing a white towel to his face. The towel had turned mostly red by the time they crossed the ice to the visiting team's entrance.

Lying on a table in the small visitors' dressing room, the ceiling, to Draper's barely focused eyes, seemed to be spinning. Blood continued to seep from his mouth and right eye socket. For several chilling moments, Draper thought he'd already lost the eye. The career he had worked so hard for, the one that seemed to have little hope when the Wings obtained him for just a $1 waiver fee after he was dumped by the Winnipeg Jets in 1993, might already be over. Several NHL players had had their careers shortened when they lost the use of an eye. Most of them might have avoided the fate had they worn a protective visor. Lemieux wore such a "shield," and, like most players who did, was ridiculed for it. Real men don't wear shields, most Canadian NHLers—including Draper—believed. Now he wasn't so sure.

On the ice, Lemieux was assessed a five-minute match penalty by McCreary, which meant his automatic ejection from the game. Believing McCreary's call to be unfair, Lemieux made a showy, petulant exit, slamming the door built into the boards behind the north-side net in the aging arena.

Red Wings defenseman Paul Coffey tied the game on the ensuing power play, and everybody on the team knew Draper was tough enough to get back in the game and help them win. When he regained full consciousness in the dressing room, the first thing Draper did was look for his gloves.

"I just felt I was going to be able to get up and go out and play, finish the game," said Draper, who did not know until the next day, when he watched a replay from his hospital room, that it was Lemieux who had hit him. "That's the one thing I remember, just: 'OK, grab my gloves and let's get back out there.'"

But while the Red Wings took the ice for the second period of a 1-1 game, team doctor David Collon gently informed

Draper his season was over. Just looking at his face was enough to know that; never mind the X-rays. They would eventually show broken bones to Draper's nose, jaw, cheekbone, and, possibly, right eye socket. Five teeth were bent inward toward his throat. A total of 40 stitches were needed to close cuts around his eye and inside his mouth. Dr. Collon knew Draper's jaw would probably need to be wired shut.

Detroit captain Steve Yzerman was the only Wings player to get a look at Draper between periods. Not until after the game did Draper's other teammates get a look. Immediately, the disappointment of losing the game, 4-1, turned to rage for some. Red Wings veteran forward Dino Ciccarelli and goalie Chris Osgood were the most vocal—particularly when they realized they had already shaken the hand of Lemieux in the traditional series-ending procession at center ice.

Ciccarelli, no stranger to controversy in his career, including a previous stint in jail for assault, would utter one of the more famous quotes in one of the most famous rivalries in hockey history: "I can't believe I shook this guy's frickin' hand. We lost and I'm pissed off. But to see Kris Draper's face makes me sick. I didn't see his face until after the game, but his face is turned sideways. If the league doesn't do something about that . . . I mean that's ridiculous. He could have broken his frickin' neck."

Down the hallway, in the jubilant Avalanche dressing room, Lemieux stood in a hot-off-the-presses Western Conference Championship T-shirt, drinking a beer and high-fiving teammates. A first-year beat reporter for the *Denver Post*—covering my first NHL team ever—I stood in that dressing room and immediately posed a question to Lemieux about Draper.

"Are you sorry about the hit on Draper?" I asked. "Apparently his injuries are pretty bad."

"Nobody wants to see a player get injured. I didn't try to hurt him, and I'm sorry he's hurt," Lemieux said.

That was as close as Lemieux would get to an apology.

There was no asking about the extent of Draper's injuries. No asking where he might be in the building for a quick visit. When some Detroit reporters pressed Lemieux about the incident, the two-time Stanley Cup champion and son of a blue-collar truck driver from Mont Laurier, Quebec, took a familiar adversarial posture.

"I don't want to waste my time talking about Detroit," he said. "They were beaten for the second year in a row. I try to hit everybody as hard as I can, just like everybody tries to hit me as hard as they can. Everything is always vicious about us, and not them. At worst, I thought it should have been a two-minute penalty. I think that was going to be his first call, but then [Mc-Creary] saw blood and decided to change his mind."

With that, Lemieux took a long last drink of his beer, crumpled the can, and tossed it in the trash. That's the end of it, Lemieux seemed to say with the gesture. No more questions about that. Move on.

Not by a long shot.

Osgood, the second-year Wings goalie who had been bested by Colorado's Patrick Roy, had to fight himself not to storm the Avs dressing room looking for Lemieux.

Osgood issued the first of many threats Lemieux would receive the next few months—many of them, from fans via fax and hang-up phone calls, threatening death.

"Our players aren't going to forget it. When he comes back to play the Wings next year, he'd better be ready. We'll be waiting for him," Osgood said.

This wasn't the first time in the series somebody wanted to physically go after Lemieux.

Lemieux was suspended for Game 4, following a Game 3 incident in which he reared back and threw a punch to the back of the head of Detroit's Slava Kozlov. That was in retaliation for Kozlov's previously unpenalized sucker punch to Colorado defenseman Adam Foote, which drove his face into the glass and drew a cut that needed 18 stitches.

"I told 'Footie,' when he got up and I saw his face, I said, 'We'll get him back,'" said Lemieux, foreshadowing in reverse the events that would take place three games later.

After Game 3, a 6-4 Detroit victory, Lemieux walked out of the south entrance to McNichols with his wife, Debbie, and baby son, Brendan—named in honor of Brendan Shanahan, Lemieux's good friend and former teammate in New Jersey.

To get to the player parking lot, the Lemieuxs had to walk past the idling Detroit team bus. Through the bus's open doorway, Lemieux heard what sounded like an older man's voice yelling his way.

"Lemieux, you gutless son of a bitch, nice sucker punch," the voice said from the front. "I hope the league suspends your ass."

Lemieux instantly knew the voice to be none other than that of legendary Red Wings coach Scotty Bowman.

"Pardon me?" said a stunned Lemieux, who walked onto the first inside step of the bus to confront Bowman.

For Lemieux, this was a first. Hockey has always been a vicious sport, but one held together by a tenuous code of moral conduct off the ice. When a game ends, tradition holds that any beefs can wait to be settled until the next game. When the game's over, it's over—no matter the injustice that might have happened on the ice. Players who tried to punch each other's lights out in a hockey game were likely to shake hands and have a laugh afterward. "That's hockey, eh?" as the Canadian saying goes.

This, however—confronting a player carrying a baby in his arms, next to his wife—was not hockey.

Lemieux heard "Get the fuck out of here" from some members of the Wings before heatedly telling Bowman, "I would expect better out of you. I'm with my family here, have some class."

"Fuck off, cocksucker," was returned in chorus upon Lemieux's exit.

The next day, prior to a practice, Lemieux walked through the same doorway into the arena. The first person he saw was Bowman, talking quietly with Colorado general manager Pierre Lacroix.

"Hey Scotty, if you want to talk, it's time to talk now. I don't have my kid now, and you don't have your entire bus behind you," Lemieux said, inching closer to the 62-year-old Bowman, a former junior player in the Montreal system whose playing career was partially derailed by a head injury suffered from a high stick by Jean-Guy Talbot in a 1951 game.

Bowman didn't want to continue the matter. "He just buried his head and walked away," Lemieux said.

Lemieux, sure enough, was suspended one game by NHL director of hockey operations Brian Burke. Convinced that Bowman's parking-lot tirade and griping about Lemieux in the media had something to do with Burke's decision, Avalanche coach Marc Crawford felt he had to return Bowman's "mind game" with one of his own.

A former fringe player with the Vancouver Canucks, at 35 Crawford was in just his second year as an NHL head coach—on paper, no match for the six-time Stanley Cup champion Bowman. But Crawford had a media savvy beyond his baby face and anchorman-stiff hairstyle.

Asked about the suspension in a morning press conference at McNichols, Crawford turned the subject back around to Bowman and the metal plate he was long rumored to have in his head as a result of his junior injury. (The rumor was untrue.)

"Scotty Bowman, he's notorious for taking an incidental factor in a game and trying to create a lot of focus around that. He does it by planting questions in the media; he does it by trying to create an awful lot of controversy," Crawford said. "He's a great thinker, but he thinks so much that you even get the plate in his head causing interference on our headsets during the game."

Crawford's wife, Helene, scolded her husband for the remarks, even telling *Sports Illustrated* it was a good thing he and the team were staying in a Denver hotel for the series—a playoff hockey tradition—because he wouldn't have "gotten any" that night at home.

After Lemieux's hit on Draper, not even Crawford believed a suspension wouldn't be coming his way.

"Claude plays the game hard, and he probably deserved the penalties," Crawford said after his team knocked out the supposedly invincible Red Wings. "But tonight's not the night to talk about it."

The day after Game 6, Lemieux knew a suspension for the upcoming Stanley Cup Finals against the Florida Panthers was a strong possibility. If anything would be a killer for Lemieux, it would be sitting out a Finals game. He was already gaining a reputation as hockey's Reggie Jackson, a Mr. October in June. He loved the pressure of big games and the boos from enemy rinks. Entering the 1996 Finals, Lemieux already had 52 goals in 136 career playoff games, with one Conn Smythe Trophy and three overtime game-winning goals with the Montreal Canadiens.

Lemieux tried to make a deal with Burke: In exchange for letting him play every game of the Finals, Lemieux would sit out half of the following regular season without pay.

No dice. "They turned me down," Lemieux said. "It was a big commitment on my part. That's how bad I want to play in the playoffs."

Lemieux was suspended for the first two games of the Finals, both won by the Avalanche. Supporters of Draper were outraged at what they said was a light sentence. Lemieux returned for Game 3, and scored Colorado's first goal in a 3-2 victory. Two nights later, in the sweaty, packed visitors' dressing room at Miami Arena, Lemieux took a long drink of champagne from the silver Cup for the third time in his career.

Having been promised by Lacroix before the season that his current four-year, $5.2 million contract would be ripped up for a richer one if things went well, Lemieux was the king of the world.

"Thank you, Father Pete," Lemieux said, hugging Lacroix.

About a thousand miles away, Draper lay in a room at Michigan's Henry Ford Hospital. While Lemieux sipped sweet bubbly from the Cup, Draper sucked down the last of his ground-up meal through a straw into a mouth that would stay wired shut for five weeks.

The 1995–96 NHL season may have ended that night, but the nastiest and best-played rivalry in pro sports for the next six years was only just beginning.

Hockeytown and a Cow Town

It was the best rivalry of its time in pro sports, and it never should have happened.

To look at the confluence of events that had to come about for there to be any rivalry between the Red Wings and the Avalanche is to be staggered by the unlikelihood of it all.

What were the odds a team in its first year in a new city, one that previously had only six years of NHL history at all, would in months emerge as the most hated team in the league to an Original Six franchise?

What were the odds a player who had won a playoff MVP trophy with a championship team—who had been with that team for years—would suddenly want out?

What were the odds that a team in one of the best hockey markets in North America, in a Canadian city not far from where the sport was invented, would suddenly find itself 1,996 miles away in the western United States?

What were the odds the most beloved player in the most celebrated and rabid hockey city of all would have a blow-up with his coach and, four days later, be on a plane to Denver, Colorado?

However long the odds, all these things happened. And here's the kicker: the Red Wings were in many ways indirectly responsible for much of how the Avalanche team of 1995–96 and beyond was built.

If Detroit had played to its capabilities in the 1995 Stanley Cup Finals against the New Jersey Devils, Claude Lemieux never would have won the Conn Smythe, and never would have tried to get out of the four-year, $5.2 million contract he had verbally agreed to with Devils general manager Lou Lamoriello earlier that season.

Lemieux's MVP award and the Devils' triumph were about the only things that went right for him in 1995. The start of the 1994–95 NHL season was wiped out by a lockout by the owners, which meant players weren't getting paid. Lemieux at that time needed money.

He was in the middle of a divorce from Carol, his wife of seven years. For Lemieux, the divorce was painful and expensive. When play resumed, the distractions of the divorce played a part in Lemieux's worst regular-season performance of his career. In a shortened 48-game season, he scored just six goals in 45 games played. In 1991–92, he had scored 41 goals in 74 games for the Devils.

With steep alimony and child-support payments to make, Lemieux approached Lamoriello about a new contract. A former coach and player at Providence College, the short, balding Lamoriello was a soft-spoken but hard-boiled man who could be a ruthless negotiator.

Still, Lamoriello liked Lemieux as a player. He got better as the games got bigger, and he was still only 29. The season before, Lemieux was outstanding in a long Devils playoff run. So, about a month before the playoffs he gave Lemieux what at the time was a pretty fair offer—four years and $5.2 million. The average NHL player salary in 1994–95 was $733,000, and Lemieux would be making nearly twice that.

In the midst of a terrible season statistically, Lemieux agreed to the deal. Trouble was, he never actually signed it. Somehow, his signature on the official hard copy of the contract wasn't there. No big deal, both parties thought. They'd get around to it.

The Devils made it into the 1995 playoffs as the fifth seed in the Eastern Conference. After a somewhat mediocre regular season, the Devils suddenly got hot, beating Boston and Pittsburgh fairly easily in the first two playoff rounds, then ousting Philadelphia in the conference finals. Lemieux iced a rubber Game 5 in the Philly series with a big, booming slap shot from the right side against Flyers goalie Ron Hextall in a 2-2 game with 45 seconds left in regulation.

But the Devils didn't have a chance against the mighty Red Wings, at least not to the pundits, most of whom predicted a sweep. And it was—in New Jersey's favor. Lemieux scored the game-winning goal in a 2-1 Game 1 Devils victory in Detroit and scored another goal in Game 3. He finished the playoffs with 13 goals in 20 games for a Devils team that won a record 10 playoff road games.

When the playoffs ended and the Devils finished their Stanley Cup parade around the parking lot of Brendan Byrne Arena, Lemieux was in no hurry to sign the contract hard copy. He was a playoff MVP, the NHL's Mr. Clutch. Show me more money, he said. Lamoriello wasn't too worried, because he had not only the verbal commitment from Lemieux but his signature to an earlier faxed copy of the deal. Lemieux consulted his agent, Boston-based Steve Freyer, who also handled Bruins superstar Ray Bourque. The deal appeared valid, but Lemieux believed since he'd only signed a faxed copy, it wasn't.

He fired Freyer in unhappiness over the deal, later hiring Howard Silber, the brother-in-law of his second wife, Debbie.

While in the Bahamas on his honeymoon, Lemieux told the Devils he wanted a better contract or he'd declare himself a Group V unrestricted free agent—which he would have been entitled to do because he was a 10-year pro and making just under the league average. That flimsy piece of fax paper was not a legal document, Lemieux convinced himself. Besides, it was smudged, hard to read.

Nonsense, said Lamoriello, and on September 19, 1995, the case headed to arbitration.

"Call it a Conn job," Devils beat writer Rich Chere wrote about Lemieux's gambit for the *Newark Star-Ledger*.

Still, Lemieux believed NHL arbitrator George Nicolau would rule in his favor, partly because another NHL player, Red Wings goalie Mike Vernon, had lost in a similar case—only in reverse.

"Vernon had received a fax offer from Detroit before the Finals, and he hadn't signed it and hadn't agreed to it," Lemieux recalled. "All of a sudden, they lose four straight and he signs the fax copy of the contract and says to Detroit, 'OK I'll take the offer.' Obviously, his leverage had gone down. Well, his case gets thrown out by the arbitrator [Nicolau], and the arbitrator says, 'Unless we have an original copy of the contract with all the five copies, whatever, of the signed contract between the player and the team, that contract is not valid.'"

Years later, Vernon said Lemieux was only partly right.

"We had the faxed copy, and the arbitrator just ignored it. Fax copy will hold in a court of law. But arbitration is different. I counted several times when the other side lied. It's a he-said, she-said kind of thing," Vernon said. "A fax is a done deal. That's why [Lemieux] lost, and I lost on several other issues I guess. I got the offer at the start of the playoffs, game day, and I told Kenny Holland 'can we talk about this tomorrow?' I guess that's what they considered as being a 'no.'

"Eventually, I was a free agent. They came back and said

they wanted me to be the new goalie. I sat down with the new president and signed a contract. I said, 'Well, I want to get what I deserve.' And they said, it would make [Red Wings owner] Mr. Ilitch look bad, and I said, 'Well, you've made Mr. Vernon look really bad.' I said, 'Well, do a signing bonus over here for this amount of money and I'll take this amount of money here.' So, I did take a little less, but I got what I wanted over here. So, I got what I wanted."

On September 29 Nicolau's verdict came in: Lemieux's deal was binding.

"That was [Nicolau's] last case," Lemieux said. "They made that basically one-page deal, verbal agreement, valid. I wasn't too happy."

A stubborn Lemieux told Lamoriello he was through with the Devils, that he wanted a trade. Lamoriello told Lemieux he would try, but Lemieux never suggested Colorado, home of the newly relocated Avalanche, as his desired location. Ironically, Lemieux had recently spent some time at the Edwards, Colorado, vacation ranch of Devils owner Dr. John J. McMullen, and marveled at the state's beauty. Still, Lemieux didn't know anything about the Avalanche, other than that the team used to be the Quebec Nordiques.

Lemieux thought he would go to another Eastern Conference team, or maybe to the team he'd just beaten, Detroit. A coach like Scotty Bowman would want a winner like him, right?

But it just so happened that during training camp of the Avalanche's inaugural season, 1995–96, Colorado GM Pierre Lacroix also had a holdout veteran forward who wanted either more money or a trade. His name was Wendel Clark, a player similar in style and size to Lemieux. The mustachioed Clark had been a centerpiece to Lacroix's first big trade with the Nordiques in 1994, coming from Toronto in a deal that sent Mats Sundin to the Leafs.

Clark had a good season for the Nordiques in 1995, but felt

the $1.05 million (Canadian funds) he was due the next year on his contract wasn't good enough and wanted to renegotiate. Lacroix, a hardheaded, take-it-or-leave-it negotiator who spent nearly 21 years on the other side of the table as a player agent, refused.

A nasty standoff ensued. Clark's powerful Toronto-based agent, Don Meehan, disparaged Lacroix in the papers. After the Avs won the Stanley Cup in 1996, Meehan was quoted saying the Zamboni driver could have won the Cup with as much young talent as Lacroix inherited in Quebec. The two would stay enemies for several years.

Finally, on October 3, 1995, the Devils, Avalanche, and New York Islanders swung a three-way deal that sent Clark to the Islanders, forward Steve Thomas to the Devils, and Lemieux to Colorado. Technically, Lemieux was traded by the Islanders to Colorado, as he was initially dealt to New York for Thomas.

"I was an Islander for about 15 seconds," Lemieux said.

Lemieux would get two days of skating in before Colorado's first game of the season at McNichols Arena. The opponent?

The Detroit Red Wings, of course.

On October 6, 1995, the NHL made its return to Denver following a 13-year absence. On May 7, 1982, McMullen, along with Brendan Byrne and John C. Whitehead, bought the Colorado Rockies for $8.5 million and moved them to New Jersey.

The Rockies had spent six miserable seasons in Denver, after a previous stint as the Kansas City Scouts. The franchise was plagued by an ownership group, led by Jack Vickers, Peter Gilbert, and Arthur Imperatore, that didn't want to be patient for its young talent to develop. Rising stars such as Barry Beck, Rob Ramage, and Wilf Paiement were hastily traded for older, bigger-name players who had seen better days.

In 1979 the team hired Don Cherry away from the Boston Bruins as head coach. Cherry, who would later find greater fame and fortune as a bombastic personality during the CBC's *Hockey Night in Canada* broadcasts, guided Colorado to a 19-48-13 record and was fired after one season.

The Rockies' best season was a 22-45-13 record in 1980–81. The team was so bad that it became best known for two personalities that never played a game. One was a wild-haired, trash-talking fan named Crazy George, who taunted opponents by their bench and clanged a cowbell that reverberated throughout the usually half-empty McNichols Arena.

The other was British glam-rock singer Gary Glitter, whose song "Rock and Roll, Part 2" became the team anthem after goals were scored. The song went on to become a staple in sports arenas throughout the world, with its familiar "Hey!" chorus.

The Denver of 1976–82 was nothing like the city it would become in the 1990s. Largely dependent on the oil and gas industries, a terrible economic slump gripped the city in the Rockies' years when the prices of both commodities went south.

Despite having a lousy team and a poor economy, Denver's hockey fans were ridiculed when the team moved. "Denver isn't a good hockey town" became a catchphrase around the league, especially in Original Six markets such as Detroit. It seemed dubious that the NHL would ever consider a return.

But starting around 1990, the economic fortunes of the city began changing rapidly. The beginnings of the American high-tech revolution had some roots in Denver, with telecommunications companies such as US West heralding new businesses that attracted thousands of upwardly mobile young professionals. Once a moribund collection of dirty, empty buildings, downtown Denver soon was transformed into a collection of sleek condominium lofts overlooking busy microbreweries, restaurants, and dot-com startups.

Thousands of twentysomethings from around the country looked at Denver as an attractive place to start a new life. People like me.

In 1991, at 26 years of age, I was laid off from my $6-per-hour job as a proofreader and part-time sportswriter at the *Concord (NH) Monitor*. I lived in my folks' basement, with no car, as I had totaled my baby blue Ford Fairmont a couple of years before on a Massachusetts highway. I relied on rides from friends and my mother to get to work—not exactly what instills a young man with macho pride. Now, along with no car, I had no job. Now what?

I had visited a friend from Colorado the year before and instantly was wowed by Denver's big, wide-open spaces, jagged mountain skyline, and milder winter weather. I remember thinking, This is a place I could live some day if I had to. Well, here was my moment of truth: What better time than now to make the move, to go west as a young man?

Without a job lined up, out I came to Denver on May 15, 1991. Purely coincidentally, my best friend from New Hampshire, Chris Spaulding, and his then girlfriend, Debbie, had moved to Denver a few months before. They agreed to take me on as a subletter to their small two-bedroom apartment that, with the rent split three ways, cost me just $160 a month. I didn't care that I had no gainful employment; it felt invigorating being in a new place where nobody knew who I was. I was tired of the *Cheers* theme-song life. In Denver I could be anybody I wanted to be, unlike back home where everybody knew my name—and baggage.

After six months of working temp jobs ranging from a bill collector for a trash company to a guy who signed people in to take tours of an open house, I started sending form letters to sports reporters at Denver's two daily newspapers, the *Denver Post* and *Rocky Mountain News*. Only two responded with phone calls—Norm Clarke of the *News* and Natalie Meisler of the *Post*—which shows you the kind of class they had. I was a nobody, sending in bland letters that read the same to everybody who got them. I had a journalism degree from New Hampshire's Keene State College, but only 12 "clips" of part-time sportswriting experience at the *Monitor*. Being a sportswriter was something I never thought I'd actually ever be able to do for a living, but it was a pipe dream I wasn't ready to give up on. I grew up reading the *Boston Globe*'s sports section from cover to cover, which was a great education in the art of good sportswriting. My writing hero was Bob Ryan, the longtime *Globe* writer and columnist. I can still recite some of his best passages, including one in which he paraphrased a line from the Beatles' "For The Benefit of Mr. Kite" to describe the heroics of Gerald Henderson and Greg Kite in a Boston Celtics playoff game.

(In 2001 I finally got the chance to meet Ryan, in the elevator at the Pepsi Center in Denver. The trouble was, the Avalanche had just won the Stanley Cup, and I was frazzled over the stories I had to write. The combination of pending work and nervousness about being with the man himself meant I choked after shaking his hand; I got all tongue-tied and barely spit out a "Nice to meet you.")

I'd recently taken a course in Denver about how to get a job in the field you want, which instructed job seekers to call a "decision maker" and ask to meet with him or her for just 10 minutes. Don't come right out and ask for a job, the instructor said—that's too threatening and looks too desperate. Just ask the person the question: How can I get to be in your shoes someday, and how did it happen for you? The purpose is to flatter the decision maker, get him to talk about his own past glories. Maybe he'll feel flattered enough to reciprocate with some kind of lead, or maybe a job offer itself. The key, though, was to get the meeting face to face, not over the phone. There was some statistic they pumped into our job-seeking brains, I remember, that you had about an 800 percent higher chance of getting a job by actually meeting with the decision maker as opposed to only talking over the phone or sending resumes cold.

To my surprise Neil Devlin, the high school sports editor of the *Post*, agreed to meet with me. On a winter night where I nervously overdressed and stuttered, we did, and he sent me on my way, thanking me for coming but saying he had no current openings. I thought it was back to the bill collection agencies for me, or else one of them would come calling *me* for the overdue electric bill. But a week later, the phone rang. It was Devlin on the line. Would I be interested in taking high school sports scores over the phone, he asked? It would only be $7 an hour, a couple nights a week, and no benefits.

I practically leapt through the phone. I knew this was the rock-bottom job in the sports department, and the odds of going from there to full-time staff sportswriter was another pipe dream. But I didn't care. I had my foot in the door of one of the biggest papers in the country. I had a sense of optimism that better things would happen—and as a lifelong Boston Red Sox fan and generally glass-half-empty kind of guy in the first place, such a feeling was unusual.

Good things did happen. I got a chance to get out of the office and write some high school sports stories, and from there was promoted to cover college sports and some "trash" pro sports, stuff like indoor soccer. Then, one day in February 1995, while I was writing a high school swimming preview story a few hours before I was to go cover a University of Denver hockey game, the phone rang in the sports department. A guy was looking for the paper's hockey writer. Having covered the Pioneers and the Denver Grizzlies of the International Hockey League, I was it.

"I hear the owners of the Denver Nuggets are looking at buying the Quebec Nordiques," this person, my own personal Deep Throat, told me. "You might want to look into it."

There had been expectations that COMSAT Video Enter-prises, a Maryland-based satellite and entertainment company that owned the Nuggets, would one day try to bring an NHL team back to Denver to play in the new arena it planned to build. But no one thought it would happen soon, and everybody thought COMSAT would wait for an expansion team, not buy an existing one.

Wrong. The tip from Deep Throat was right on the money. I got the biggest scoop and lucky break of my career when the paper announced "COMSAT Bids for Nordiques, Source Claims" across its front page the next day. That was a bit bigger a story than the swim preview and DU game story that appeared in the same edition.

The Nordiques, which entered the NHL in 1979 after seven years in the old World Hockey Association, could no longer stay financially competitive playing in Quebec City. The team needed a new arena, but the bigger problem was a lack of heavy-weight corporate support, the kind that could fill the $100,000-a-year luxury suites that were fast becoming the new cash cows of professional sports.

Nordiques majority owner Marcel Aubut tried to get the city to build a new arena with a casino inside, all the profits of which would go to the Nordiques. Mayor Jean-Paul L'Allier said, "*Non.*" At the time, the provincial government was closing nine hospitals in the area because of budget cuts, making a tax-payer-sponsored bailout of a hockey team politically and practi-cally unfeasible.

Quebec premier Jacques Parizeau did offer a last-minute package worth $21 million (CDN) over three years to protect against the Nordiques' losses of between $10 million and $15 million a year, but it wasn't enough. Thus, on May 25, 1995, in a conference room in Bethesda, Maryland, Aubut sold the Nordiques to COMSAT for $75 million.

"The team is ours," I remember former COMSAT spokesman Paul Jacobson telling me over the phone the night before the announcement was made.

A few days later, *Post* sports editor Mike Connelly gave me a full-time job as the team's new beat writer. I still can't believe it happened.

Although the price paid was, at the time, the most ever for an NHL team, those in the hockey know considered it a bargain. It was going to be a great team, they said. Years of horrible records meant high draft picks, and former general managers such as Pierre Page, Maurice Fillion, and Martin Madden had presided over some shrewd choices, such as Joe Sakic, Adam Deadmarsh, Adam Foote, Owen Nolan, Mats Sundin, and Eric Lindros. On June 30, 1992, Page engineered a controversial trade of Lindros to the Philadelphia Flyers for established players Steve Duchesne, Mike Ricci, Kerry Huffman, and Ron Hextall, along with the rights to the Flyers' 1991 first-round draft pick Peter Forsberg, Philadelphia's first-round pick in the 1993 draft, future considerations, and a staggering $15 million in cash. At the same time Page was making the trade with the Flyers, however, Aubut was making a secret deal with the New York Rangers for Lindros. It took an arbitrator named Larry Bertuzzi (uncle of controversial future NHL star Todd Bertuzzi) to declare the Flyers the winner in the Lindros trade, but history would prove the Nordiques—and later, the Avalanche—got the best of it.

It was a trade that, combined with Quebec's own growing young talent, would later help transform it into an NHL powerhouse.

When the Nordiques came to Denver, the team had no new nickname. At first, COMSAT CEO Charlie Lyons—a slick-talking, sandy-haired young man and big fan of extreme sports—wanted to call it the Rocky Mountain Extreme. Marketing plans were drawn up around the name—a rare collectible sought after by Avs fans today is an initial advertisement with the words "Extreme Hockey" around it—but they were promptly canceled after the *Denver Post* caught wind of it and printed it—and fans reacted overwhelmingly against it.

At the team's first public appearance before the fans of Denver, at a rally at McNichols, all players wore generic white t-shirts that read, "Colorado NHL." Only the most hard-core hockey fans knew who any of the players were. In fact, when Colorado governor Roy Romer introduced captain and long-time NHL star Joe Sakic, he called him "Joe Kasic."

After COMSAT held a "feedback forum" in which the public could choose from eight proposed names, Avalanche became the landslide winner. A new logo was introduced, which was ridiculed by some for looking like melting soft-serve ice cream with a puck attached. But Denver's kids thought it was cool, and before long the logos were all over the Mile High City.

When the Red Wings came into McNichols Arena for the first game in the newly named Colorado Avalanche's history, they carried with them nearly 70 years of NHL tradition. Formed in the fall of 1926, the team was originally made up of transferred players from the Victoria Cougars of the Western Canada Hockey League. In fact, the team was first known as the Detroit Cougars, and they played not in Detroit, but across the river in Windsor, Ontario. In the team's first season, it finished last and lost a then princely sum of $84,000 at the gate. It didn't help that the Great Depression was nearly upon the country; according to a *Detroit News* account, "Detroit Mayor Frank Murphy held a charity game and one fan showed up with five sacks of potatoes for admission. He was given a standing room spot."

In 1927 the team moved to Detroit to play in a gleaming new building, the Olympia. Later nicknamed the Old Red

Barn, the building could hold 16,375, counting standing admission, and would serve as the team's home until 1979. In 1930 the Cougars were renamed the Falcons, but in 1932, after the team was purchased by industrialist Jim Norris, the name was changed again, this time to the Red Wings. In the land of Henry Ford, where the automobile was revolutionizing the country, a "winged wheel" became a natural choice as the team's new logo.

The team was coached by a loud, brash man named Jack Adams, who became known for a browbeating style with his players and any referee who dared make a call against them. Under his tutelage, the Red Wings gradually improved to the point where the team won its first Stanley Cup in 1936, captained by Doug Young and featuring other stoutly named players as Ebbie Goodfellow and Bucko McDonald.

The Red Wings would win two more Cups under Adams in the next seven years, and in 1946 signed an electrifying young player from Floral, Saskatchewan, named Gordie Howe. A strapping young man with sloping, muscular shoulders and a neat, parted haircut, Howe was a combination of strength and finesse that the game had never seen. He could stickhandle a puck through a crowd, or he could drive an opponent through the glass with a big body check. Despite an aw-shucks, Canadian prairie boy nature off the ice, Howe had a mean streak on it. He never forgot a slight, no matter how minor, almost always responding with his fists or "lumber." In fact, a term was coined in honor of Howe's skill and toughness: a "Gordie Howe hat trick" is a goal, an assist, and a fight in the same game.

Howe would play alongside teammates Sid Abel and Ted Lindsay on a line so dominant offensively it became known as "the Production Line." It was a perfect nickname for a line in the increasingly more automated world of automobile assembly in the Motor City. The Production Line led the Red Wings to Stanley Cups in 1950 and 1952, and even without Abel, Detroit went on to two more in 1954 and 1955. The team had a terrific new goalie named Terry Sawchuk, who would go on to set a record for most career wins with 447. The Red Wings made the Finals five more times in the next 10 years, but were beaten each time.

Then, starting in 1967, the NHL expanded from 6 to 12 teams. The dilution of talent weakened the Red Wings, who missed the playoffs 9 of the next 10 seasons. The team got even worse by the early 1980s. Even after moving into the then swank new Joe Louis Arena, adjacent to the Detroit River downtown, the team soon became known as the "Dead Wings." In 1980–81, the team finished with a 19-43-18 record, "improving" to 21-47-12 the following season.

By 1982, after 50 years of ownership and dwindling crowds, the Norris family sold the Red Wings to a Greek pizza baron named Mike Ilitch. Previously a purveyor of fish and chips with a chain of restaurants named London Derby and owner of some Wendy's franchises, Ilitch brought the same hustling personality he gave to his Little Caesar's pizza chain to the increasingly moribund team.

With attendance only in the four figures for many games at the Joe, as the arena was known, in his first year as owner Ilitch began an audacious promotion to attract more fans. For every home game in the 1982–83 season, Ilitch gave a new car away to a lucky ticket holder. As Ilitch told the *Detroit Free Press*, "There was nobody in the place. We had only 4,100 or 4,200 season-ticket holders. We were nationally recognized as the Dead Wings. I got our sales group together and said, 'We've got to do something to get some attention.'"

What the fans wanted more than a car, though, was a winning team. Finally, with the arrival in 1983 of a slick-skating youngster from Ottawa named Steve Yzerman, the Red Wings started to get better. The team made the playoffs from 1983 to 1985, and after a horrendous 17-57-6 season in 1985–86, advanced to the conference finals the following two seasons.

In the summer of 1993 Ilitch hired 59-year-old William Scott "Scotty" Bowman as head coach. It wasn't long before the Red Wings would get to the next level under Bowman, who was already a legend, with six Stanley Cups as coach with Montreal and Pittsburgh and another as director of player personnel with the Penguins.

Bowman guided the Wings to the Cup Finals in 1995, and Detroit was the runaway favorite to win in 1995–96.

No way did it seem likely that the newly relocated Nordiques, now the Avalanche, would give the Red Wings much trouble in the Western Conference. And no way in the world would anybody who watched the first meeting between the Red Wings and Avalanche guess the teams would become mortal enemies by season's end.

It was a tame affair, won by the Avalanche 3-2 in front of 16,061 fans. There was a serious injury when Colorado defenseman Uwe Krupp, a 6-foot-6, 235-pound player from Germany, was checked into the boards by Martin Lapointe and suffered torn ligaments in his knee. He would miss the rest of the regular season.

But, as hockey games go, this was a like a game of touch football. The Avalanche won on a late third-period goal by the stylish Russian left wing Valeri Kamensky, who spoke almost no English and could not describe his actions to reporters afterward. Assisting on the goal was Lemieux, continuing to bedevil the Red Wings as he had months before in New Jersey.

Kamensky also scored the Avalanche's first goal, and after he did a fan threw a Rocky Mountain trout onto the ice. It was Colorado's nod to a long tradition in Detroit of throwing an octopus onto the ice during the start of the playoffs. On October 15, 1952, two brothers named Pete and Jerry Cusimano, who owned a Detroit fish market, threw a dead octopus onto the ice as a gesture of hope for their Red Wings after their first goal in Game 3 of the Finals against Montreal. In 1952 it took only eight victories to win the Stanley Cup—the same number of tentacles on an octopus.

Following that first game, niceties toward the opposing team flowed from both dressing rooms.

"They're a great hockey club, with lines that are four-deep and their coach is probably the biggest legend in all of coaching," said Colorado coach Marc Crawford.

Bowman talked less about the loss than he did about how nice it was to see Denver back in the NHL.

The Red Wings packed up their gear and walked peacefully out to the team bus, past the Avalanche dressing room. Some players, even Lemieux, exchanged pleasantries with their opponents. Lemieux chatted briefly with Detroit goalie Vernon, presumably about their recent arbitration cases, and Avalanche Russians Kamensky and Alexei Gusarov talked warmly with Red Wings countrymen Vladimir Konstantinov, Igor Larionov, and Viacheslav Fetisov.

Avalanche fans didn't know what to make of their new team, many still having trouble naming players without a program. While making his way to the dressing room following his victory in net for the Avs, goalie Stephane Fiset received a salute from a somewhat inebriated fan.

"Hey, FIZ-zet . . . Fishnet . . . hey, whatever your name is . . . WAY TO GO!" the fan yelled.

It wouldn't be long before a new goalie named Patrick Roy would arrive in Denver to replace Fiset. A winner already of two Stanley Cups and two Conn Smythe Trophies with the hallowed Montreal Canadiens, Roy was lovingly known by fans as "Saint Patrick."

If any player at the time seemed destined to stay with the same team his whole career, it was Roy. But on December 2, 1995, he would be embarrassed in a game to the point where he would stomp over to the Canadiens' president, sitting behind the team bench and inform him, "I've played my last game in Montreal."

If one team hadn't been so hot that night as to put nine pucks past him in an eventual 11-1 rout at the Montreal Forum, chances are Roy would not have left Montreal that season and certainly wouldn't have been traded to Colorado just four days later. If that team had just eased up a little, Roy would probably never have been able to alter the balance of power in the Western Conference with his inclusion on the Avalanche.

That team, of course, was the Detroit Red Wings.

"I've Played My Last Game in Montreal"

The Red Wings came into the Montreal Forum for the final time on a frigid Saturday, December 2, 1995. The fabled building would be abandoned by the Canadiens following the 1995–96 season in favor of a new arena, the Molson Centre.

While the Wings were on their way to a record-setting season for victories, the Canadiens were well into a period of decline. The team won the Stanley Cup in 1993, thanks to the brilliant goaltending of Patrick Roy. He won an incredible 10 games in overtime during the run to the Cup. It was his second Cup; he'd backstopped the Habs—short for *Les Habitants*—to a previous one in 1986, and both seasons he won the Conn Smythe Trophy.

He was nicknamed Saint Patrick by longtime *Montreal Gazette* hockey writer Red Fisher following the 1986 championship over Calgary, and was easily the most popular and famous athlete in all of Quebec.

But the Canadiens missed the playoffs in the lockout-shortened 1994–95 season, for the first time since 1969–70. Roy struggled with a 17-20-6 record, the only losing season of his

19-year career. The Canadiens fired coach Jacques Demers, a former Red Wings coach who had a reputation for favoring Roy over other players. Roy sometimes got practices off that were mandatory for the rest of the team, and it was Roy, Demers' critics said, who dictated his own playing schedule—not Demers.

Demers was replaced by former Canadiens forward Mario Tremblay, who had no previous head-coaching experience.

Roy was upset at Demers' firing, and did not think Tremblay was the right man for the job. The 1995–96 Canadiens got off to a slow start, losing their first five games, including a 7-1 opening-night loss to Philadelphia. Personality conflicts were starting to infect the team, with a simmering feud between Roy and defenseman Mathieu Schneider. Between periods of a game the year before in Philadelphia, Roy stood up in the dressing room and gave what sounded at first to be a motivational speech, but was intended instead as a dig at Schneider's play.

"Don't worry, boys, we're only a couple goals down, we're right there, everybody's playing good," said Roy, who then looked over toward Schneider's locker and said, "Except one guy."

Incensed, Schneider shot back, "Just shut the fuck up and stop the puck."

Roy responded by throwing a cup of Gatorade at Schneider, and the two had to be separated by teammates.

Roy led Montreal to wins in 12 of the next 14 games, but by the night of the game with Detroit, the Canadiens were on a four-game winless streak. The only game of the four that wasn't a loss was a 2-2 tie at home with the Avalanche, November 25, in which Sandis Ozolinsh scored through Roy's "five-hole"—the space between a goalie's pads—in the final minutes of regulation.

The Red Wings hadn't won at the Forum since 1988, but it quickly became apparent their 0-7-1 streak would end this night. Roy was having one of those nights where it seemed the puck was the size of a Tic Tac. He couldn't stop anything. Detroit's Slava Kozlov finished with four goals, while fellow Russians Sergei Fedorov and Igor Larionov combined for another nine points.

Larionov, a longtime member of some great Soviet Red Army teams, opened the scoring at 3:10 of the first period. Kozlov added two and Nicklas Lidstrom and Greg Johnson had one each for a 5-1 Wings lead after one.

When Kozlov scored at 2:52 of the second, the notoriously fickle Montreal fans began to turn on Saint Patrick. They started giving mock cheers for every save he made, which made Roy furious. He responded by sarcastically raising his arms, mocking the fans right back. Four of the nine goals he allowed in the game, on 26 total shots, came on the power play—hardly the goalie's fault.

But what made Roy the most furious—and his teammates the most incredulous—was the fact he was still in the game at all. Much like a pitcher who doesn't have it and gets a second visit from the manager, a goalie who has given up his fifth or sixth goal of the night usually gets a seat on the bench, especially if the score isn't close. It's more out of professional courtesy than anything else by that point.

But even after the Red Wings had made it an 8-1 game on another goal by Johnson, Tremblay still hadn't sent backup Pat Jablonski out for relief. Roy cursed under his mask, almost trembling with rage. Tremblay was trying to show him up, he believed: trying to show who was boss to his new team.

"It just kept going and going and going, with Patty still out there, and we were like, 'Are you kidding me?'" remembered Mike Keane, the Canadiens' captain at the time. "I don't know if [Tremblay] was trying to do the alpha dog thing, but he was out of his league. He didn't know what to do."

Finally, after Fedorov made it 9-1 at 11:57 of the second

period, Tremblay made the move. Roy skated like a power skater back to the bench. Initially, he wanted to walk over to Tremblay and knock him over. That would show him. Instead, he got up from the end of the bench and trudged over with his familiar seesaw walk, past Tremblay and over to where team president Ron Corey was sitting, right behind the bench. The glass behind the bench was low enough for Roy to stand over it and quickly and firmly declare, in French, to Corey, "I've played my last game in Montreal." Shocked looks on the faces of Corey and others in the front row were evident as Roy made his way back to his seat on the bench. On the way, he glared back at Tremblay, who wore a look that seemed smug and defiant. Roy said to Tremblay, "As-tu compris"—do you understand?

"Mario had a hair-trigger temper," said Fisher, who began covering the Canadiens on March 17, 1955, the night of the infamous Rocket Richard riot at the Forum and throughout Montreal after the great Richard was suspended for the playoffs by NHL president Clarence Campbell for punching linesman Cliff Thompson. "He played that way, he talked that way. He was the boss, and nobody was going to tell him how to coach that hockey team. So there was a wall between the two. Roy manipulated Jacques Demers. He tried that stuff on Mario, telling him how to coach. It didn't work."

Roy stewed on the bench the rest of the game, and quickly left the Forum afterward. Some of his teammates tried to find him, to calm him down and talk him out of his statement to Corey. Nobody knew where he was except Keane, who learned he was at the home of his agent, Bob Sauve, a former NHL goalie. Before he found out Roy was at Sauve's, Keane visited Roy's sprawling suburban Montreal home. Keane ended up taking Roy's oldest son, Jonathan, with him to Sauve's house.

"It was like out of a movie," Keane remembered. "I didn't know how to get to Sauve's place. So there I am, after a game in the car with Patrick's son, trying to find a house in the middle of the night."

Keane eventually found the house after pulling over at a gas station to ask for directions. Once inside, Keane found Roy drinking a beer, still visibly unsettled but otherwise fairly calm. Meanwhile, Sauve's phone was ringing off the hook, with teammates and the rabid Montreal media seeking him out for information on his client.

"It was just a madhouse," Keane said. "He was upset, obviously, at the whole thing. But he was pretty quiet, and the thing I remember was that he probably wasn't going to change his mind about what he told Corey. Once Patty makes up his mind on something, that's usually it."

Indeed, there was no going back. Roy told Keane he couldn't play for Tremblay, and had already instructed Sauve to formally request a trade out of Montreal.

The next day, Canadiens general manager Rejean Houle announced that Roy was suspended from the team, and that a trade would soon be made.

When he saw the news accounts of what had happened in Montreal, Claude Lemieux quickly stopped by the office of Avalanche general manager Pierre Lacroix.

"I said to him, 'Hey, I probably don't need to tell you this, but we gotta get this guy,'" Lemieux said.

It had been a few years since he'd played with him, but Lemieux probably knew Roy as well as anybody in the league. The two came up with the Canadiens together as rookies in 1986, and were teammates on the 1985 Sherbrooke Canadiens team that won the American Hockey League's Calder Cup championship. Roy won MVP honors, with Lemieux finishing runner-up.

In 1986, the two were again the top two postseason performers, this time in the NHL playoffs for Montreal. Roy went 15-5 with an incredible 1.92 goals-against average (GAA) and bested Calgary's Mike Vernon in a six-game Final. The 20-year-old Lemieux scored just one goal in 10 regular-season games for Montreal, but potted 10, along with 6 assists, in 20 postseason games. Included was an overtime goal to the top shelf of Hartford's Mike Liut in Game 7 of the Adams Division finals, and a goal on Montreal's only shot of OT in a victory over the Rangers in the following series.

"Patrick and I were very close; we went through the same things together," Lemieux said. "In Montreal, it was like breaking a union when you came in as a young player. It was tough."

Now, nearly 10 years later, Lemieux was in a brand new city and hoped Roy would join him. The Avalanche of early 1995–96 clearly had some great young talent, but the question mark was always the goaltending tandem of Fiset and youngster Jocelyn Thibault. Neither had any record of playoff success, and even though some wondered if Roy wasn't already on the downside of his career, he still was probably the league's most feared goalie in big games.

Lacroix needed no prodding from Lemieux. For a man who loved the thrill of making deals, who once admitted to having trouble driving past a house with a for-sale sign without wanting to pull over and talk to the owners, the Roy situation was a dream scenario for him. The night after Roy's tirade, Lacroix had a message on his phone from Houle.

"It said something like, 'You probably know why I'm calling. Call me back if you want to discuss a deal,'" Lacroix said.

Lacroix thought he had several advantages over other teams who might want Roy. First was his French-Canadian heritage. He could converse more comfortably than other GMs with the francophone Houle. His team had a stockpile of young, inexpensive players to offer, some of whom weren't getting the ice time they wanted and probably deserved on the talented Avs.

And, not the least of which was his relationship with Roy himself. Before Lacroix took over as GM of the Nordiques, Roy was a client of his JanDec player agency. When Lacroix took the job with Quebec, he sold the agency to Sauve.

Surprisingly, Lacroix found few competitors in the hunt for Roy. Philadelphia was interested, but not enough to part with much of its young talent or draft picks. And Roy had never played well against the Flyers.

Chicago offered a package that included goalie Ed Belfour, but Houle wanted a young francophone to replace Roy, and saw promise in the younger Thibault.

"Thibault was the player that really put the deal over the top for Montreal," Lacroix said. "That was what made the deal happen."

In reality, the Avs liked Thibault but had questions about his mental and physical toughness. Time would prove them correct. Lacroix knew Houle would want more than just Thibault, so he gave him a list of four forwards and told him he could take any two. But as one condition, Lacroix said, he had to have the veteran Keane in return.

At the time, Keane was on the outs with Canadiens fans over his refusal to learn French. Keane was the first captain in Canadiens history who spoke no French, and the francophone Montreal media made a big deal out of it.

The Canadiens liked the potential of two of the young forwards on Lacroix's list: Andrei Kovalenko and Martin Rucinsky. Although Lacroix took immense satisfaction in keeping his dealings secret from the media, going to almost Nixonian lengths in his paranoia of the press, rumors ran rampant in Denver that Roy might soon join the Avalanche.

On December 5, the Avalanche played San Jose at McNichols, and between the first and second periods, *Denver Post* columnist Mark Kiszla and I climbed the stairs up to Lacroix's makeshift luxury box at the top of the arena. Through binoculars, Kiszla and I could see Lacroix talking on the phone through most of the first period, and our hunch was that he wasn't calling Domino's to order a pizza. Standing on top of the back row of seats, we shouted up to Lacroix to ask about a possible Roy trade. As he almost always did, Lacroix played dumb, saying, "I haven't heard." We both knew better, but without anything concrete, we couldn't really write much in the paper the next day. Still, the first paragraph of my December 6, 1995, story about the game, a 12-2 rout of the Sharks, read, "One thing is for sure: The Colorado Avalanche wouldn't have needed Patrick Roy last night."

At 3:30 a.m. EST, Lacroix and Houle agreed to a deal. At 6 a.m. the Avalanche put out a press release saying it had acquired Roy and Keane in exchange for Thibault, Rucinsky, and Kovalenko. On paper, it looked like the steal of the century. History would prove that it pretty much was.

The rest of the league, including Red Wings coach Bowman and general manager Jimmy Devellano, was stunned. Had Rejean Houle lost his marbles?

"We just hoped he'd be traded to a team out East that wasn't so formidable," Devellano said. "We had two pretty darn good goalies in Mike Vernon and Chris Osgood, so we weren't in the hunt for Roy. Maybe Roy was a little past his prime, and maybe he was a little bit of a dingbat, too, you know? But we knew he was a good goaltender. It just wasn't our need, so to speak, but maybe in hindsight we should have tried a little harder for him. We were responsible for making Colorado better, in a perverse kind of way."

Bowman was not pleased to learn the young, talented Avalanche had just added Roy. He was unhappier when he read that Keane was part of the deal.

"The worse part is, why did Montreal have to throw in Keane?" Bowman recalled. "I don't know why they would have to pay a premium. That was inexperience on the trading front by Montreal, and emotion. They should have just been patient. They never really recovered, until [goalie Jose] Theodore came along. Houle bypassed Detroit, because he knew we had Vernon. But it put Colorado over the top."

Roy, 30 at the time, thrived on proving people wrong. He absolutely loved it when somebody said something negative about him. It gave him something to dedicate himself to, to make the doubters admit they were wrong.

One of the things being whispered was that the Red Wings had his number, not only with the 11-1 thrashing that drove him out of Montreal, but a later regular-season game with Colorado in which Detroit beat him, 7-0.

Detroit had exposed Roy as washed up, the whisperers went. They would be silenced by season's end.

62 Wins—For Nothing

Patrick Roy did look finished after Detroit's 7-0 whitewash on March 22, 1996, at the Joe. It was Colorado's third straight loss to Detroit after the opening-night win. With the playoffs only a few weeks away, any thought that the Avalanche might be able to beat Detroit in the postseason seemed absurd.

On the short bus ride back to Detroit's Atheneum Hotel, the team bus got stuck in traffic. In a foul mood already, Avs coach Marc Crawford told the bus driver to open the door. He stormed out, and the rest of the team joined him in hoofing it the last couple of blocks.

At 34, Crawford had been the youngest coach in the NHL when he was hired by Pierre Lacroix to coach the Nordiques in 1994. Again, his looks were deceiving; he had the face of a choirboy, but the mouth of an angry truck driver. He did not suffer fools gladly, which he had to do a lot with the Denver media in the early days.

I still remember the sting of his dismissive chuckle when he noticed I called high-powered agent Don Meehan "Tom Meehan" in my very first story from Avalanche training camp. Although Denver had long had college hockey, had once had an NHL team, and had a championship International League team in 1994–95, most in the Denver media didn't know a wrist shot from a wrist watch when the Avs came. Thinking back to some of my first stories—despite having grown up watching Bobby Orr and covering the teams I did—I was probably one of them. You have to watch the game on a night-in, night-out basis to truly know the sport's many nuances.

Crawford would sometimes roll his eyes at the neophyte questions he'd receive. One time during the 1996–97 season, an older reporter who worked for an obscure radio station in town asked, "What about Uwe?" during Crawford's postgame talk, after a game in which defenseman Krupp had no bearing one way or the other on the outcome.

"What *about* Uwe?" Crawford asked back rather snappishly, and the reporter slumped in his chair, unable to follow up.

Despite his youth and lack of NHL coaching experience, Crawford made clear to his players that none would take advantage of it. He had no fear of tearing into established players and, with perhaps the exception of Roy, gave no special treatment. After one early Avs practice when Kovalenko was still with the team, he was literally chased into the dressing room by a cursing Crawford over his lack of work ethic. At one practice after a loss, Crawford went down the roster and summed up their performances: "No heart," Crawford told defenseman Adam Foote; when Adam Deadmarsh's name came up, Crawford said, "Deader—no-show."

Crawford was born on February 13, 1961, in Belleville, Ontario, and grew up in Cornwall. His father, Floyd, played junior and some minor pro hockey and later coached in the Ontario Hockey League with Cornwall and Guelph.

Crawford got his scrappy side growing up in a family of eight other brothers and sisters, where there literally were fights for the last piece of chicken or biscuit on the dinner table. This propelled him, despite having less skill than many players, to a 176-game NHL career, all with the Vancouver Canucks. Crawford played for the Canucks from 1981–87, scoring 19 goals and 50 points, but never spent a full season there. Each season saw some time playing for Vancouver's minor-league club, the Fredericton Express of the American Hockey League.

After his playing career ended with the Milwaukee Admirals of the International Hockey League in 1989, Crawford was hired as head coach of Cornwall in the OHL, where his father had coached only four years before. Despite a combined two-year record of 47-80-5, Crawford's coaching ability caught the eye of Toronto Maple Leafs GM Cliff Fletcher, who hired him away to serve as head coach of Toronto's top farm team, St. John's of the AHL. After three winning seasons, including one trip to the Calder Cup Finals in 1992, Crawford was considered a rising young star in the coaching ranks. New Nordiques GM Lacroix made Crawford his first hire, a risky move in a primarily francophone city.

Crawford's first season was delayed because of a lockout, and he spent the off time learning French. In only a couple of months, he became proficient enough to do interviews with the French media, which was appreciated by them and the Nords' rabid fans.

Crawford won NHL Coach of the Year honors in 1995 after leading Quebec to a 30-13-5 record in the shortened season, first overall in the Eastern Conference. The Nordiques were eliminated in the first round of the playoffs, however, by the defending Cup champion New York Rangers.

Even with Roy and Keane on the Avalanche, most experts said it would be a good season for Colorado if it could win one playoff round in 1996, two at best. The Avs had a respectable 31-18-6 record with Roy after his acquisition, but the team was still considered too green and a little soft, with too many questions surrounding Roy's current ability.

Besides, nobody was going to beat the Red Wings.

Coached by the inimitable Bowman, Detroit was a deep, balanced team that destroyed the competition in the regular season. Its 62 wins remains the most in NHL history. The Wings had the "Russian Five" of Igor Larionov, Viacheslav Fetisov, Slava Kozlov, Sergei Fedorov, and Vladimir Konstantinov. The five were frequently on the ice together, and sometimes it was a sight to behold. Brought up with the Russian hockey values of sharing the puck and the ability to curl away from defensive pressure, they sometimes resembled hockey's version of the Harlem Globetrotters and their famous keep-away acts. The best of the five was probably Fedorov, a flashy, good-looking center who dated and briefly married tennis heartthrob Anna Kournikova. Fedorov won the Frank J. Selke Trophy that season as the league's top defensive forward and led the team in scoring with 107 points.

"It was sick sometimes," Red Wings goalie Mike Vernon said. "I mean, there were times when I could have left the net and gone out for a pizza, and the other team still wouldn't have the puck from those guys when I got back."

The Wings had eight players with 70 or more points and seven who scored 20 or more goals. Vernon and Chris Osgood combined for eight shutouts, and won the William M. Jennings Trophy, awarded each year to the goalies of the team that allowed the fewest goals. The team also had the intangible of hunger on its side, having lost in the Finals the year before.

Along with loads of talent and desire, however, there was also pressure—not only to win the Cup for the first time since 1955, but to break the record of 60 regular-season wins set by Bowman's 1976–77 Canadiens.

With the regular season winding down, Bowman, in his zeal for the record, refused to cut back much on his top players' minutes. The top seed for the Western Conference playoffs had long been sewed up by Detroit, but Bowman kept pushing as if the Wings were fighting for the eighth and final spot.

The Avalanche had had the number-two seed long secured as well, and went into the playoffs with its best players better rested.

Even though they eventually met in the Western Conference finals, neither the Red Wings nor the Avalanche had an easy time in their first two playoff rounds. The Wings were extended to six games in the first round by the Winnipeg Jets, a franchise in its last days in the city. Roaring, white-clad crowds at the Winnipeg Arena, desperate to keep their team from leaving, spurred the Jets on to victories in Games 3 and 4 to tie the series before Detroit won the last two.

In the second round, the Wings ran into a hot St. Louis Blues team, which had a pair of forwards named Wayne Gretzky and Brett Hull. Detroit won the first two games, but veteran goalie Jon Casey, playing in place of injured Grant Fuhr, led the Blues to three straight wins, with Game 6 back at the Kiel Center. Detroit dug deep to pull out a 4-2 win, but St. Louis appeared to have the Wings on the ropes in Game 7. Casey had blanked Detroit through regulation, and the winning goal appeared to be on the stick of Blues veteran Shayne Corson with seven minutes left in the first overtime, but his point-blank chance was stopped by Osgood.

The game went through a scoreless first overtime, and, perhaps because of the regular-season record push, some of the Wings were starting to look out of gas. That's when Wings captain Steve Yzerman came to the rescue, stealing a puck from the Great One, Gretzky, and beating Casey with a slap shot to the stick side, from just inside the blue line, at 1:15 of the second overtime. The Joe's familiar loud, long foghorn blast reverberated, and the Wings were on to the conference finals. Bowman was one of the first people on the ice, running to the pile of players on Yzerman and showing much more emotion than usual.

In Denver, meanwhile, the Avalanche battled through two tough rounds itself. The first, against Vancouver, was marked by Canucks coach Pat Quinn saying the Avalanche's defense had some "marshmallows back there," and a confrontation between Crawford and Avs tough guy Chris Simon at practice following a Game 2 loss at home. Before the series, Avs coaches handed out individual handbooks to players, spelling out what was expected of them. Simon's made clear that it was assumed he would outplay Vancouver's enforcers, Gino Odjick and Joey Kocur, who combined for fewer than Simon's 16 goals in the regular season. Plus, Simon was not to let either get away with any "liberties" against his teammates. But Odjick scored the game-winning goal in Game 2, and laid more than a couple heavy hits against Avs players. At practice, with the team gathered around, Crawford laced into Simon, saying, "Either you're with us or you're not, Chris. What will it be?" Simon, whose fierce, long-haired Ojibway Indian looks and scary left-hand punch hid a shy, sensitive nature, later sank to his knees and buried his head into the ice, looking like he might be crying.

But Simon and the Avs recovered. Thanks to a fortunate call from referee Paul Stewart in Game 5, which gave Colorado a 5-on-3 power-play advantage it used to tie the game in the third period, the Avs beat the Canucks in six games.

The second round brought on the veteran Chicago Blackhawks, and a weird, wild series ensued. Chicago won Game 1 in overtime, which led to immediate skepticism that Roy—who wasn't great in the Vancouver series—could win the big OT games anymore. The Avs won Game 2, but lost Game 3 in OT in Chicago after defenseman Craig Wolanin turned the puck over to Chicago's Sergei Krivokrasov, who scored on a shot that deflected off Wolanin's stick.

In the Avs dressing room, Claude Lemieux tore into Wolanin in front of the team. "Get your fuckin' head out of your ass," he yelled, which produced the opposite effect in Wolanin than Lemieux was trying to get.

"I wanted to rock the boat," Lemieux recalled. "I felt that was a good time to rock the boat. Sometimes you have to have some guys go at each other in the locker room to wake the whole team up. Usually hockey guys after a game like that will respond in a much more aggressive way, and get in an F-you contest. But it didn't happen that way."

Indeed, Wolanin, an exceedingly warm and friendly person, dissolved into tears in his stall. He broke down again in televised interviews soon after. If, as the movie saying went, there was no crying in baseball, there surely was no crying in hockey. Fair or not, Wolanin's emotional reaction did not sit well with some in the macho hockey environment, including the steely Roy and Crawford. Wolanin would never play again for the Avs, watching the rest of the playoffs in street clothes.

"I have mixed feelings, but those are the things sometime that need to happen. I remember [Devils captain] Scott Stevens and me getting emotional just before a playoff run in New Jersey, in practice at the morning skate," Lemieux said. "We went toe-to-toe in the room, verbally and almost swinging at each other. But that got us closer than ever, because we had to spend time together to work things out. That got the whole team closer. But Woolly is a great guy, a fantastic guy, and I obviously felt really bad about it right after."

The Avalanche won the next three games to capture the series, two of which went to OT. In the triple-OT Game 4, the Avs again benefited from a referee's curious judgment; this time, veteran Andy Van Hellemond, who had blown a call the year before that cost Quebec a playoff game, perhaps tried to atone for it with a non-call when Chicago's Jeremy Roenick broke in alone on Roy in the first OT. Roenick was blatantly hooked from behind by Colorado defenseman Sandis Ozolinsh, an obvious infraction that probably should have resulted in a penalty shot. Instead, Van Hellemond swallowed his whistle, and the Avs went on to win on a Joe Sakic goal against Chicago's standout goalie Ed Belfour.

Belfour would miss Game 5 under mysterious circumstances. The team said he was ill with the flu, but several players said the real culprit was food poisoning from some bad lyonnaise potatoes eaten the night before at Denver's Morton's of Chicago (the restaurant said it had no other complaints from patrons that night). The Avs lit up substitute goalie Jeff Hackett for an easy win, and won game 6 in OT on an Ozolinsh goal. Chicago's best defenseman, Chris Chelios, missed Game 6 after being injected with Novocain in the wrong spot in his leg by the team doctor. Chelios tried to shake off the numbness by skating before each period, but couldn't do it. The Blackhawks hilariously listed Chelios as being out all night with an "equipment problem."

Lining the streets of Detroit prior to the 1996 Red Wings–Avalanche conference final were banners proclaiming "I Want Stanley." The Red Wings even crafted a playoff theme song with that title, based on the 1982 hit "I Want Candy" by Bow Wow Wow.

Downtown Detroit had seen its population cut roughly in half from a height of about 1.85 million during the industrial boom of the 1950s. It was a far stranger sight along Michigan Avenue to see a storefront with people inside instead of boards across the windows. A city once teeming with jobs and business saw the majority move to the suburbs, taking the educated, more prosperous workers with them. "White flight," while a racially insensitive term, is nevertheless an accurate one to describe what happened in Detroit. In 1967, five days of rioting that left 43 dead and 1,189 injured stained the city's image and accelerated the population exodus. According to the 2000 census, 81.6 percent of Detroit's population was African American, with a median family income of $39,480. For whites in Michigan, the average was $71,460, and in the 1950s whites made up roughly half of Detroit's population.

African Americans traditionally have made up only a fraction of hockey's player and fan base, but that didn't stop Wings owner Mike Ilitch from dubbing Detroit "Hockeytown" in 1995. While many of Detroit's downtown residents at the time didn't care about hockey and couldn't name one Red Wings player (our paper, in fact, did an informal survey confirming it), the sport was booming around the rest of the state. By 2004 nearly 4,000 Michigan high school students played on varsity hockey teams, and other youth and adult leagues had waiting lists in the hundreds.

Local television ratings for Red Wings games, helped some by the hockey-loving population across the Detroit River in Windsor, Ontario, were often the highest of any team in the NHL. National TV ratings in Michigan were equally high.

By Game 1 against Colorado, Hockeytown was in full infatuation mode with its Wings and dismissive of their opponent's chances. So too, it seemed, were Red Wings players.

Before the series began, Detroit's Larionov was asked by reporters what was the biggest thing to fear about Colorado. From the shower room nearby, a voice said, "Barry Beck," a reference to the former Colorado Rockies defenseman.

"They didn't respect us," Keane said. "They were pretty arrogant in that series. Even when we'd beat them, they'd just kind of snicker and think it was luck."

For a team that wasn't supposed to give them any trouble, however, the Red Wings seemed to go to some bizarre lengths to rattle the Avalanche. Lacroix said the team was subjected to "bomb-sniffing" dogs by arena personnel on the team bus prior to practices and Game 1 of the series.

Then the Avs were awakened at 3 a.m. the day of Game 1—an afternoon game—by a fire alarm at the team's hotel. Not only that, a fresh coat of paint—and all its noxious fumes—awaited the team in the visitors' dressing room.

Lacroix suspected Bowman was behind every inconvenience.

"To me, that's when the rivalry really started," Lacroix said. "For some reason, they seemed very worried about us, to go to those extremes. They wanted us to respond or get mad and lose our cool. I said, 'No, we're not going to even let them know we cared about it, like nothing happened.' I think that threw them off instead."

The Red Wings took a quick 1-0 lead in Game 1 on a goal by Paul Coffey, an offensive defenseman who still had blazing speed at age 34. It looked like another blowout in the making for the Red Wings against Roy, but it didn't turn out that way—thanks in part to Coffey.

In the second period with the score still 1-0, Avalanche third-line center Stephane Yelle made a harmless-looking crossing pass from the corner to the front of the Detroit net. Nobody but Coffey and Wings goalie Osgood was anywhere near the puck. All Coffey had to do was take the puck and he'd find vast open space to skate with it. But the three-time winner of the Norris Trophy inexplicably shot the puck right into his own net. It was as if he'd temporarily forgotten which team he played for, because there was nothing accidental looking about his shot.

The goal stunned the sellout crowd, and Coffey looked up at the roof with a disbelieving look. He would later say he didn't realize he was so alone in front of the net that he felt hurried to clear the puck away. This was the kind of break the Avs were looking for, and they started taking it to Detroit. While the Wings were a record-setting team at the time, the Avs coaching staff felt Detroit had a couple of exploitable weaknesses: the first was the team's defense, which Colorado thought had some age issues. D-men such as Coffey, Fetisov, and Mike Ramsey were well into their 30s and still logged regular minutes.

The Avs also felt they could wear down Detroit physically with continuous hitting and younger, fresher legs. Still, nobody gave the Avs a real shot at victory.

"We knew we'd have to play perfect games to beat them," Colorado assistant coach Joel Quenneville said. "But we [coaches] got a chance to watch their Game 7 with St. Louis at Joe Louis Arena. I think we picked up a few things that helped us."

Indeed, Colorado had five days off before the start of the series, while Detroit had only two. A tone was set early in Game 1, when young Avalanche star center Peter Forsberg delivered a devastating hit on Swedish countryman Nicklas Lidstrom. Other Avs such as Simon and defenseman Adam Foote hit anything that moved with a winged wheel on the front.

The Avalanche took a 2-1 lead on a goal by Deadmarsh, one of the many recent talented first-round draft picks harvested from the franchise's awful years. Deadmarsh had no fear of anything or anybody, which is partly why his career was cut short years later after numerous concussions from fights and big hits. Deadmarsh literally dove into a pile of bodies in front of Osgood to score the go-ahead goal, a lead that appeared safe with Roy in net and Colorado on the power play in the third period.

But Coffey scored a short-handed goal, and Wings fans believed order was restored. In fact, Larionov looked to have the game won in the last minute of regulation, but his doorstep chance was blocked by Roy's diving save to send the game to overtime. Then, with 2:29 left in the OT, Keane fired a long, innocuous-looking wrist shot at Osgood. It would be an easy save, and the game would go to another OT. Except the puck somehow eluded Osgood's glove and fluttered to the back of the net. It was the kind of goal the otherwise solid Detroit netminder would have an unfortunate tendency to allow throughout his career.

Nobody could believe this was the shot that ended it. Years later, Keane would take more credit for the goal than his surprised expression at the time showed.

"That shot was heavy," Keane said, laughing. "I mean, heavy."

Keane and Roy shared a long hug afterward. For both, it was their first victory over the Red Wings all season, after five ugly losses. The two had become exceptionally close, driving to the rink together and having each other's families over for dinner.

Both men were also exceptionally superstitious. Roy never, ever skated on the blue lines on the ice, always doing a little hippety-hop over them while heading to the dressing room between periods. He skated over the goal lines marking his crease after each period, and always had the same pregame meal: steak, mashed potatoes, and maybe a little salad. He also slowly skated from the blue line to his net before every game, mentally shrinking the goal down to the size of a postage stamp.

During the first round against Vancouver, Roy and Keane were driving to McNichols for a game and Keane accidentally knocked over an orange pylon set up in the players' lot. The Avalanche won the game, so of course it had to be the lucky fallen pylon that did it. For the rest of the playoffs, Keane had to knock over a pylon with his truck before every home game.

For the playoff Avs of 1996, there were other acts of divine providence. Along with some fortunate calls, they benefited from injuries to some of their opponents' best players. In the Vancouver series, superstar forward Pavel Bure was out with a broken leg. Against Chicago, Chelios and Belfour missed key games, and talented winger Tony Amonte was lost early in the series to a knee injury after being checked into the boards by Foote.

In Game 1, Detroit lost captain Yzerman in the second period to what was listed as a groin strain (in keeping with the playoff tradition of misleading the media—and the opposing team—about the nature of a player's injury, the injury was more to his knee than groin). Yzerman missed Game 2 as well.

Colorado took advantage of Yzerman's absence with a 3-0 win to take a stunning two-game series lead. Roy was magnificent, making 35 saves, while Osgood was beaten on shots by Sakic, Ozolinsh, and fourth-line winger Warren Rychel.

For the first time in the rivalry, some smack talk was hurled between the teams and cities following the game. It was no surprise that it was started by longtime *Denver Post* sports columnist Woody Paige, a Tennessee native and distant relative of legendary Confederate cavalry general Nathan Bedford Forrest. Paige spoke with an easygoing southern twang, but his written words could bite to the core.

"The Wingnuts here traditionally throw slimy octopi on the ice. Last night they should have been hurling calamari. The Avalanche reduced the Detroit Red Wings to fried squid. Pass the cocktail sauce," wrote Paige. "If the Avalanche can win two games in Denver . . . the Red Wings will become The Greatest Gagging, Heaving, Choking Team In The National Hockey League."

"Like I said all along, the playoffs are the playoffs. It's totally different," Roy told reporters. "It's a different season."

Suddenly, any psychological advantage the Wings thought they had on Roy was gone. Bowman knew it, but he couldn't help taking a shot at Roy in hopes of flustering him. At this point, Bowman hadn't yet learned not to give Roy any bulletin-board material to use as motivation.

"It's not like there were any great saves," said Bowman, which was hardly true.

"It's not like there were any great shots," countered Paige.

The Avalanche as a whole was starting to get that championship feeling. Crawford knew he had two of the best young centers in the NHL in Sakic and Forsberg, and proven veterans who loved big-game pressure in Roy and Lemieux.

Lemieux hadn't yet severely injured Kris Draper, and was still a game away from punching Kozlov and earning a suspension, but he was already a distracting nuisance to the Wings with his play on the ice and his words off it.

"I don't think there's anyone in here shocked that we won the first [two games]," said Lemieux, which wasn't exactly true. "And it wasn't a shock last year [with the Devils]. It was a shock to the people here and it was a shock to the Detroit press, but it wasn't a shock to us and it isn't now, either."

Shocking or not, the Avalanche closed out Detroit with wins in two of the next four games, including a crucial 4-2 win in Game 4. Lemieux watched in street clothes, still simmering from being accosted two nights before by Bowman in the parking lot.

"Scotty Blowhard didn't hold up the Dead Things' bus last night," wrote Paige in the *Post* after the Game 4 Colorado win. "Coach Blowhard may be able to control the spineless, gutless National Hockey League, but he can't Zamboni the Avalanche. The NHL suspended Lemieux for last night's game and fined him a thousand bucks—because of Blowhard's complaints. But all Blowhard did was cause an avalanche. With an aroused, passionate crowd and a Colorado team intent on becoming Avengers, Blowhard and the Dead Things were drawn, quartered and run out of Denver. Octopi R Squared. Blowhard may lord over the Detroit media—which was drooling over the Dead Things as the greatest team in the history of hockey until it lost two straight at home to the Avalanche. But he is nothing but a losing Chinook windbag in Colorado."

Even after losing Game 3, Roy felt he had gotten inside the heads of Detroit's players. The one he distracted the most was probably the veteran Dino Ciccarelli. Known for his ability to stand in front of the net and withstand physical abuse to score goals, Ciccarelli was a master of tip-ins and screens of the goalie and an overall pain in the neck.

As usual, Ciccarelli had himself planted in front of the net when Roy decided to be just as big a pain in the neck to him—or, more accurately, to his groin.

As the series wore on, Roy occasionally jabbed his stick into Ciccarelli's crotch from behind. Surprisingly, the referees let him get away with it, which infuriated Ciccarelli to the point of swinging back. All that did was send Ciccarelli to the penalty box, which figuratively got him off his game while literally getting him out of it. Ciccarelli was assessed a team-high 12 penalty minutes in the series, most from retaliation on Roy.

As the final minutes ticked down in Colorado's 4-1 Game 6 series-clinching victory, the crowd at McNichols became incredibly loud.

"Loudest in a building I've ever heard it in hockey," said Quenneville years later.

After the game, Bowman credited the Avalanche, but also the Denver media, for the team's success.

"You people are really behind your team," Bowman said.

The worst thing a sportswriter can be called is a "homer" (it was a charge that would nevertheless be hurled back and forth among Detroit and Denver writers several times in the future), but Bowman seemed to truly believe the Denver press played a role in the victory.

"Feel the tremble. Hear the roar. Look out! There's a roar in the Rocky Mountains. It's the Avalanche," wrote Paige.

When the season ended and the Avalanche got the first major pro sports championship in Denver history, many believed some kind of reconciliation would happen between Lemieux and Draper.

But a couple of things exacerbated the situation, and it didn't happen. After Lemieux's relatively light suspension and subsequent Colorado sweep of Florida in the Finals, bitter feelings ran deeper among Red Wings players and fans. Perhaps a loss by Colorado, caused in part by Lemieux's suspension, would have cooled the anger among Winged Wheel faithful.

But first Lemieux's smiling with the Stanley Cup for a second year in a row, followed by his public lack of concern about Draper's condition, fueled Detroit's rage to where Draper's mother and a Michigan legislator got into the act.

Draper's mother, Mary Lynn, threatened to file a civil suit against Lemieux on her son's behalf, and Michigan state representative Kirk Profit tried to get the Colorado attorney general to file assault charges. Neither legal threat came to fruition.

Feeling everybody was going overboard with the situation, Lemieux responded with snickering sarcasm.

"That was their best scenario because they had something to talk about all summer instead of why they lost," Lemieux said, after playing for Canada in the 1996 World Cup of Hockey tournament. "Detroit has this incident in mind more than their losses two years in a row."

Lemieux was hounded by the subject. At the World Cup, he drew scorn from much of the Canadian media, including barbs from Don Cherry and longtime *Vancouver Province* columnist Tony Gallagher, known for his poison pen. Lemieux countered Gallagher, calling him a "skinny piece of shit."

"It just shows his disappointment of Vancouver not being able to go any further and another Canadian club not going past the first round of the playoffs (last season). Instead of writing what he's really mad about, he writes about me," Lemieux said.

What probably enraged the Red Wings most, though, were comments by Lemieux that he "made Draper famous" with the incident, and that "nobody would ever have heard about him" otherwise.

"That was what really did it, those kinds of things he said," Darren McCarty recalled. "Just the lack of remorse, the lack of any sympathy at all."

The paradox of it all was that few NHL players were as sympathetic to the fallen and disadvantaged in life as Claude Percy Lemieux.

Pepe

Born in Buckingham, Quebec, on July 16, 1965, Claude Lemieux grew up in the northwestern Quebec town of Mont Laurier, bordering the Lievre River. The river and surrounding forest made Mont Laurier a favored tourist destination, and the town had fairly healthy agricultural and transportation economies. The rumble from mighty steel logging trucks competed with the mooing of dairy cows, whose milk yielded some of the finest cheeses in Canada.

Little Claude was the second child of Gabriel and Rachel Lemieux. To feed his family, Gabriel worked as a truck driver six or seven days a week, hauling logs and whatever else the three or four local companies he worked for could stuff in his truck. Rachel worked as the manager of the small restaurant inside Mont Laurier's hockey arena. Hot chocolate, grilled cheese, and hot dogs on grilled buns were the restaurant's specialties among a clientele whose appetites were big and their tips small.

"We didn't have much," Lemieux said. "It was a below middle-class upbringing. We were poor. It wasn't to the point of starving or having decent clothes, but we had one family vacation in 15 years."

That vacation, Lemieux remembers, was to a campground in Quebec not far from where Gabriel was born. The family took their meager savings, packed their lone beat-up automobile and mostly spent the vacation visiting relatives. At the beginning and end of the trip, they camped in the rugged woods along the river, roasting hot dogs on sticks and telling stories.

"It was a big deal for all of us, but especially my father," Lemieux said.

The only member of the family who couldn't make it was Lemieux's younger brother, Serge. Stricken with cerebral palsy at birth, Serge Lemieux would never know his brothers, Claude and Jocelyn, or his sister, Carol. Unable to give Serge the kind of care he needed, his parents reluctantly committed him to government care.

Young Claude would put on a brave face and try to smile his way through the semiannual family visits to Serge's barren, institutionalized setting, but inside his heart broke in a million pieces every time.

"He couldn't talk, he couldn't walk," Lemieux said. "We visited him every year at Christmas and Easter. Those moments should have been happy, but they weren't. It felt awful looking at him. You'd ask yourself, 'Why is he like this?'"

Claude wondered how he could be so big and strong, much more so than other kids his age or even older, and his brother so utterly incapacitated. He would never understand this mysterious way of life, and forever feel guilty it was he who had been so physically blessed, but not Serge. Throughout his NHL career, Lemieux tried to compensate for his guilt with countless unpublicized visits to sick kids, often doling out large sums of money to help. In 1997 Lemieux visited the bedside of a 12-year-old Denver girl named Brittany Lamb, who suffered severe injuries in a car accident that claimed the life of her aunt. Lemieux had heard the girl was a fan of his, and one day, only a couple of hours before the Avalanche were to play the hated

Red Wings, he sat and told stories to her and left a roomful of gifts. Later, he scored two goals, "in her honor."

Lemieux was heavily involved in various DARE antidrug programs in the cities he played, and in 1999, following the Columbine High School shooting massacre, he paid for various household services of a grieving family.

He always knew that he couldn't help others if he didn't take care of himself first, though, which is why Lemieux maintained a maniacal zeal for personal success.

Hanging out at his mother's restaurant after school, sneaking the uneaten French fries from departed diners' plates, Claude noticed the skaters, young and old, on the arena ice. It looked easy and fun, and it wasn't long before he pestered his mom for skates of his own.

On the tight family budget, new skates were out of the question. But Rachel scraped up the five dollars necessary for a pair of used skates from a five-and-dime store and by age six Claude was a regular on the many outdoor shinny games in his neighborhood. The local boys would play all day on a favorite pond, whose waters were frozen by November or so and would stay that way until late March.

Almost immediately, Claude stood out from the rest. As a child, he had thick, strong legs that powered him ahead of others in races for the puck. But it was not at forward that he first started out as a player; he was a defenseman until age 13.

"But I was always trying to score goals, always way up the ice. It made the coaches figure I'd be better off up front," Lemieux said.

Lemieux played for an organized team at around age seven, in a local outdoor league. He again needed hockey equipment that was beyond his parents' financial reach. Luckily, some neighbors had kids a little older, and the Lemieux borrowed and bought their used equipment. Within a year or two, Lemieux was good enough to make the traveling team, quite a plum for someone so young. The travel wasn't far for most league games, but it was for some of the tournaments in which Lemieux's team was invited to participate.

"I remember the tryouts as an 8-year old. I thought I'd make the house league, and within two or three games I got a call from the travel coach and he said they'd been watching me," Lemieux said. "That coach was the father of Jose Charbonneau, drafted by Montreal two years after [in 1985] I was drafted by Montreal."

All the Mont Laurier boys dreamed of being future Canadiens. Lemieux, however, believed it was destiny. He never lacked confidence as a player; one day, while playing street hockey with brother Jocelyn and others from the neighborhood, Lemieux bragged that one day he would drive a white Cadillac with money from his first NHL check. (He chose a white Grand Prix instead.)

Lemieux found that opponents often were intimidated by his size—and the size of his mouth. He knew almost by instinct who could take his verbal taunts and who couldn't. Those who couldn't, he'd zero in on. The more players he could mentally get off their games, he thought, the better his team's chances of winning. It would be a trait he'd take with him all through his NHL career, although sometimes it would backfire comically, such as the time in New Jersey he yelled at Philadelphia Flyers captain Eric Desjardins, "What's that 'C' for, 'selfish'?"

Indeed, Lemieux was not blessed with superb English skills, which he knew he'd probably need someday for a career in the NHL. He was one of the worst students in his high school English classes; he had a hard enough time with his native French. But Lemieux would eventually learn to speak fine English, much of which he credits from watching *The Price Is Right* in his later teen years.

Lemieux was not as bad a student in other subjects, such as

math. Like his father, he was also good with his hands fixing things, especially cars and trucks.

"My dad was always in the shop working on cars, so I would hang out with him and learn from him," he said.

Lemieux even took a few professional courses in auto mechanics, just in case the hockey thing didn't work out.

But it would. At 17 Lemieux was good enough to play for the Trois-Rivieres Draveurs of the Quebec Major Junior Hockey League. That meant leaving home and living with a billet, or host family, in Saint Bruno. Living with billet families is a long tradition for Canadian major junior players, who are too young to live on their own, and couldn't, anyway, on the modest salaries they are paid. Lemieux did not bother with high school in his year at Trois-Rivieres, which didn't thrill his parents. But he felt he needed to put all his focus on hockey, that schoolwork would only slow him down.

Lemieux was lucky; his billet family lived in a nice section of town, nice enough, in fact, that a few players from the Canadiens also lived there. One of their neighbors was Canadiens forward Pierre Mondou and down the street from him lived the team's former equipment manager, who was now a scout named Pierre Meilleur and who "bird-dogged" local players for the Canadiens.

"One of his best friends was Serge Savard, and the year I got drafted by Three Rivers, Serge became the GM of Montreal. It gave me a big advantage at being drafted by Montreal," Lemieux said.

After just one season with Trois-Rivieres, Lemieux was taken by the Canadiens in the second round (26th overall) of the 1983 NHL draft. Many players, when they are first drafted, become so overwhelmed by the unreality of it all that they never make it into the pros. Not Lemieux; he set a plan to make it full-time to the Canadiens within two or three years, and told himself over and over not to be awe-struck by Canadiens stars now sharing the same dressing room, such as Bob Gainey and Larry Robinson. You're just as good as anyone else, Lemieux reminded himself. No—better.

In the 1983–84 season, the Canadiens played Lemieux eight games, in which he scored one goal and one assist. The goal came in Buffalo, one Lemieux doesn't remember well because "it was a crappy goal, a tip-in or something where I didn't even know I scored until I got to the bench."

Lemieux spent the rest of the season with Verdun of the QMJHL, scoring 41 goals in 51 games. Some of those goals were scored on a skinny netminder named Patrick Roy of the Granby Bisons, a team with a terrible defense that sometimes allowed 60 or 70 shots a game. Roy, in fact, faced an average of 43.4 shots a game for the Bisons that season.

"I loved playing against them. We'd pepper them," Lemieux said.

Lemieux thought the big year at Verdun and his eight solid games with Montreal would all but guarantee a full-time roster spot with the Canadiens the following training camp, but it didn't happen that way. He didn't make a great showing at camp, and was sent back to Verdun. He played only one game for Montreal in 1984–85, getting an assist and seven penalty minutes. With Verdun, he scored a whopping 58 goals and 124 points in only 52 games, and it was clear that he was too good to be wasting his time in junior hockey anymore.

But Lemieux was worried about his hockey career for the first time in his life. He worried he didn't fit into the Canadiens' plans, especially for the 1985–86 season, that they had their minds set on sending him to their top AHL affiliate in Sherbrooke. Lemieux worried he might be buried in the minor-league system forever. Maybe he'd get some bad injury down there, and never make it to the NHL full-time.

Sure enough, Lemieux wasn't given much of a chance to make the Canadiens at training camp, and was shipped off to

Sherbrooke along with another Habs rookie—Patrick Roy. Players at Sherbrooke made an average of about $26,000 (CDN), a far cry from the big-money contracts Lemieux dreamed of as a kid. Still, he was getting paid to play hockey, and Lemieux vowed once and for all to show Canadiens management the error of their ways in not keeping him with the big club.

He averaged nearly a point a game in the regular season for Sherbrooke, and improved his defensive play with a more physical style. Sherbrooke went on to win the Calder Cup, with Roy winning MVP honors and Lemieux finishing runner-up. When Sherbrooke's season was over, the Canadiens recalled Lemieux and Roy toward the end of the NHL season.

Neither would ever look back. Lemieux played 10 games for Montreal, only getting one goal and two assists. But he impressed Canadiens coach Jean Perron with his better defense and grit, which Perron thought might be useful in the playoffs.

Lemieux and Roy were added to Montreal's playoff roster, and what followed was straight from the Canadian version of Hollywood. Lemieux scored in overtime in Game 7 on Mike Liut to knock Hartford out of the playoffs, then got an OT winner in Madison Square Garden to beat the Rangers in a game of the Prince of Wales Conference finals. Lemieux just kept scoring, finishing the playoffs with 10 goals and 16 points in 20 games.

Roy was even hotter in the Montreal net, going 15-5 with an amazing 1.92 GAA. The underdog Canadiens beat Calgary in six games for the Stanley Cup. Like at Sherbrooke just a couple months before, Lemieux probably would have been named MVP of the playoffs if not for Roy. He didn't care, though; with about $35,000 in bonus money from the AHL playoffs and another $60,000 or so from winning the Cup, Lemieux had a lot of unexpected money in his pocket. More important, his name would be on the Stanley Cup forever. So too, he hoped, would he be with the Canadiens for the rest of his playing days.

But he would spend the majority of the remainder of his long career with other teams.

It never really worked out for Lemieux in Montreal after that magical 1986 playoff run. He posted good scoring statistics for the Canadiens the following three seasons, but the Habs failed to win another Cup for their demanding fans. Perron was fired after the 1987–88 season, and Lemieux became frustrated with his successor as coach, Pat Burns.

"He just didn't think I should play as much as I wanted to play. I felt I should be on the power play, in penalty killing, not just my regular shift," Lemieux said. "I got tired, too, of the pressure of the media and everything else, and wanted a new challenge."

Lemieux wanted more of a leadership role with the Canadiens, perhaps even the captaincy left vacant when Gainey retired in 1989. Instead, Burns named Guy Carbonneau and Chris Chelios as co-captains. Lemieux was hurt by the snub, and his 1989–90 season was made worse by an abdominal injury that required surgery and limited him to 39 games and just eight goals. That season, Lemieux went to GM Savard and asked for a trade. Savard said he would try to deal him by the start of the following season's training camp.

On September 4, 1990, Lemieux was sent to the New Jersey Devils for Sylvain Turgeon. Lemieux saw in the Devils a young, up-and-coming team on which he could be a leader. He was out of the insane media pressure-cooker of Montreal, where it was not uncommon for media numbering in the double digits to travel with the team. For the first time in a few years he felt he could exhale a little.

"Everything in Montreal just always happened so slow, with

all that tradition attached to everything," he said. "It becomes stifling after a while to players. I thought it would be the perfect place, coming from near there and everything. But really, all that does is put all kinds of expectations on you from everybody, everything from winning every single game to getting tickets for a friend of a friend of a friend. I needed to break out on my own."

The 1990–91 Devils featured the newly acquired Lemieux along with three players who would later play with Detroit for several years—Brendan Shanahan, Slava Fetisov, and Doug Brown.

Of the three, Lemieux would grow closest to Shanahan. A rugged winger with leading-man looks and a wicked one-timer, Shanahan spent the first four years of his career in New Jersey. Taken second overall in the 1987 NHL draft, the native of Mimico, Ontario, was the kind of power forward coaches dreamed of. Shanahan had many Gordie Howe hat tricks in his career, and Lemieux instantly bonded with him.

Lemieux finished with a career-high 30 goals for New Jersey, and Shanahan scored 29. But the Devils had only a 32-33-15 record, and lost in the second round of the playoffs. Shanahan, who became a free agent at the end of the season, left for St. Louis.

Lemieux was upset the Devils didn't try to keep Shanahan, but GM Lou Lamoriello wouldn't budge on owner John J. Mc-Mullen's strict budget. Players who tried to use financial leverage from other teams when their contracts were up were always viewed with disdain by Lamoriello and McMullen. It was a sign of disloyalty—even though Lamoriello tried to have it both ways with many players: unless you took a big "hometown discount," you were gone, but where was the loyalty from management for a job well done?

Five years later, Lemieux and Shanahan were teammates again, this time on the Canadian World Cup team. Debbie Lemieux was pregnant, and they knew it would be a boy. But what to name the child?

"He told her that, you know, he played with this guy in New Jersey named Brendan and he liked the name," Shanahan recalled. "So, I got to know the whole family, and obviously I knew Claude well from New Jersey. He and I were good friends in New Jersey."

Without Shanahan, the Devils managed to improve, going 38-31-11 in 1991–92. In each of Lemieux's first three seasons with Jersey, however, the Devils never made it past the second round. It wasn't his fault, as he scored 10 goals in 19 playoff games those years and scored what would be his high-water mark for goals in the NHL—41—in 1991–92. By 1993–94 the Devils were a serious threat in the Eastern Conference. With an outstanding rookie goalie, Martin Brodeur, and the 1991 addition of rock-solid defenseman Scott Stevens, who came to New Jersey as compensation for Shanahan, the Devils by 1994 came within one game of making it to the Stanley Cup Finals. But a Stephane Matteau double-overtime goal in Game 7 of the conference finals for the New York Rangers knocked out New Jersey, and the team blew a 3-2 lead in a series made famous by the Rangers' Mark Messier guaranteeing a win in Game 6.

Not long after his marriage to Carol crumbled, Lemieux met Debbie on a double date with Devils teammate Mike Peluso. The two sensed an instant chemistry, and Lemieux phoned her for a date when he heard she and Peluso were no longer an item.

By now, Lemieux had a well-established reputation for being a pain to everyone not wearing his team's uniform (and occasionally to his own teammates, too). Opponents thought he was a "diver" on the ice, embellishing contact to draw penalties.

Sports Illustrated hockey writer Michael Farber wrote that Lemieux played two positions: "right wing and prone."

He was hated in Boston, not only for some big goals but for his constant heckling of star Bruins forward Cam Neely. In 1994 Neely had a bit role in the hit movie *Dumb and Dumber*, and the following season Lemieux yelled at Neely, "Which one were you, Dumb or Dumber?"

As bad as the taunts could sometimes be, Lemieux never meant anything too personal by them. In fact, he often sought out the players he was verbally nastiest toward to shake hands when the games were over. But on the ice, any and all of an opponent's personal life was fair game to be used as psychological warfare.

Lemieux took plenty of verbal abuse as well. His nickname was Pepe, a less-than-friendly reference to the 1950s Looney Tunes cartoon character Pepe Le Pew—a skunk with a French accent who, among other things, made the females run from his stench.

Lemieux also took a lot of kidding for his enormous head and face. He had a big, wide forehead and a voice that was even bigger. Early in Lemieux's career, when most NHL rinks had press boxes that hung directly over the ice a fairly short distance away, Lemieux's voice could clearly be heard by reporters. Whether he was calling for the puck or giving it to an opponent, Lemieux's pipes rang loudest. In fact, Lemieux loved to sing. He often sang current pop tunes in the showers, on the buses, or at karaoke bars. When he played in Denver, Lemieux liked to belt out songs at an upscale cabaret-style bar called Sing-Sing. Patrons remember Lemieux singing the 1998 Cher tune "Believe" with particular gusto.

Lemieux was one of the most impatient people ever. On the team bus, he would often fret that the driver was going too slow. When a traffic light turned yellow, Lemieux would yell, "Run it" and was anguished if the driver stopped. Like the

Holly Hunter character in *Broadcast News*, Lemieux obsessed over the quickest routes the bus driver could take to the rinks, often calling out directions.

Like many hockey players, Lemieux was a golf fanatic. On off-days on the road, he frequently played with Roy, an even bigger golf fanatic. Once on a rainy day in Southern California, Lemieux and Roy chartered a jet to play at a course in nearby Palm Springs for a match.

Coming from a poor background, Lemieux had the common tendency to overcompensate when he came into money. He spent great sums on things like cars and jewelry and was always on the lookout for a good stock tip—some of which didn't pan out. He constantly railed against the high taxation rate for earners in his income bracket, and any mention of US president Bill Clinton was enough to earn his wrath for the rest of the day.

But his 1995 Conn Smythe performance, marriage to Debbie, and trade to Colorado made 1996 a great year for Lemieux, and he was rewarded with a brand-new multiyear contract extension worth more than $2 million per season following his second straight Cup.

The 1996–97 season, however, would be one big headache for Lemieux—literally and figuratively. The Red Wings were out for two things: the Stanley Cup and some of Lemieux's blood.

"Pretty, but Not Gritty" No More

Kris Draper's first days following the hit from Claude Lemieux were spent at Detroit's Henry Ford Hospital. His broken jaw was wired shut, and it would stay so for five weeks. He was able to eat only through a straw, mostly protein shakes.

But in some ways he was lucky. The right orbital bone was not broken, as first feared, and doctors said there was no loss of vision. The fractures in his nose and cheekbones would heal, and his concussion symptoms gradually diminished. Draper was told he would play hockey again the following season, which brought palpable relief.

But his teammates and Red Wings fans remained angry at Lemieux. One of his most frequent visitors in the hospital was Darren McCarty.

"I was drinking then, so I might have said something like, 'I'll get him,' but I don't remember for sure," McCarty recalled. "But I do remember reading some of Lemieux's comments about it that summer. It was something you stuck in the back of your mind."

Of more concern to Red Wings management that summer

was how to bring the Stanley Cup back to Detroit. The Wings were gaining a reputation as a team that couldn't win the big ones. For that to change, coach Scotty Bowman thought, two changes had to be made: his team had to get bigger and tougher, and it had to start playing defense.

"I think people thought of the Red Wings then as pretty, but not gritty," McCarty said.

At training camp, the Wings promoted 6-foot-2, 225-pound defenseman Aaron Ward to a more regular role and gave more ice time to forward Martin Lapointe, a rugged winger with a talent for getting under opponents' skin.

But the big move made by Detroit for the 1996–97 season was the acquisition of Brendan Shanahan from the Hartford Whalers for Paul Coffey, Keith Primeau, and a first-round draft choice. The deal was consummated a few days into the season, on October 9, and would prove to be a coup for Bowman.

Getting Shanahan wasn't Bowman's first priority in the deal. Even though he wasn't the GM—Jim Devellano was—Bowman engineered the trade.

"It was to get rid of Coffey," he said. "He had a huge contract, and he wasn't the player he [once] was. But Mr. Ilitch really liked Primeau a lot. He was his kid. He didn't want to do anything. But I went in and told him, 'We may take a bit of a hit in the long run on Primeau, but getting rid of that contract might be the best thing that ever happened to you.' Shanahan was a big part of it, too."

The Wings no longer were a team of pretty skaters that lacked toughness and a great finisher. Shanahan was a pure goal scorer who could also grind along the boards and put home rebounds in front of the net.

Later in the season, the Wings signed veteran tough guy Joey Kocur, who was playing in a local beer league. Kocur's presence alone made the Wings a lot meaner. Meanwhile, the opposite was happening with the new archrival Avalanche. The team traded probably the league's premier enforcer, Chris Simon, to the Washington Capitals after he held out of training camp for more money. In his place came Brent Severyn, who had the physique and raw strength of a bodybuilder, but who hated fighting. Severyn would fight for the Avs, but it always seemed as if he was punching a time clock instead of his opponent. When his fights were over, he would race to the penalty box, appearing almost relieved.

The Red Wings may have solved their size and grit problems, but Bowman knew his team ultimately had been beaten the previous few years from a lack of defense. Namely, it didn't have a good enough system. Too many players, he thought, played hard at the offensive end only. At the top of his list was the captain, Steve Yzerman.

Bowman had been nagging at Yzerman to improve his defense since a lunch meeting with him following Detroit's shocking first-round playoff defeat to San Jose in 1994. Bowman still didn't think Yzerman was buying into his program following the Finals loss to the Devils, and whispers began to emanate from Detroit that Yzerman was on the trading block.

Bowman's former housemate and coaching partner in Pittsburgh, Pierre McGuire, heard the whispers and relayed them to management of his new team, the Ottawa Senators.

"We were the ones who proposed that deal to Detroit. It was going to be Yzerman for Alexei Yashin," said McGuire, then a pro scout with Ottawa. "I was sitting in the car with Brad Marsh, Ray Shero, [GM] Randy Sexton and myself. We had just watched our team play a preseason game, and we were driving back to Ottawa, and Marsh had been a teammate of Yzerman's, and at that time he had yet to win a Stanley Cup. The question asked to Marsh was whether Yzerman was a winner, and the answer was unequivocally yes. Can he help our franchise win a Cup, and the answer was yes. We all agreed we should explore this, and try to get him."

The deal never happened, however. "They'll deny it, but at the end of the day I think that was more to stimulate Steve than to really help the Ottawa Senators," McGuire said.

By the start of the 1996–97 season, perhaps still shocked that the Wings had even thought of trading him, Yzerman was finally ready to buy in to more of a two-way game. More important, he was ready to sell his teammates on Bowman's plan of a left-wing lock defensive system, basically a variation of the neutral-zone trap that was becoming in vogue in the NHL. Nobody was more respected—and feared—in the Detroit dressing room than Stevie Y, whose dark glare was all it took to get teammates in line.

But it may have been Red Wings goalie Mike Vernon who was most responsible for getting his teammates—and Bowman—to believe that the best way to win a championship was with defense. A former Stanley Cup winner with a keen analytical hockey mind, Vernon was never afraid to say what was on it.

"I went up to Scotty after one of the exhibition games my first year and I said, 'Scotty, you don't need a goalie, you need a system.' He said, 'What do you mean?'" Vernon recalled. "I said, 'Well the puck goes in the corner and everybody seems to go at it. It's like Mighty Mite hockey. All you need to do is just play a little zone defense.' I said, 'You got beat out last year because you didn't know how to play defensive hockey. Defensive hockey with the ability you have, I mean that's a no-brainer.' I think what he said to Steve was that we need a commitment to defense from the whole team, and I need you to buy into this and the team to buy into this. I think they both came to the realization they had to do this. I remember Stevie saying to me, 'We got beat out by San Jose last year because we just couldn't keep the puck out of our own end.' I said, 'Well, play a zone defense, it's simple, and try to take the middle of the ice away and keep everybody on the perimeter.' And Stevie was committed to that. He knew that. Then, everybody else bought into that, and we went on from there."

But could anybody beat the defending-champion Avalanche? For the first half of the season, the answer seemed a resounding no. By January 27, Colorado had won or tied 38 of its first 50 games, even with injuries to Lemieux and superstar Peter Forsberg.

In the second game of the season, at Dallas, Lemieux stepped in one of the many ruts in the terrible Reunion Arena ice and tore an abdominal muscle. As a result, he missed the first rematch between the Wings and Avs, November 13 in Detroit, a placid game won 4-1 by Colorado. Shanahan griped afterward that his team "can't show them that much respect," that they played like they were admiring the Avs' Stanley Cup on their bench.

Lemieux also missed the second meeting between the teams, December 17 in Denver, but the Wings didn't show much respect this time.

Alexei Gusarov was about the last player one would expect the Red Wings to target physically. A tall, wiry Russian whose parents had been residents of Leningrad during the German siege in World War II, Gusarov was a finesse defenseman who sometimes incurred the wrath of fans for playing too "soft."

Gusarov was a jokester who never would allow himself to be quoted in the papers but always promised reporters to "talk tomorrow." He smoked the occasional cigarette between periods, and would feign a lack of English comprehension to out-of-town reporters—then tell a joke in perfect English the next minute. Gusarov's real age was also something of a mystery; a parlor game among reporters was to joke that Gusarov could be seen in the background of various Russian hockey photos dating back to the time of Lenin.

Gusarov rarely hit anybody harder than with the most routine of checks, so it was a shock when the Avs defenseman was sent flying into the boards by Detroit's Lapointe in the December 17 game at McNichols. Lapointe probably outweighed Gusarov by 40 pounds and slew-footed him to get him off balance before shoving him into the glass.

Gusarov fell backward, hitting his head hard on the ice. The impact caused his tongue to roll inward, obstructing his airway. Gusarov's eyes also rolled back, giving him a sickening, ghostly look. Avalanche trainer Pat Karns first feared the worst when he got to him on the ice.

"His wrists and fingers were rolled back, a sure sign of possible brain damage," Karns said.

Luckily, Gusarov would suffer no lasting damage and resume his career. But Colorado's Rene Corbet also suffered a head injury in the game, after a hard hit into the boards from Detroit's Aaron Ward, and Avalanche GM Pierre Lacroix was furious after the game, even though his team won 4-3 on a tie-breaking goal by his son, Eric.

At McNichols, the visiting dressing room exited into a hallway that conjoined with one leading to the pressroom. Reporters could walk right past the dressing-room door and hear things between periods or after games they typically can't in today's modern arenas.

Lacroix was lurking between the pressroom and the Wings dressing room when he spotted Lapointe and unleashed a profane tirade in French to the francophone Lapointe. Lacroix broke off into a few sentences in English as well, which could be plainly heard by reporters down the hall.

The Red Wings, Lacroix shouted at Lapointe, "would never win a fucking game," a rather odd putdown against a high-powered team. He accused Lapointe of a cheap shot on Gusarov, and turned away yelling, "You're going to remember me, kid."

BLOOD FEUD

As he did, Red Wings associate coach Dave Lewis started toward Lacroix.

"Don't you fucking talk about our guy after what your fucking guy did," Lewis yelled, referring to Lemieux's hit on Draper.

Seeing Lewis blow up was nearly as surprising as the Wings going after Gusarov. Known throughout the league as one of the nicest men around—a tag that would be used against him nearly a decade later when he was fired as Red Wings head coach—Lewis's face turned beet red screaming at Lacroix. Arena security quickly stepped in to end the fracas, but it became clear that the Draper incident hadn't been forgotten by the Wings.

"It was very, very satisfying to come back and win and shove it up their ass, the way they played the game," said Colorado's Scott Young, whose goal with 9:12 left tied the game 3-3.

"As far as I'm concerned, they can't moan about the Draper hit anymore," said Avs defenseman Adam Foote.

But nothing was settled in the minds of Detroit players. Lemieux missed this game as well, still recovering from abdominal surgery. That night, Lemieux talked to *Post* columnist Woody Paige from his cell phone on the way to the game. His words did nothing to dim Detroit's hatred of him.

"I may have saved a lot of people's jobs with the Red Wings last year. I took the heat off Bowman. What happened with me diverted the attention in Detroit away from the team's downfall in the playoffs. All the Detroit press and the fans wanted to talk about was cheap shots. What if they were talking about their team? Scotty took the situation and ran with it. And they can't get over it," Lemieux said.

On January 4 against Philadelphia, Lemieux returned. The Avalanche was well on its way to the Presidents' Trophy for the NHL's best regular-season record—which had become something of a jinx in recent years, best exemplified by Detroit the previous two seasons. Colorado looked like a solid choice to break the jinx, though. Patrick Roy was superb in goal, finishing with a league-best 38 victories. Despite injuries to Joe Sakic and Forsberg that limited each to 65 games, the team just kept winning.

Detroit didn't seem as good anymore. The Red Wings would finish 10 points behind Dallas in the Central Division, winning 24 fewer games than the previous season. Detroit fans grumbled about goalies Mike Vernon and Chris Osgood, even though they would allow the fewest combined goals (197) in the Western Conference by season's end.

Vernon couldn't win the big ones anymore, critics said, while Osgood was too much of a flopper and not mentally tough enough. Star center Sergei Fedorov's goal production dropped by nearly half, from 56 in 1993–94 to 30, and he was "too soft." Bowman's coaching quirks were alienating his players, the griping went, and the Detroit media started to openly wonder if perhaps a new coach was the cure for the Wings' slide.

On March 16 the Red Wings traveled to Denver for a third meeting of the season with the Avalanche. For the first time since the hit on Draper, Lemieux would be on the ice against the Wings. The Denver and Detroit media hyped the game as a "showdown" and anticipated a bloodbath.

Draper's physical injuries had since healed; his psychological ones had not.

"The hardest part for me to handle is he never apologized or admitted I was in a vulnerable position," Draper said the day before the game. "If he'd said that, that would have gone a long way."

Draper remained bitter about what he felt was the light sentence given to Lemieux by Brian Burke and NHL commissioner Gary Bettman, saying, "(They) contacted my mother, which I appreciated because my mom had the hardest time handling this. But I still wouldn't give them the time of day."

Lemieux was not in a conciliatory mood the day before the game. He repeated some of his stock lines about the Red Wings exploiting the issue. He also noted Draper's subpar statistics at the time and wondered if he, too, was tiring of the attention.

"It's certainly not his seven goals, four assists and minus-9 that's going to get him attention," Lemieux said.

Upon hearing Lemieux's remarks, Draper responded, "That sickens me to hear that. The best thing for me to do is go out and have the best game of my career. I've been thinking about this game for a long time. I'm going to be nervous."

About the rivalry to that point, Draper added, "They hate us, and we hate Colorado. It's the best rivalry in pro sports right now."

The game was again won by the Avalanche, 4-2, which gave Colorado seven victories in its previous nine games with the Wings. There was indeed a confrontation between Lemieux and Draper. But it was hardly a bloodbath.

At 19:38 of the first period, the two became entangled by the side of the net after a whistle. With Lemieux's back turned, Draper reached over and pried his helmet off. The two exchanged words for about 20 seconds, but no punches were thrown.

"I said, 'If you want to settle the issue, let's do it now,'" Lemieux recalled. "Nothing happened. He didn't say anything. He wasn't going to do anything."

Both were given 10-minute misconducts and that was that; there were no major incidents afterward.

In the Avalanche dressing room, some players, including Lemieux, came close to openly mocking the Red Wings.

Denver Post columnist Mark Kiszla wrote, "The most hated man in Detroit walked away grinning. Claude Lemieux's head was squarely on his shoulders, not on a platter, as the Red Wings had prayed. A vengeful team and town waited 289 rancorous days to get Lemieux, and the biggest chunk the Wings could take out of the Colorado winger was a small scratch on his nose.

"'That's as much as they could've gotten out of me,' said Lemieux, absolutely no worse for wear after the Avalanche's 4-2 victory against Detroit on a Sunday night full of spite."

Kiszla wrote further, "Detroit so hates Lemieux it can taste the bile. But the Red Wings can't hurt him, can't intimidate him, can't touch him. So the motor mouths of the Motor City have sputtered to a stone-cold silence. After being reminded once again that the Avalanche can take Detroit's best shot and just skate away . . . it's a rivalry only in Detroit's spiteful dreams. The fact is the Red Wings can't find a way to beat Colorado with finesse or brawn. . . . Everything Detroit has done to change its team in the past 12 months has been designed to find the strength to stand up to Lemieux. And what do the Wings have to show for it? Nothing. Detroit can tell itself that what happens in the regular season doesn't matter. But that would be a lie. After his chance for personal redemption was gone, Draper walked from the locker room to Detroit's team bus without so much as a whimper. He couldn't have said less if his jaw were wired shut. As a member of the New Jersey Devils, Lemieux ended a Detroit dynasty before it started in 1995. As a member of the Avalanche, Lemieux took a championship the Wings thought sure was going to be theirs in '96.

"Bowman can't beat him, and Draper can't bloody him.

"'I don't think,' Colorado goalie Patrick Roy reported with sarcasm as dry as a stiff martini, 'Claude Lemieux is going to be intimidated by Draper or anybody else.'

"For 289 days, the Red Wings have been itching to rumble with Lemieux. And the best they could do is knock his helmet askew?

"'Show's over,' Lemieux said."

Not by a long shot.

March 26, 1997: Payback

On March 25, the Avalanche improved to 46-19-9 with a 4-0 shutout over the Whalers in Hartford—the club's final appearance in the Insurance City.

Eight games remained in the regular season, one of which was the following night in Detroit. Colorado coach Marc Crawford might have rested players such as Patrick Roy and Claude Lemieux, as the playoffs were nearing and it was the second night of back-to-back road games.

But the Avalanche was still in a fight with Dallas for the Presidents' Trophy, which would give it home-ice advantage through the playoffs. Two more points against the Red Wings would go a long way toward ensuring that goal. So the decision was made to play Roy, Lemieux, and the team's other regulars.

This was to be Lemieux's first game in Detroit since the hit on Kris Draper, and the Avalanche knew there was potential for trouble. Lemieux was still receiving occasional death threats from anonymous sources, so the decision was made by the club to provide him with a bodyguard in Detroit.

The bodyguard was stationed outside Lemieux's room at the Atheneum Hotel, near the heart of Detroit's Greektown area.

There was a police escort for the team from the airport to the hotel, with additional security personnel stationed outside.

On that March 25, *Detroit News* columnist Bob Wojnowski went to the Red Wings practice to gather material for his column the next day. Wojnowski wanted to write about Lemieux's return and make the larger point that the Red Wings had done too much talking—whining, even—about the hit on Draper, and not enough action.

"I was talking to McCarty and presented that to him the day before I wrote that column, and he shrugged and said, 'Yeah,'" Wojnowski recalled. "My thought was, 'Shut up and stop talking about it, and do something about it.'"

In the course of his conversation with Darren McCarty, Wojnowski induced a comment that would be much discussed 48 hours later.

"I was taught the best time to get revenge is when they're not expecting it," McCarty said. "He's played long enough, he knows eventually something will happen. The trump card is, he doesn't know when."

In the prescient column that appeared, under the headline "A Time for Revenge," Wojnowski made an impassioned case that the time was now, that night.

"There are rumors (the Avalanche) plans to bring along their snippy little towel boy, Claudia Lemieux, but this cannot be confirmed," Wojnowski wrote. "There are reports Lemieux will arm himself with his standard gear—visor, sharpened stick, extra padding, girdle and that phony sneer that supposedly makes him intimidating. . . . Lemieux is a nuisance, a dirtier Bill Laimbeer, if there is such a thing. He's an agitator, certainly, but he's intimidating like a carjacker is intimidating. You don't know when he'll strike, but you can bet it'll be from behind followed by sudden flight."

Wojnowski cited McCarty as a prime candidate to rearrange Lemieux's face, and wrote, "Wings fans shouldn't shower him with octopi tonight. They should honor him with turtles, because when danger lurks, Lemieux retreats."

Next to the column, *News* editors made a graphic that showed Lemieux's mug shot in a "Wanted" poster that read: "Wanted—Claude Lemieux. Height: 6-foot-1. Weight: 215 pounds. Distinguishing characteristics: No. 22, wears wimpy mask to cover his face. Modus operandi: Likes to attack from behind; when players square off, he looks for the nearest European player; during fights, he likes to lead with his stick; instead of apologies, offers jokes; always blames his opponents; seldom stays with one team more than two years. Last seen: Tuesday in Hartford."

At the Atheneum, the night before the game was uneventful. The tired Avs slept in, most opting out of the morning skate at Joe Louis Arena. Lemieux did not read the Wojnowski column, but probably would have shrugged it off if he had. Being in the villain's role was nothing new, and he and the Avs felt they were so superior to the Red Wings that they weren't much concerned about them anymore. They felt no team could beat them in the playoffs, with Dallas being their top threat in the West.

The Detroit fans and media continued to be down on the Red Wings. Goalie Mike Vernon's name was fodder on the talk radio shows as the team's biggest disappointment. Entering the game with Colorado, in which he would start, Vernon carried just an 11-9-6 record, with a 2.48 GAA. In his previous start, at Chicago, Vernon allowed three goals on four shots before being pulled. In stark contrast, the three-time Stanley Cup champion Roy was 36-13-7, a possible Hart Trophy candidate as NHL MVP. Long gone was the supposed mental edge Detroit had over him. Now it seemed the other way around.

Depressed about his play and unsure whether he would even start in the playoffs, Vernon remembered thinking one thing might help turn around the fans' opinion of him: "A fight. I was kind of on the outs, because Ozzie was kind of getting to be the No. 1 goaltender. I said to myself and my wife, 'The only way that I'm going to be able to win these fans back is by maybe getting in a fight.' That was kind of bizarre, because I'd never had a fight in my NHL career to that point. I had a tussle with Kirk McLean before, but that was it."

But who could Vernon fight and not get killed? Vernon was listed at 5-foot-9 in the Wings media guide, but he was probably closer to 5-foot-7. He was listed at 175, but that might have been 15 pounds too generous. Nobody ever called Vernon a wimp, however. He packed a fierce temper into his small frame, and was highly intelligent. He would sometimes grow impatient with reporters over their clichéd questions and let them have it. "Take the cock out of your mouth and ask your question," Vernon sniped once at a Calgary reporter.

Vernon would have loved to drop the gloves with Lemieux, but he knew such an opportunity probably would not come up and that he probably wasn't the best physical specimen to tackle the job. Usually, goalies only fight other goalies, but how likely was a bout with Roy? Roy, too, had a legendary temper—as his exit from Montreal made evident. But he also hadn't been involved in any NHL fights to that point.

On the day of the game, some Wings fans wore t-shirts made by a local radio station that read, "Screw Lemieux." A Denver radio station was not to be outdone in tastelessness, buying a billboard ad that showed Draper's face in a broken-up puzzle, and on-air promos with a baby crying that purported to be Draper.

In the Detroit dressing room prior to the game, McCarty said, there was no open talk about any plan to get Lemieux.

"It was quiet," he recalled. "Really, there never was any official talk among any of the guys about what to do. It was just an unspoken thing. Guys didn't really have to say anything. We knew we had to do something. After a certain point, it becomes a question about your manhood; how much are you going to take?"

Vernon certainly had no idea what might be coming.

"They usually don't include the goalie in those kinds of conversations," he said.

Up in the press box, Wojnowski took his seat, not far from a small contingent of Avalanche management, including media relations director Jean Martineau and GM Pierre Lacroix. The press box itself at Joe Louis Arena is a long, skinny aisle featuring stools with little room between them and the wall behind. It isn't uncommon to be bumped into by passersby numerous times during a game.

Along with Wojnowski, the *News* was represented by Wings beat writers Cyndi Lambert and John Niyo, while the competing *Detroit Free Press* had first-year beat writer Jason La Canfora, hockey columnist Keith Gave, and renowned general sports columnist Mitch Albom.

The *Free Press* and *News* writers generally loathed each other, particularly Lambert and Gave, who was distinct for never wearing socks and the overwhelming scent of cologne that gave away his presence well in advance.

La Canfora, in his early 20s at the time of his hiring, earned enmity from competing beat writers when it was revealed in a Detroit alternative publication that *Free Press* editor Gene Myerson told staffers La Canfora would "own the beat" after just three weeks on the job.

Representing the Denver papers were Terry Frei of the *Post* and Rick Sadowski of the *Rocky Mountain News*. I happened to be at home, as Frei took a handful of road trips each season and this was one of them. He'll never let me hear the end of it, either.

Lemieux, of course, was booed heavily when he took the ice for warm-ups and on his first shift of the game. A few minutes into the game, however, it was already looking like another anticlimactic night, like the one 10 days prior.

The Avalanche took an early 1-0 lead on a pretty one-timer by Valeri Kamensky off a faceoff. Lemieux, playing on his usual line with Kamensky and Peter Forsberg, was already a plus-1 and the Avs were dictating play with their speed.

Around the middle of the first period, however, the hits started getting bigger. It wasn't long before the first fight of the game happened, but Lemieux wasn't a party to it. Colorado's hulking Brent Severyn squared off with Detroit defenseman Jamie Pushor and manhandled him along the glass. Minutes later, Rene Corbet and Detroit's Kirk Maltby briefly went at it.

The Avs would have guys like Severyn and Corbet fight all night if that's what the Red Wings wanted. But with the clock winding down in the first period, the seasons of both teams would be altered for good, the pendulum of the rivalry swinging back to Detroit with one swing of McCarty's fist.

It all started with two of the game's most unlikely combatants—Colorado's Forsberg and Detroit's Igor Larionov, at 18:22 of the period. Forsberg, though a brilliant player, was quiet and humble. Larionov, nicknamed the Professor, wore eyeglasses, spoke in complete sentences, and had a cerebral air.

Forsberg was the atypical European forward, however, in that he would give back as much rough stuff as he would take. He relished making big, payback hits to whoever might have slighted him earlier. Still, Forsberg was rarely involved in anything nastier than a big check or some minor pushing and shoving.

Near the Detroit bench, along the blue line, Forsberg became entangled with Larionov. They fell to the ice, and Forsberg gave Larionov a slight punch to the head. Larionov fought back, and they began wrestling for a few seconds until a linesman interceded. The other players on the ice looked on, while grabbing onto one another, as is the hockey custom. Kamensky and Nicklas Lidstrom held onto each other, while Russians Alexei Gusarov and Vladimir Konstantinov clutched in amusement and Brendan Shanahan was tied up with Adam Foote. The only two players who weren't paired up were Lemieux and McCarty.

McCarty was entangled with linesman Ray Scapinello, and Foote also had a hand on his sweater. Lemieux, standing a few feet away from McCarty, looked on at the Forsberg and Larionov tussle.

It was then that McCarty swatted Foote's hand away and broke free of Scapinello. He whirled around to face Lemieux, who had his hands down and was still watching Forsberg and Larionov. After a pause of a second or two, during which McCarty looked directly at Lemieux, McCarty threw a right-hand punch that got Lemieux flush on the right side of his head. Lemieux went down instantly, clutching his face with both hands.

"Oh, that's awww-ful!" Avalanche radio play-by-play man Mike Haynes yelled into his microphone. "Oh my goodness, Darren McCarty jumps Claude Lemieux!"

Haynes, an excellent announcer who nevertheless subscribed to the broadcasting school of thought that the home team can do no wrong, reveled in calling fights. He would give detailed descriptions of each punch, sometimes throwing punches into the air himself as he called them.

"You'd see his tie swinging back and forth with each punch," said Haynes's broadcast partner, Norm Jones.

But there were no punches by Lemieux for Haynes to describe here. Lemieux tried to get to his feet after the initial blow, but was pushed down as McCarty came back for more.

Lemieux knelt facedown, covering his head, as McCarty threw left-handed punches to the back of his head and back.

Surprisingly, Scapinello did not try to break up Lemieux and McCarty. Usually when a player is down and appears hurt, a linesman intercedes immediately. Referee Paul Devorski also played spectator to the unfolding chaos. Seeing that Lemieux was getting no help from anybody, Roy charged out of his net.

He skated toward McCarty with the intent of getting him off Lemieux. Seeing this, Shanahan broke free of Foote and skated toward Roy to try and cut him off. What happened next was a midair collision between Shanahan and Roy, who both left their feet trying to stop each other. Roy would hurt his left shoulder in the collision, later telling Shanahan at the 1998 Olympics that it "was never the same again."

"It all happened so fast," Shanahan recalled. "Mac was yelling for me to come help him get loose. So I came over and grabbed Foote's arms. Darren shook loose and took off. Patrick came charging out and Darren had his back turned to Patrick. So I let go of Adam and took off, and Adam I'm sure had no clue where I was going. I don't know if Patrick saw me, but at the end he did because we both kind of jumped. It was a WWF move. I didn't throw any punches at him. I was just trying to keep from a third-man-in situation."

As Roy came out, so did Vernon. Foote grabbed Shanahan after he collided with Roy and tried to pull him aside. Vernon and Shanahan grabbed Foote and began simultaneously spinning him around. Roy looked over at Lemieux, who by now was being dragged over to the Detroit bench by McCarty.

Roy decided to go help his roommate, Foote, who still had Vernon and Shanahan on top of him. Roy grabbed Vernon and the two squared off at center ice.

"Patrick Roy, Mike Vernon, trading punches!" Haynes screamed. "Left by Vernon, a right by Roy, a left by Vernon, a right by Roy, they dance at center ice, a left by Vernon, Patrick

Roy at center stage! Oh my goodness. Man oh man. A full-out brawl at Joe Louis Arena. But it was Darren McCarty with as cheap a shot as you'll ever see. Jumped Claude Lemieux, when he shouldn't have! Terrible, cheap, unsportsmanlike play by Darren McCarty. It's disgusting!"

Vernon was almost knocked down by a hard right hand thrown by Roy to start the fight, but stayed on his feet and hit Roy with a surprising left that opened a cut over his right eye.

Vernon remembered what his brother, Kevin, told him when it came to fighting.

"He said, 'Throw 'em, just keep throwin' 'em,'" Vernon said. "And try to duck and bury your face and come up and keep throwin' em. That's all I can remember when I started with Patty was, 'Just don't stop.' If I stop, I'm going to get clobbered here."

Roy landed the most punches in the fight, but Vernon won the wrestling match to the ice, which drew a thunderous roar. He instantly felt like a player transformed, to himself and the fans.

"It kind of turned everything around. It really kind of gave me a lot of confidence, that 'I'm still here, I'm still going to fight for my job, still battle,'" he said. "It just carried on from there. I gained more confidence from that, even though I didn't play that well that game.

"But I've never been so exhausted in my life. I'm serious, I was exhausted. I'd throw one and he'd throw one, and I'd try to cover by putting my head into my armpit. Patrick was hitting the top of my head, obviously, with the height thing. I was kind of jumping up trying to punch back. I just kept throwin' 'em. And then, for some unknown reason, I was so tired with my right arm that I threw a left, and I think I surprised him. And I think that's the punch that kind of, I think, cut him."

While Roy and Vernon fought, a bloodied Lemieux remained in a crouch position by the Red Wings bench. McCarty threw more punches and then kneed him in the head. Looking on from the Wings bench, with Lemieux right below him, was Draper. Finally, Scapinello broke things up. Lemieux staggered to his feet, blood pouring from his face, the back of his jersey bunched up near the top. He skated to the Avalanche bench and into the dressing room, where trainer Pat Karns would apply 10 to 15 stitches to close a cut.

Lemieux would always refer to McCarty's initial assault as a sucker punch, even though video of the incident clearly shows McCarty looking Lemieux in the face right before.

"Some said it was a sucker punch, but it wasn't. I cold-cocked him," McCarty said. "He was standing back, watching Igor and Forsberg rassle. I got him pretty good with the first punch. I was pretty mad. I tried to get him some more, but only got the back of his head."

In the dressing room, Karns described Lemieux as calm but slightly dazed.

"I think he said something like, 'I should have seen that coming' or something close," Karns said. "But he wasn't seriously hurt or anything. We knew he'd return to the game."

The blood of Lemieux, Roy, and Forsberg stained the Joe Louis ice. Forsberg, who had sustained a cut earlier in the game from a collision, had it reopened in the tussle with Larionov and missed the rest of the contest.

The sellout crowd at the Joe roared with approval. Finally, their Red Wings had stood up to the Avalanche and, literally and figuratively, smacked them in the mouth. A sizable number of Wings fans were made up of autoworkers from the surrounding manufacturing plants. In only a couple of minutes, the formerly "pretty, but not gritty" Red Wings had been cast more in their image: Tough. Blue-collar. An eye for an eye.

It took nearly 10 minutes for order to be restored by officials. At first, it seemed a no-brainer that McCarty would be kicked out of the game. He had instigated a fight while another was going on, grounds for a game-misconduct penalty. At minimum, he would be assessed a fighting major and a 10-minute misconduct.

Amazingly, Devorski only assessed McCarty a double-minor penalty for roughing. Avs coach Crawford was incredulous.

"No fucking balls!" Crawford yelled at Devorski, while putting his hands by his crotch. "No fucking balls!"

Eight years later, Devorski admitted he blew it by not tossing McCarty from the game—something the game's other linesman, Dan Schachte, told him right after the incident should have been done.

"We were at the penalty box, and Schachte said, 'Devo, you've got to get rid of McCarty,'" Devorski said. "And I'm going, 'Well hang on here.' I had Forsberg and this guy going at it, I had the two goalies going at it and Shanahan, and I said I really didn't see much what Lemieux was doing. I was trying to plead my case and Schachte just said, 'Devo, you've got to get rid of him.' Now that I look back, if there was ever a five[-minute major] and a game-misconduct, that was it."

In the Wings dressing room, Vernon figured there was no way he'd be allowed to stay in the game, either.

"I was sitting in my stall, and I'm thinking I got kicked out, and Osgood comes in and says, 'You've got to go back out on the ice,'" Vernon said. "I said, 'I can't, I've got to get kicked out for that!' I was so exhausted. Sat on my stool to catch my breath, and I had to get back out there. Thank God I think they only had one or two shots after that."

Devorski also admitted Roy and Vernon technically should have been tossed from the game for being second-men-in fighters, "but back then, you just never, ever threw the goalies out."

When play finally resumed, Adam Deadmarsh and Konstantinov fought, with the Wings' Russian defenseman taking the worst of it. The period finally ended with Colorado still holding its 1-0 lead.

In the Red Wings dressing room, there was an unspoken feeling of satisfaction. Lemieux had finally gotten his. The Wings were no longer "Mac" from the Charles Atlas comic book ad, always getting sand kicked in his face.

"It was weird, though, because nobody said anything still," McCarty said. "It would have seemed like it was no big deal to somebody looking in who didn't know the situation. But we knew it was bigger than that."

Four seconds into the second period, Foote and Shanahan dropped the gloves. It would be the first of several fights between the two in the years to come. Throughout the second period, several Colorado players went out of their way looking to get even for what happened in the first. Deadmarsh squared off with McCarty, but any hopes of bloody revenge for what he did to Lemieux failed to materialize, as McCarty more than held his own.

Later, Severyn squared off with Detroit's Aaron Ward. In the process, Severyn lost his jersey and shoulder pads, leaving him to look like John L. Sullivan in a turn-of-the-century boxing ring. The barebacked Severyn wore a raging, out-of-control look as he swung away at Ward.

"I thought, 'Oh damn, why did I have to pick Sevvy?'" Ward said. "That was a little bit of a mismatch there."

Severyn and Ward would soon be ejected from the game for reaching their fighting limit. Meanwhile, Lemieux had returned to the action, stitched up but otherwise looking fine. He did not go out of his way to confront McCarty, however, something that might have earned back some lost machismo and respect from teammates.

"I think to a point, he wasn't prepared. But I think if you're 220 pounds, you fight back. I told him that myself. That's his choice," Mike Keane said. "Thing is, he wasn't that bad a fighter. I'd seen him fight in Montreal, and he was pretty tough. But some players like to do it, some players don't. Some can't."

Indeed, Lemieux would later lament that he dropped his guard too much for such a game.

"I should have been more on the lookout for something like that," he said. "Obviously, there could have been five suspensions on that play. I got kneed, I got hit in the boards. There's no chance when you get drilled like that. So, I didn't have too much respect with how that took place, but that happened and I took it."

Keane would fight Detroit's Tomas Holmstrom in the second period, in another one-sided bout. The redheaded Keane wasn't overly big, but possessed expert fighting skills honed from years in the rough-and-tumble Western Hockey League with the Moose Jaw Warriors. Keane, who had the Warriors' logo tattooed on his arm, had been something of a bodyguard for star scorer Theo Fleury, who would later play with Colorado.

On the ice, the Avalanche maintained a 4-3 lead after two periods.

Up in the press box, Colorado's Lacroix decided to head downstairs to watch the rest of the game in the visiting coach's office. That narrow passageway may or may not have been too much for Lacroix to navigate by the time he got to the seat of the *News'* Wojnowski.

"I was sort of standing there instead of sitting on my stool. This was after all the fighting," Wojnowski recalled. "Lacroix just came barging through, and it wasn't that there was no room to get around. He just rammed his shoulder into my side and I'll never forget what he said. He said, 'Get out of my way, you fucking prick.' I just went, 'What, what?'"

For Lacroix, it was not out of the ordinary to have a run-in with a newspaper reporter. In his earlier years as a GM, Lacroix was not yet used to the daily scrutiny of his moves by the media and he sometimes reacted to criticism with mockery, profanity, or outright threats.

At the *Post*, columnist Mark Kiszla and I were often at the wrong end of his ire. Lacroix would sometimes say I was only cut out to cover the "kennel club" as a sports writer, and he once held a press conference in the middle of the McNichols Arena parking lot on a sweltering summer day to denounce Kiszla as "unethical." When Kiszla was around the arena looking for stories, Lacroix sometimes held his nose and mused aloud, "What smells?"

Lacroix could also be very charming, and one learned not to take his eruptions personally. He could browbeat you one minute, then admire wallet pictures of your children and ask how the rest of the family was doing the next. He was always a gentleman around women, and he doted on his wife of more than 40 years, Colombe, or "Coco." The two were best friends with singer Celine Dion and her husband, René Angelil, with Lacroix the best man at their wedding, much of which Colombe designed herself. In many ways, Lacroix was just like Scotty Bowman, a self-made man who learned to play hardball in business but had a soft side.

When Kamensky achieved the hat trick to make it 5-3 in the third period—a goal assisted by Lemieux—the game seemed over. Roy didn't blow many third-period leads, and there was no doubt he had extra motivation after he and his teammates had shed their own blood.

But Detroit's Martin Lapointe scored his second goal of the game with 11:33 left to make it 5-4, and Shanahan tied it soon after with a backhand shot from behind the net that banked in off Roy's leg.

The game went to overtime. It was only a regular-season game with nothing on the line, but the winner might gain a huge psychological advantage over the other come playoff time. If the Avs won, they could say to all of Detroit, "We took all your best shots, and you still couldn't beat us on your home ice." But if the Wings could win, their players knew the bully—in their case the Avalanche—would lose the intimidation factor.

"I think we had to win that game," Shanahan said. "I think if we had won it and there's no fight, it wouldn't have been as big a deal. And if we fought and lost, it's not as big a deal."

Shanahan would help see to it Detroit would win. Shortly into the five-minute overtime, he spotted a teammate open across the ice and fed a pass for an easy one-timer past Roy. The teammate was none other than McCarty, whose shot into the net, with Lemieux trailing the play, sent the crowd into a frenzy.

Perhaps the person who least wanted to see McCarty score at that moment was Devorski.

"I'd just realized he should have been gone, and then that bites me in the ass with him scoring," Devorski said. "I was there going, 'You're killin' me McCarty, you're killin' me.' I told him later, 'You owe me a game.'"

McCarty had personally avenged Draper, and now had beaten Colorado with his stick.

"It was like out of a movie," McCarty said. "For us, Hollywood couldn't have scripted it any better. It was perfect. It changed our team."

When McCarty scored, teammate Ward was watching in street clothes behind the Colorado goal. He immediately dashed for the Red Wings dressing room, which at the Joe meant passing the doorway to the visitors' room, in the hallway.

As he got to the Avalanche door, Ward was intercepted by Crawford, who was on his way to the officials' room to give them a piece of his mind.

"All of a sudden, I felt an elbow into my side," Ward said. "I look back and it's Crawford." Ward and Crawford exchanged profanities, and not for the last time. Crawford denied bumping into Ward, telling a Denver radio station the next day, "I wouldn't know Aaron Ward from the equipment boy."

McCarty was called back onto the ice as the game's first star, and his legend was born. *Free Press* columnist Albom led off his next day's column, "Darren McCarty will never pay for another meal in this town again."

The headline of the March 27 *Free Press* sports section said, "Bloody Good," with a picture of Roy's bloodied face front and center. "The Wings showed guts, skill and an undying resilience," La Canfora wrote.

In the Avalanche dressing room, Keane belittled the Red Wings as "a bunch of homers" and "gutless" with "no heart." Keane wondered why the Wings had played "soft" when the games were in Denver, forgetting about the big hits on Gusarov and Corbet in December.

McCarty called the game "old-time hockey" and downplayed his actions against Lemieux, who perhaps not surprisingly had little to say to the media himself.

"If you believe in the Bible," McCarty said, "it's an eye for an eye. Fist on fist."

Vernon immediately noticed more of a Three Musketeers attitude on his team.

"We tested each other, relied on each other, and we rose to the occasion," he said. "It made us all believers that we can do this, we can battle. The confidence within the dressing room after that for the rest of the season was different. Detroit fans, they like their fighters, the Joey Kocurs and Bob Proberts. After that, the fans, when I came back out onto the ice from the dressing room, they were chanting my name. It was just a whole different feeling. The radio shows were saying all of a sudden I was the No. 1 goaltender, and it kind of turned everything around."

The Avalanche tried to act like nothing had changed; all

that happened was they lost a game, players said. But many knew different.

"That was the turning point," Severyn said. "Our team was so close, but what happened with our team, we went in two different directions after that."

In Denver, columnist Woody Paige tried to stoke the rivalry with a blistering column about the Wings and the city of Detroit two days following the pivotal game.

"In 1805, Detroit was destroyed by a fire. Must have been the first year one of the city's pro teams won a title. Regrettably, Detroit was rebuilt," Paige wrote in the *Post*. "But every time (which is not often) The Automobile & Enema Capital of America gets a championship team, as in 1984 when the Detroit Tigers prevailed in the World Series, the downwardly mobile citizens try to burn it to the ground again.

"Can't blame them.

"So Claude Lemieux should be praised—not assailed, attacked and assaulted—in Detroit.

"The Detroit Fire Department ought to present him with a lifetime achievement award. He saved Detroit from itself.

"If it weren't for Lemieux, Detroit would be charcoal. His New Jersey Devils defeated the Red-faced Wings in the 1995 Stanley Cup Finals (and Lemieux was MVP), and his new team, the Colorado Avalanche, flagellated Detroit in the 1996 conference finals. Denver celebrates with champagne, Detroit with Molotov cocktails.

"However, there will be no firestorms in Detroit this year.

"The Red Wings are Dead Things again. Let them enjoy their one trifling victory over the Avalanche.

"That collection of thugs, lugs, mugs and slugs (reflecting the city they represent) won't be around in the playoffs to inconvenience the Avalanche. Too bad. The Avalanche would love to face and face off against the Detroit Teamsters. But the Gooners are goners. Scotty Bogeyman attempted to reshape his club so he could beat the Avalanche, but all he has is a team that could beat up on the fatigued Avalanche in one regular-season game.

"No wonder the Dead Things were mad. Even with the overtime triumph, they have to stay in Detroit. To keep up with the number of fights and penalties, the Blood Wings didn't need a stat crew. They should have brought in a Lestat crew. Talking to a Detroit player was like an interview with the vampire.

"Oddly enough, the Detroit media and radio stations and vassals have been so intent on exacting their revenge on Lemieux, they've ignored that the Dead Things are gagging, choking dogs. A typical scum-vacuuming sports columnist in Detroit claimed McCarty's action 'was a punch that had to be thrown, if not now, then never.'

"He is right. McCarty had to do his fist-on-head now. Because he will never get the opportunity in the playoffs. But the Avalanche's cry next year when Detroit comes back to Denver will be: 'Remember The Maim.' And Detroit does a slow burn."

The playoffs were only a few weeks away. To meet again, both teams would probably have to win their first two rounds again. The Avalanche made sure it would get home-ice advantage by wrapping up the Presidents' Trophy, while Detroit went in as the number-three seed.

Colorado had little problem with Edmonton and Chicago in the first two rounds, while Detroit again beat St. Louis and Anaheim.

On May 15, the stage was set for the most anticipated hockey playoff series in years. Colorado versus Detroit, once again in the Western Conference finals. It would end as one of the most intense six games in hockey history.

"You're All a Bunch of Pussies"

Scotty Bowman went into the 1997 Western Conference finals looking for an edge. Which meant he entered the series with a pulse and other vital signs.

Probably no other coach in hockey history thought from as many different angles as Bowman. If he thought a TV camera's lights were a potential distraction to just one shot by one of his players at a practice, the cameraman was ordered out. If he thought a reporter wanted to ask a player possibly tough questions that might at all detract from his concentration, he might lurk in the background or simply make the player unavailable.

He knew every single NHL beat reporter's name and what they looked like, and most of the columnists, too. He would cajole some, charm others, and browbeat the rest: anything to get an edge for his team. Perhaps he could even glean a little inside information out of the unsuspecting reporter about the opposition.

I still remember very clearly standing in the hallway outside the media room of McNichols Arena prior to Game 4 of the 1996 Western finals. I'd had a story in the paper the day before saying the Red Wings would send a tape of Claude Lemieux's punch on Slava Kozlov to the NHL offices for review and a possible suspension.

A voice called out from near the visiting coach's room: "I'm looking for a guy named Dater." It was Bowman. It was my first one-on-one encounter with the man I'd grown up watching on TV and hating when he coached the Montreal Canadiens against my Boston Bruins. I'm not ashamed to admit a lump gathered in my throat upon hearing his call. I walked slowly down the hall, with a "who, me?" look.

"You don't have to send the tape in during the playoffs," Bowman told me, with a slight tone like that of a teacher disappointed in a student. "It's automatic. The league's already here. They look at everything."

Whoops. For any reporter, having a mistake in the paper— and worse, pointed out—is like dying a small death. Lord knows I've made my share, but they never get any easier to take. Bowman, of course, was right. The league reviews any controversial incident from a playoff series itself, while in the regular season teams usually must send in a tape for review.

For me, though, Bowman's chiding had a strangely uplifting effect. I'd just gotten chewed out by the great Scotty Bowman, I thought. He actually read my story! Still, I vowed never again to make a mistake involving him or his team. And that, I'm sure, was always a big secret to Bowman's success: he made you never want to screw up again. He made you want to please him the next time, to be able to say, "See, I did it right this time. See, see?"

During the next game, in Detroit, I walked up to Bowman in the press dining room and told him I appreciated his correcting me. A little small talk ensued, and I told him I was from New England and a big B's fan growing up. He immediately recounted a couple of series between his Canadiens and Boston, saying it was "great hockey" and went out of his way to praise a workmanlike Bruins forward from the day, Don Marcotte.

From that day on, and especially after Bowman retired, he and I kept up a fairly regular correspondence. He gave me all his phone numbers, said to call any time. Many hours of talk—mostly all about hockey, but much about his life in general—took place. It was, and still is, a thrill talking to, for my money, the greatest coach of all time in any sport.

But when he coached, Bowman kept his distance from pretty much everybody except his wife, Suella, and his five children. Everything was about getting that little edge to win, and when the Avs-Wings 1997 series began, Bowman was focused on a piece of wood.

Bowman was convinced the visitors' bench at McNichols was too close to the boards, making it uncomfortable on his players' knees. He also thought it wasn't regulation length. He was probably right on both counts, but despite his complaints to the league offices, nothing was done. For Bowman, this was the kind of distraction that could drive him—along with the people at the other end of his endless complaints—nuts.

So, after consulting with one of his assistant coaches, Barry Smith, he came up with a solution: The Red Wings would have a six-and-a-half-foot bench made for them by one of Smith's friends in Colorado Springs with some expertise in woodworking. If the league wouldn't fix the bench at Big Mac, Bowman would show them.

Starting in Game 1 on May 15, the Red Wings trotted out their makeshift bench. No longer would three of his players have to sit on metal chairs, and maybe lose a second getting over the boards for their next shift because the bench wasn't long enough. For Bowman, that second might make the difference. He immediately went into the series feeling like he had an edge on Colorado he'd been missing the year before.

"It was a disadvantage on line changes. We were a team that

used to match up quite a bit. We had a lot of players," Bowman said. "Maybe it had no effect on the series, but the one thing that bothered me was that the league kind of pushed it under the table. If somebody would have been aboveboard and said, 'Look this isn't right, the benches have got to be fixed.' . . . it was more gamesmanship, but it did affect changing on the fly a little bit. Their bench was bigger and longer, and we had guys sitting on the second tier. It was jammed in there. It was an awful bench. The coach nearly tipped over on the players. Guys had to climb over each other."

After Game 1, it appeared that Colorado's Patrick Roy still had the ultimate edge on Detroit. Colorado won, 2-1, on a game-winning goal by Mike Ricci, set up by Lemieux. Despite the humiliation at Joe Louis on March 26, Lemieux entered the series as the playoffs' leading goal-scorer with 10, and his 19 points were tied for first. He was still Big Game Claude.

The Red Wings outshot Colorado 35-19, but Roy was magnificent. Not much credit was given to him or the Avs in the Detroit papers the next day, however; *Free Press* hockey columnist Keith Gave spent most of his copy trashing Big Mac and Denver hockey fans.

On a stormy Denver night, a half hour before the game, a small electrical fire triggered a power outage in McNichols, delaying the start and leaving the lights dim most of the game.

"The McNichols crowd [is] inarticulate at best and routinely bordering on moronic," Gave wrote in a column headlined, "What a Dump: This Game Deserved Better."

"Well, excuse us for living," countered the *Post*'s Woody Paige the next day. "Why doesn't NHL commissioner Gary Bettman just call off the rest of the Western Conference finals and award the series to the Red Wings because people in Colorado are no-account, light-hearted, dim-witted, mountain-mutton, trailer trash, loft litter and condo compost? Unlike Detroit, we don't know anything about hockey or automobiles, but we do know this: Since the 1957 Chevy, the classic car most coveted by collectors, was introduced in Hockeytown, the Avalanche was won one more Stanley Cup than the Red Wings."

Added the *Post*'s other columnist, Mark Kiszla, "Throw another victim on the scrap heap at The Dump."

Unlike the previous year's series, however, Roy was not quite in the heads of the Red Wings. Just keep playing the way we did in Game 1, Detroit players told themselves, and we'll get them this time.

"We were playing a lot better than the year before," Mike Vernon said. "We had control of the puck a lot more. We were dictating the style of play. We lost the first game, and it didn't feel good, but we still felt good about ourselves."

For Game 2, the Avalanche flew in a University of Alaska hockey player named Erik Drygas as a guest. The previous November, at a Chinooks practice, Drygas suffered a broken neck that left him paralyzed. Before the game, Lemieux and Ricci brought Drygas into the Avs dressing room and players signed his jersey and talked.

The Red Wings won the game, 4-2, a close score in a game that was not close at all. Detroit again badly outshot the Avalanche, this time 40-17. Only Roy's superb goaltending gave Colorado any chance at victory, and it was still a 2-2 game with five minutes left in the third period.

With four minutes remaining, Steve Yzerman banked a shot in off Roy's leg from behind the net to make it 3-2. Darren McCarty added an insurance goal, and Detroit was even and headed home.

That morning, McCarty was awakened in the wee hours by a Denver hard-rock station that had gotten his hotel room number. It ruined his sleep, but the good-natured and music-loving McCarty played along on the air, albeit half in a daze.

Some of the other things heard on Denver radio weren't so funny. Throughout the series, a Denver all-sports station played the same baby-crying promo that mocked Kris Draper. Many Avalanche fans and a few players ridiculed Draper for not fighting his own battles since the hit from Lemieux. Draper was a whiner, they said, hiding behind his teammates, having them fight his battles.

After the loss in Game 2, the typically mercurial Kiszla belittled the Avalanche for not fighting back enough. The Red Wings had been allowed to become the bullies since March 26, he wrote, which was probably true. Chris Simon wasn't around anymore to pummel anybody who laid a glove on Joe Sakic and Peter Forsberg, and the huge Uwe Krupp was lost in the series to a back injury that later required surgery.

"For the first time in their NHL reign, the champions have been revealed as vulnerable skaters who can be physically manhandled at the blue line," Kiszla wrote. "In Game 2, Forsberg and Sakic put only a single, lousy puck on net between them. Every time a ref turns his head, it's painfully obvious the Red Wings intend to mug Forsberg and rattle his brain."

Paige, however, was still taunting the Wings and their entire fan base: "Even if the Red Wings win the series, people in Denver won't be forced to live in Detroit. What? Avalanche worry? No team in the league ever has won a playoff series 1-1. (Although one might have thought the Wings had Saturday night by listening to the freaky reactions of the articulate TV and newspaper types from Detroit when the Red Wings went ahead.)"

When the series shifted to Detroit, the Avalanche talked about playing with more passion and hunger. But those things were missing, and everybody knew it. No matter how hard championship teams talk about the evils of a "Stanley Cup hangover," it is difficult to avoid. A year's worth of pats on the back and being the guests of honor around town can morph into a toxic combination of self-satisfaction and lethargy. While the Avalanche clearly had not succumbed by getting this far again into the playoffs, it was obvious the Red Wings were the hungrier team. Despite three straight years of playoff disappointment, Detroit felt they were not only the best team in hockey by this point, but the baddest and toughest, too. The night of March 26 had a lot to do with that.

"We just didn't feel like a pretty team anymore," McCarty said. "We felt like a bunch of hardasses now. We felt we could pound Colorado on the boards now, where I'm sure they felt that way against us the year before."

Another big problem for Colorado in the series was a virtual disappearing act by Forsberg. He would finish the series with no goals and one assist in five games, the worst playoff showing of his career. As would be a problem throughout his career, Forsberg got hurt in the previous round. He was slew-footed by Edmonton's Bryan Muir, resulting in a nasty concussion.

Forsberg was a total dichotomy as a person and player. He was shy and quiet off the ice, rarely speaking above the softest of decibels. He was difficult to get to know, usually preferring the company of a select few lifelong friends from Sweden whom he would often fly out to Denver for days at a time.

For the first few years of his career, he found a close friend in Adam Deadmarsh. They were usually inseparable around the rink, always trying to one-up each other with practical jokes and good-natured insults. They would have loud, protracted video game battles on the team's charter airplane, usually some kind of golf game or Doom. The winner would wear a mythical championship belt and lord it over the other until the next battle.

Deadmarsh had a serious girlfriend, Christa, his first couple years in Colorado, and he later married her. Forsberg, on the other hand, was single and liked it that way. And he had no shortage of female admirers in Denver and elsewhere. When

Forsberg walked into a room, women seemed transfixed by his bright blue eyes and wavy blondish hair.

The first year or two in Denver, Forsberg and Deadmarsh often went to a country-western dance club named Stampede—and that's exactly what the women did when they saw Forsberg in a pair of cowboy boots and tight Wranglers.

(In 2001 the Avalanche traded Deadmarsh to Los Angeles, right after Christa gave birth to premature twin girls after a difficult pregnancy. Forsberg was so upset, he told Avalanche management he would never sign another contract with the team. But he did, staying another three years.)

On the ice, Forsberg was a killer. He was the rarest of European forwards in that he played with a mean streak. Any hit on him above the routine level would be duly noted, and he would patiently wait for a chance to freight-train the offender in a subsequent shift. His open-ice hits could be as scary as those of the biggest and meanest defensemen. He ended the careers of two Dallas players, Brian Skrudland and Craig Ludwig, partly because of injuries from his hits. He broke the ribs of another Dallas player, Joe Nieuwendyk, with a monster hit.

Forsberg took plenty of big hits, too, which created a vicious cycle of retaliation all the time. And that's why he suffered so many injuries. He took numerous cheap shots from lesser-skilled players over the years. It was the only way he could be stopped. With a puck on his stick, Forsberg was magical. He had a low center of gravity while skating, which made him virtually impossible to knock off the puck. His stickhandling ability was right up there with the best who ever played the game. Perhaps only Wayne Gretzky was ever a better pure passer than Forsberg. With his passes, he was like the 20-game-winning baseball pitcher in that he was a master of changing speeds; he could make the long, hard pass up the middle or the perfect drop pass to a teammate 20 feet behind.

With a game on the line, Forsberg's eyes turned wild looking in their intensity. He thirsted for the clutch moments, especially, for some reason, on the road. He scored numerous crowd-silencing goals to win games for Colorado. Afterward he would revert back into his aw-shucks persona, never bragging about anything, never giving himself any of the credit. But there was always an understated level of confidence around Forsberg that made it clear: yeah, I'm The Man.

The Red Wings won Game 3 at the Joe, 2-1, on two Slava Kozlov goals. Kozlov could speak almost no English, but he always said, "Hi-de-ho, boys" after a goal. There was a party atmosphere to the aging arena; indeed, the song by Kid Rock played right before the opening faceoff of every playoff game said, "There ain't no party like a Detroit party, cuz the Detroit party don't stop."

The Avalanche probably outplayed Detroit, but not in goal, as Vernon got the best of Roy. Marc Crawford was upset at a few of his players for a lack of intensity, especially Valeri Kamensky. Forsberg and Deadmarsh weren't doing enough, either, and veteran Mike Keane stood up in the dressing room after the game and laced into the team, saying it had too many "passengers" so far.

Near the team bus a little later, Keane, Roy, Lemieux, and Sakic huddled together. The conversation got animated at times, with Roy throwing his hands in the air and pacing back and forth. By that point, a slight division in the Colorado dressing room had taken hold, and it would come and go over the coming few years.

The addition of Eric Lacroix, the general manager's son, helped create tension in the room that would come to a head two years later. Soon after the Avs won the Cup in 1996, Pierre Lacroix traded backup goalie Stephane Fiset to Los Angeles for his son. On paper, it seemed like a logical move, as Lacroix was a needed power forward with some goal-scoring ability. But it was always an awkward situation, and as time went on he became an easy scapegoat among players for the team's troubles. Some of it was fair, and some of it wasn't. Eric went six games with only one assist in the 1997 series with Detroit, however, and some in the room felt he was being treated with kid gloves by Crawford and management overall. Crawford would lace into veterans such as Kamensky and Deadmarsh, the grumbling went, but always seemed to spare the GM's son.

"We were a little tight as a team in that series, no question," Keane recalled. "We knew we weren't playing as well as Detroit going into it. We were hoping to win too much, as opposed to expecting to win."

Still, the day before Game 4, Roy took part in a press conference that got a little surreal in its machismo.

There were two off-days before the game, and on the first, Crawford spent much of his press conference complaining about Detroit defenseman Vladimir Konstantinov. Crawford took a page out of Bowman's book with references to an opposing player's alleged tactics, hoping it might result in a call down the road.

"He could have a penalty every shift he's on the ice," said Crawford, who also, and probably rightly, complained Forsberg wasn't getting any calls for the slashing he was taking.

On the second day, Roy, perhaps sensitive to the growing criticism that the Avs were whining and playing too soft, thumped his chest at the Red Wings.

"Let's play," Roy said, grabbing a microphone off a table and pulling it to his face. "We don't care what's happened so far. It's what happens now until the end of the series that matters. It's time for us to play. As a team, we've got to be more physical and more tough on their players. I think everybody is ready for Game 4, and to see if Detroit is ready to pay the price. That's what I want to see. We haven't shown them nothing so far. We haven't seen how bad they want to pay the price, because I know my team and I know how bad we want to win, and I know this is far away from being over. I know that we're going to come out stronger than we ever done so far in this series. We're going to be in their face. We're not going to do cheap shots, but we're certainly going to prove to them that we want to win the Stanley Cup as much as they do, and probably more."

Post columnist Kiszla seemed unimpressed.

"Strap your helmet on tight," he wrote. "Because never has Roy's big mouth put Colorado on such dangerously thin ice. Now the Avalanche will be forced to find out the truth about the great, unanswered question of the 1997 NHL playoffs: Do all these pretty skaters from Colorado really have the strength or the stomach to win a brutal hockey war?

"With his team on the run in the Western Conference finals, Roy did something incredibly bold: He spit on Detroit.

"In no uncertain terms, Roy questioned the heart of the Red Wings. He arrogantly dismissed Colorado's 2-1 deficit in the best-of-seven series as irrelevant. The Avalanche goalie vowed his troops would take the fight to Detroit in Game 4. And he fully expects the enemy to fold. Since joining the Avalanche, never has the cocky Roy made a speech with such potential for humiliation. Here's why: No goalie can be a team's goon. And the hardest lick anybody on the Colorado roster has delivered all series is the blind-side shot Roy gave Tomas Sandstrom on the way to the locker room during Game 3.

"Although Roy fears no man in the whole NHL, his Avalanche teammates scare absolutely nobody. Want to know the sad truth? The Red Wings are laughing at the Avalanche. Asked Wednesday if Colorado was tough enough to play dirty hockey, Wings enforcer Vladimir Konstantinov responded by chuckling for a full five seconds. Detroit bullies are taking the NHL rulebook and rubbing Peter Forsberg's nose in it. Konstantinov thinks Colorado coach Marc Crawford is a naive fool for whining about Detroit's cheating.

"'If you're not cheating,' Konstantinov said, 'you can't win.'"

By Game 4's end, Roy had an omelet on his face. Detroit won, 6-0. It was a total smoke show from beginning to end. Detroit outshot Colorado a stunning 14-2 in the first period, building a 2-0 lead on goals by Larionov.

Despite Roy's tough talk that his team would punish Detroit physically, it would be Forsberg who would have to walk stiff-legged to the team bus afterward, following a low-bridge hit by, of all people, Draper. Forsberg would miss the next game and barely be able to play Game 6.

Roy allowed five goals before being pulled for backup Craig Billington.

"Yo, Patrick," wrote the *Free Press*'s Gave. "You were curious to find out how much Detroit was ready to play Thursday? How does 6-0 Red Wings sound, buddy? For all the talk you and your coach were doing this week, this was the best you could bring? Well, how does a 3-1 deficit in the best-of-seven series sound, pal?"

Wrote *Free Press* Wings beat writer Jason La Canfora, "The Avalanche complains. The Red Wings persevere. The Avalanche moans. The Red Wings score. The Avalanche whines. The Red Wings win."

Years later Detroit's Brendan Shanahan remembered Colorado's Lemieux talking trash to him when the game started.

"He looked at me and said, 'You're a loser, you've never won a Stanley Cup,'" Shanahan said. "Just, like, after a scrum in front of the net. I'm not much of a talker on the ice, but I know enough to know that when Claude says things on the ice, that . . . well, it was stupid at the time. Because, you talk about me focusing in and making sure I prove him wrong. We were playing well at the time, but it was even more incentive to finish out the series. It was a lesson to me, that no matter who I was playing or what I thought about them or how I wanted to get him off his game, that was a bad thing to say to somebody. It was just all the more incentive. Adam Foote said it to me, same thing, in Game 1. It was all good to hear."

Lemieux was as reviled in Detroit as ever, but by now had become more a source of mockery than anything. Handmade signs reading "Claude the Fraud" and "Turtle Lemieux" were everywhere in the arena.

The Denver and Detroit media kept playing up the Lemieux-Draper angle for all it was worth. Before Game 4, a Denver all-sports radio station somehow managed to get one of the Detroit newspapers to accept an advertisement that pictured Lemieux putting together a puzzle—a puzzle of Draper's face.

A Denver rock station came up with an anti-Red Wings parody, set to the music of Eric Clapton's "Cocaine." Here's a sample:

> When all of your stars are from the USSR
> Red Wings
> At the game all your fans have octopus in their pants
> Red Wings
> Gonna send Claude Lemieux to break a jawbone or two
> Red Wings

Meanwhile, up in the Avalanche radio booth, play-by-play man Mike Haynes needed police protection for the games at Joe Louis. Detroit radio stations played some of Haynes's more incendiary calls over and over, leading to more outrage. Haynes and his color analyst, Norm Jones, had to do their broadcasts mingled among fans in the stands because of a lack of room in the main press box. The taunting of Haynes was nonstop.

"They were screaming at us and yelling at us, but we had a

couple of huge security guards. These guys were huge. But it got a little personal. I would get so many e-mails from people," Haynes said.

Haynes always responded to nasty e-mails from Detroit fans the same way: with a picture of Draper being hit into the boards by Lemieux. That was it. No words with it, just the picture. Haynes had a fiery Irish temper that sometimes got him in trouble, like the time one summer night in 1998 when he pursued a burglar from his Denver home and wound up on a hospital operating table with stab wounds after catching and scuffling with him. On the operating table, Haynes was assured by the surgeon that "we're all Avalanche fans in here."

With Game 4 nearly over, during a stop in play, Crawford complained to a linesman about something. Paul Devorski stood nearby, the referee for the game. Trying to hear what Crawford was saying, Bowman wandered over to the small area separating the teams' benches and lent an ear.

What followed was one of the best-remembered but more misunderstood episodes of the rivalry. Crawford slowly but steadily launched into a profanity-laced tirade at Bowman and the entire Red Wings team that left him red-faced and bug-eyed by its end. Some of what was said was accurately reported and much of it not, but nobody ever got the full transcript. Until now.

Those with sensitivity to certain profane words might want to skip the following passage. And it should be made clear: Crawford's words should not be taken as an indictment of his character. Profanity is the language of choice in the sport. It's hockey, not tiddlywinks.

A video camera caught the incident, along with most of the language. It has never before been aired publicly.

After Bowman said something to the linesman, Crawford got things started with a comment about the alleged plate in his head: "You don't have one? Well, whadda you got in there?"

Bowman: I knew your father before you did.

Crawford: Yeah, yeah. And he thinks you're a fuckin' asshole, too.

Bowman (to linesman): He just wants a rallying point.

Crawford: Thinks you're a fuckin' asshole, too.

Bowman (to Crawford): You just want a rallying point. You want a rallying point, that's all. It's over.

(muffled)

Crawford: You got your rallying point. You got yours, we got ours now. We got ours. You gonna apologize? (louder) Are you gonna apologize?

Wings associate coach Barry Smith (to Bowman): Scotty, let him go, please.

Linesman: We're gonna get the game goin', all right?

Crawford comes back and stands over glass, leaning over to the Red Wings bench.

Crawford (leaning forward, inches from Bowman's face): Are you gonna apologize for that? Are you gonna apologize for that, you fuckin' old cunt?

Bowman: For what?

Crawford: You fuckin' old cunt.

Bowman: For what?

Crawford: For fuckin' Shanahan. (muffled)

Bowman makes a dismissive face.

Avalanche assistant coach Mike Foligno: That's fuckin' bullshit Scotty. He's fuckin' down, he's fuckin' pounding his head on the ice.

Crawford (to Bowman): Fuck you, you fuckin' asshole, you're a fuckin' loser.

Bowman: No, he did nothing.

Crawford (looking over to Red Wings players): Are you gonna apologize for that? Are you gonna apologize for that? Are you gonna apologize for that? Are you gonna apologize?

Aaron Ward: Fuck off. Sit down.

Crawford (looking over at Ward): Come on Ward. Come on (motions with his index finger). Any fuckin' time boy, any fuckin' time. Any fuckin' time, ya fuckin'—you're all a bunch a pussies. Especially you, you little fuckin' . . .

Crawford moves forward a bit and starts shaking and pointing his finger at Bowman, who has moved farther down the bench, in the middle.

Foligno: Hey, he took a fuckin' swing at him. The trainer took a fuckin' swing at him.

Crawford (shrieking): I'll fuckin' kill you. I will. I'll get you, you cocksucker.

Beer from the stands sprays on Crawford. He looks back briefly, nearly loses his balance. Somebody grabs his left arm. The crowd is yelling "Craw-ford." Crawford tries to gain his footing.

Crawford: I'll fuckin' get you.

Linesman: Don't. Crow, don't! (to Foligno) Get him down.

Crawford (with Foligno restraining him): You fuckin' old cunt. You fuckin' asshole. I'm gonna get you. I am. I will.

Foligno (to Crawford): Come on.

Stephane Yelle and Foligno hold Crawford back.

Crawford: Your time has come, and I'm gonna get you.

Crawford walks away momentarily. Barry Smith and Steve Yzerman look at Crawford in disbelief. Crawford drops a few more F-bombs to no one in particular and talks to the linesman briefly, then walks back over to the glass partition. The crowd is yelling "Craw-ford, Craw-ford."

Crawford (to Smith): Whose fuckin' ass ya kissin' now Barry, whose ass ya kissin' now? Whose ass ya kissin'?

Smith, Yzerman, and Draper look at Crawford as if witnessing a car crash.

"I said to Scotty, 'Scotty, what the hell did you do to Crow?'" Devorski recalled. "Scotty looks at me and says, 'Paul, I don't think I said anything.'"

"We just wanted to let him go," Smith said eight years later. "I think, at that moment, we knew we had them."

A total of 232 penalty minutes were assessed by Devorksi in Game 4, 204 in the third period. The March 26 game had 148. The tough-talking Avalanche had been made into fools. Crawford was only semiapologetic afterward, saying, "The emotions got a little out of line at that particular time."

Roy, as always, was unapologetic for his challenging of the Wings. That didn't stop the dagger-penned Kiszla from ridiculing him.

"With foolhardy words meant to inspire, Colorado Avalanche goalie Patrick Roy wrote the obituary for the defending Stanley Cup champions," Kiszla wrote. "By declaring war on the Detroit Red Wings, Roy blindly led his team to doom. When this NHL season is history and Colorado is left with nothing but regret, the disrespectful words Roy uttered 24 hours before this 6-0 slaughter in Joe Louis Arena will come back to mock and haunt the Avs. What the yapping goalie saw Thursday night was the shameful, painful undoing of a hockey champion. It was an ugly sight, for which Roy owes his team and his town an apology. Nonetheless, Roy is far too vain to admit he made an irrevocable mistake by baiting the Wings with a string of Wednesday afternoon insults that questioned Detroit's heart, and arrogantly laughed at any suggestion the Avs were in danger of losing their NHL title. Thursday, his yapping even cost Roy a 10-minute misconduct call for insulting referee Paul Devorski. But he stubbornly refused to apologize for anything. If pride is one of the seven deadly sins, then the cause of the Avalanche's demise must be assigned to Roy."

Post columnist Paige gave up on the Avs, now down 3-1: "Game Four was the Cup de grace. So long, Stanley. Denver vs. Detroit Thursday night turned out to be an ice cube against a blowtorch."

The next day, Crawford was fined $10,000 by the NHL. He was a much sorrier sounding person.

"You have a responsibility as a head coach in a prestigious league like the NHL to carry yourself with a lot more dignity than I did," Crawford said. "For that, I am sorry. I embarrassed the league, and more important, I embarrassed my team with my actions. There's no way you can justify anything like that."

Years later, Crawford and Bowman became good friends.

The two worked in tandem to establish an informal NHL coaches association, where they agreed to share salary information. It wasn't long before salaries for coaches began to rise significantly.

Bowman is able to laugh off Crawford's outburst now, perhaps because memories of it remind him how his team had gotten the mental edge on the Avalanche.

"I like Marc, and I always liked his father," Bowman said. "When I started to coach, a junior team, we barnstormed around. Crawford's father played for the Belleville MacFarlanes. He wasn't a big guy, but he played right defense and he had a little chip on his shoulder, although he was a stylish player. Marc is a little like that, too. But I never took any offense to what he did."

The Avalanche had one last champion's punch left in them in Game 5. Colorado won by a shocking 6-0 score, with Avs players touching Drygas's wheelchair with their sticks beforehand for good luck.

"We believe again," said Lemieux, who scored two goals.

Even Paige had renewed hope.

"The Bonhomme Richard had been stunned, shell-shocked and shot to shreds by the Royal Navy's Serapis and was swiftly sinking when Capt. John Paul Jones, up to his brass in seawater, declared something like: 'I have not yet begun to play my game,'" he wrote. "Saturday night, 218 years later, the U.S.S. Avalanche—in the tradition of Bonhomme Richard and Maurice Richard, but not Little Richard—stayed afloat and fights on. The battle is not over; it is joined. The 'Lanchers, who had to sync or swim, finally began to play their game in the Western Conference finals."

The Avalanche would play only one more game. Detroit closed out the series in Game 6, 3-1. Martin Lapointe beat Roy with a long slap shot in the second period for the game's first goal and Sergei Fedorov got the second. Forsberg could barely play with a bad charley horse and Detroit outshot Colorado one final, whopping time, 42-16.

"Av-venged," read the headline in the next day's *Detroit Free Press*.

The series was over and the Avalanche said all the properly gracious things afterward, but there was still the matter of Lemieux, McCarty, and Draper. Would they shake hands in the traditional procession when it was over?

The answer was no. McCarty and Draper brushed past Lemieux, nobody making any eye contact. This battle was over. But the war between the Avalanche and Red Wings was hardly finished.

"Nothing is sadder than two men who let pride get in the way of peace," Kiszla wrote in the *Post*. "Colorado's Claude Lemieux couldn't look at his victim's face. And Detroit's Kris Draper refused to shake his attacker's hand. The hate between the Avalanche and Red Wings refuses to die. In the most telling, dramatic moment of these NHL playoffs, Lemieux and Draper couldn't find the courage to put an end to the nastiest, bloodiest feud in hockey."

Scotty

For a hockey war, there was no better general than Scotty Bowman.

Throughout his five decades as a coach in the NHL, there was a lot of psychoanalysis done on Bowman by sports writers. Every year his team was in the Finals, you could always depend on several "What Makes Scotty Tick?"–type stories and columns by the knights of the keyboard.

Much would be made of his affinity for electric trains or that he didn't live with his wife, Suella, during the hockey seasons in Detroit. What did it all mean?

But figuring out the method to Bowman's coaching style isn't that tough. It was from the military school of thought, that in order to build up a soldier, he must first be torn down to size. If he can take the abuse, chances are he'll build himself up stronger than before. If not, well, he just didn't have what it took.

While Bowman never served in the military, his uncles did and he liked to read biographies on some of history's great leaders and the battles they fought, including generals George S. Patton and Douglas MacArthur.

But Bowman's biggest influence in life did not come from a book. It was his father, John. A man with hands almost as strong as the iron and steel he forged in 32 years as a black-smith, John Bowman grew up in Scotland and was a very good soccer player as a youth.

"He was on a championship junior team," Bowman said. "He had pretty strong legs. I kind of inherited the same kind."

Indeed, looking at a picture of John Bowman when Scotty was five is to look at the exact image his son would become, right down to the same mesomorphic physique, hairstyle, and somewhat crooked smile.

John Bowman fell in love with and married a pretty Scottish girl named Jean, and the couple immigrated to Canada in 1930. They settled in the bilingual, blue-collar town of Verdun on the Island of Montreal, and on September 18, 1933, Jean gave birth to her second child, a son they would name William Scott, in honor of his maternal grandfather. The couple had three other children, Freda (the oldest), Jack, and Martin. Scotty's uncle Martin was killed in action fighting for Scotland in World War I. John Bowman had been too young to enlist for the First World War, and was 38 by the start of the second.

John had no formal education, which meant scraping out a blacksmith's living.

"He would shoe horses. Not an easy job, they can bite you back, you know," Bowman said. "He was a strong guy."

John would later earn a better living as a foreman in a fur-nace factory, and with Jean's job as a grocery store clerk, the Bowmans led a decent lower-middle-class life. It didn't matter that his father was not a champion of industry; what would pro-vide the bedrock template for the rest of Scotty Bowman's life was seeing his father's incredible work ethic every day, year after year.

"He never missed a day of work in 32 years," he said. "Peo-ple in those days started working when they were 14. He worked hard. No schooling, but he was self-taught. Even until the last few weeks of his life, he was always reading and did his crosswords."

Young Scotty started work at age 11, as a newspaper delivery boy. He also delivered bread and by 17 or so, he worked at a dairy. He delivered milk and cheese with a horse and wagon, the clomping of the horse's shoes possibly coming from his father's handiwork.

A lifetime following his father's lead as a skilled laborer might have been just fine with Scotty. Certainly there was no shame in what his father did. But as a teenager, he became intrigued by the game of hockey. He would never lose the passion for it. He loved the raw strength it took to play, but also the finesse required to handle a puck with a stick while on skates. But to Scotty, even at an early age, hockey was a thinking man's sport. The game was a combination of timing, speed, geometry, endurance, and patience. To succeed, one had to be able to think quickly and observe detail—two of his best traits. In Montreal, where the modern game was born, Scotty was just one of thousands of kids who played street hockey into the evening, the only light coming from the dim city lamps.

With his thickly muscled legs and low center of gravity, Scotty had the perfect hockey body. He was a strong skater, with decent hands and overall skill. By his later teenage years, a junior hockey team named the Montreal Junior Canadiens drafted him. A career in the NHL as a checking left-winger seemed a real possibility. But on a cold March night in 1952 at the Montreal Forum, Bowman's playing career took a serious blow.

It happened on March 6, 1952, during a Junior Canadiens play-off game with the Trois-Rivieres Reds.

The Junior Canadiens won the first three games of the best-of-nine series and had a 5-1 lead late in the game when Bowman came in on a breakaway on Reds goalie Gilles Boisvert. As he was about to shoot, Bowman was slashed from behind by the stick of Reds defenseman Jean-Guy Talbot. The blade of Talbot's stick opened a five-inch gash to Bowman's scalp, requiring 14 stitches. Talbot received a 10-minute major penalty and a game-misconduct. Talbot would later be suspended one full season by the Quebec Amateur Hockey Association for the incident, although Talbot said it was because he refused to report to a minor pro team owned by Montreal. The suspension was lifted in January 1953.

(Bowman and Talbot would go on to be friends, with Bowman acquiring him as a player when he coached the St. Louis Blues.)

Plenty of myths abound about what happened next, many of which clung surprisingly well to Bowman's biography into his later coaching years. Myth number one was that Bowman's skull was fractured and that doctors inserted a metal plate in his head. It never happened.

Numerous jokes, as we've seen from Crawford already, were made at Bowman's expense over the years at the "steel plate in his head." He couldn't make it through airport metal detectors, people said. He had a special medical card that informed airport personnel of his situation, and was able to bypass the detectors. It was all horse-hockey, to quote Colonel Potter.

"It was one of those things that got started about me and didn't quit I guess," Bowman said.

Myth number two is that Talbot's slash ended Bowman's playing career on the spot. In fact, Bowman played for the Junior Canadiens in the same series with Trois-Rivieres after missing just the one game. He would play two more years of junior hockey for the Montreal Junior Royals.

The truth is, Bowman probably just wasn't good enough to make it as an NHL player, slash or no slash. But what is also true is that Bowman never felt quite right on the ice after his injury. He had occasionally severe headaches, and some blurred vision. He would vomit from nausea the blurry vision produced. He lost weight and strength.

"I just didn't feel the same as a player," Bowman said.

So with his junior eligibility up and his pro prospects dim, Bowman quit as a player after the 1953–54 season. At first, he wasn't sure what he'd do next. He didn't have much of an education, not much to offer the business world. Thankfully, former NHL star Frank Selke, now working in management with the Canadiens, offered Bowman a job coaching one of the local park league teams the Canadiens were establishing. Plus, Selke offered Bowman some tuition money to take college-level business courses.

"When I was playing junior, I had a scholarship offer to go to a big school [Rensselaer Polytechnic Institute]," Bowman said. "Ned Harkness was recruiting a lot of Canadians, but I wasn't interested. I wanted to be an NHL player. I didn't go and then I got injured. The Canadiens offered for me to go to school and I took a business course for two years and I coached in the park leagues."

He thought about a career in business, maybe an accountant. He was pretty good with numbers, organization. Maybe get a job in an office and make a decent living. Where was the harm in that? While Bowman took courses and coached in the park league, he also worked as a paint salesman for Sherwin-Williams.

"I worked at Sherwin-Williams for two years, and in the summer of 1956, Sam Pollock came up and said, 'We're moving the Junior Canadiens from Montreal to Ottawa,' because they weren't drawing," Bowman said. "He said, 'Would you like to come and be my assistant, as coach and assistant manager—you can learn the business.' It was a big decision, because I wanted to get into hockey, but I had to leave my job. So I got a year's leave of absence from Sherwin-Williams and went to Ottawa."

Pollock, the Canadiens' director of player personnel and future GM in their 1970s glory days, remembered Bowman for his work ethic as a player and sensed a keen hockey mind. At only 23 years of age, Bowman was an assistant coach with the Hull-Ottawa Canadiens. He coached there from 1956 to 1958, helping lead the team to a Memorial Cup in the 1957–58 season.

Bowman then went to Peterborough, Ontario, to coach yet another of Montreal's junior teams. At 25, Bowman was now a head coach as well as general manager. Bowman coached Peterborough to the 1959 Memorial Cup finals before losing to Winnipeg. He coached Peterborough until 1961, when Pollock told Bowman the Canadiens wanted him to be a scout.

"I became their head Eastern scout," Bowman said. "I was only 28 and single, and it was an old man's job. So much traveling and there was no social life. I mean, I got to see Bobby Orr when he was 13 and things like that, but it wasn't quite what I wanted. I did that until '63 and then I went to them and said I wanted to get back coaching."

The Canadiens obliged, but sent him to Omaha, Nebraska, to coach a Montreal affiliate in the new Central Professional Hockey League. Pollock would be the team's general manager, but ran things from Montreal.

"We won our first six games on the road and we were coming home, and I got in a big dispute with the two owners," Bowman said. "They wanted us to go by bus, and all the other teams were going by train. So I told them to shove their team up their ass."

Bowman said he couldn't tolerate it in Omaha, and a sympathetic Pollock told him to come back home, but to go back to scouting for the Canadiens. After a month, the Canadiens told Bowman to serve as interim coach for one of their Junior B teams, the Notre Dame de Grace (NDG) Monarchs.

"They had some good young players, guys like Larry Pleau, Serge Savard, Carol Vadnais, Rogie Vachon, and Craig Patrick," Bowman said.

Bowman coached the Monarchs for one successful year before getting a better offer, in 1965, to coach the same Junior Canadiens team he once played for. Pollock, now the NHL Canadiens' GM, rewarded Bowman for his unquestionable coaching success everywhere the team had placed him.

Across the hall from his new office at the Montreal Forum was that of the NHL Canadiens' coach, Toe Blake. To Bowman, Blake was the epitome of what a coach should be: tough, not always fair, sometimes feared but always respected by his players. Bowman soaked up every word of advice Blake offered, and studied him much harder than any of those boring business textbooks.

"I got along good with him. He was a wonderful guy," Bowman said. "I could go to him any time I wanted. What he'd always say to me was, 'Well, Scotty, you gotta do it your way, but here's the situation that I encountered, very similar to yours, and here's what I did.' He never told me, 'You should do it this way.' He was one of the first coaches who really had a handle on matching players. He really taught me to have the right players on the ice at the right time."

In 1967 the NHL expanded from 6 to 12 teams, with one entire division, the West, added that included teams in Philadelphia, Los Angeles, Minnesota, Pittsburgh, Oakland, and St. Louis.

The expansion St. Louis Blues hired Lynn Patrick as their first coach and general manager, and Patrick took a flier on the 34-year-old Bowman to be one of his assistant coaches and overall managing aide. Patrick had heard about what a good coach Bowman was from his son, Craig. Bowman got an offer of $15,000 to coach in St. Louis, quite a jump from the $7,000 he was making with the Junior Canadiens.

Not long into the 1967–68 season, though, Patrick tired of the grind doing both jobs and decided to spend all his time upstairs in the GM's box, and looked to Bowman as his successor. The Blues were in last place and expansion teams have always been a kind of graveyard for coaches; no matter how good a coach is, the record is almost never above .500 and most of the time he's only setting the table for the next coach to come along and take all the credit. *Montreal Gazette* hockey writer Red Fisher knew Bowman from his Canadiens years and was in St. Louis the night before Bowman was hired to replace Patrick.

"When we got there, who was in the lobby but Scotty Bowman, assistant coach of the Blues. We were in some dump of a hotel. He knew right where we were, even though it wasn't our scheduled hotel," Fisher said. "He was there waiting for me and Pat Curran, who covered the team for the *Gazette*. Scotty wanted to take us out on the town. We said, 'Sure.' We went out to dinner, out to some area in town where they had street artists, and some guy who did cartoons. Scotty actually paid a buck for some caricature that a guy did of me. All night long, all the guy talked about was the St. Louis owners wanted him to take over as coach. They weren't drawing shit. I said, 'What's the holdup Scotty?' He said, 'I wouldn't coach those dogs. They can't play, they can't do anything.' This went all night long. We didn't return to the hotel until 2 in the morning. At 7 in the morning, the sports news came on and the first thing was 'Scotty Bowman is the new coach of the St. Louis Blues.' Of course, he knew that all along. He wanted to kiss our ass."

In the words of one St. Louis writer, Bowman looked like Al Capone behind the Blues bench, with his wide-collared jackets and slicked-back hair. Some of his players soon might have felt the same about his personality. One oft-told Bowman story is of him walking into a bar frequented by Blues players, and putting a nickel into the jukebox to play Fats Domino's "Kansas City," with its verse, "Kansas City, here I come." The Blues' minor-league affiliate was in Kansas City, and Bowman didn't want his last-place players getting so comfortable they stopped worrying they might be sent there on the next bus.

Being only 34 at the time of his hire, Bowman naturally gravitated toward some of the Blues' older players as allies, players such as Glenn Hall, Dickie Moore, and Al Arbour. Because they could help teach the younger ones and allow him to focus more on Xs and Os, Bowman would continue to favor older players throughout his career, particularly when it came to filling certain key roles such as penalty killers or fifth and sixth defensemen.

Blues players such as Bob Plager were the first to get a dose of the Bowman coaching method. In his later years, Bowman got his messages across through a lack of communication; in St. Louis and later in Montreal, Bowman was more more likely to play verbal games to motivate his players.

"He'd walk in the dressing room before a game and say something like, 'Big, tough, Noel Picard. You know what the word in the league is now? Noel Picard's a talker.' Noel would yell, 'Who says that? I'll kill him,'" Bob Plager said in *Tales from the Blues Bench*.

"Scotty would say to us, 'There, he's talking again.'"

"Noel would say, 'Hey, I'll kill anybody who says that!'"

"Scotty would shrug his shoulders and say, 'See, talking again.'"

Picard went out and hit anything that moved that night, just to prove to Bowman nobody could push him around. Tear a guy down; watch him build himself back up. That was the Bowman method.

Bowman guided the Blues to three straight Stanley Cup Finals appearances, but the team was swept in four games each time. Even though the West Division wasn't very good, it was still a remarkable, unprecedented feat by a coach in any pro sport. Along the way, he met a St. Louis nurse named Suella, to whom he soon proposed.

After year three with the Blues, however, Bowman started to have some friction with the Salomon family, which owned the team. They argued about personnel changes, and in the end Bowman was fired, although he would term it a "mutual parting."

Luckily for him, the Canadiens were having some trouble with their own coach, and would look to Bowman for help.

In 1971 Bowman was hired by Pollock to replace Al MacNeil as head coach of the Canadiens, despite the fact MacNeil led Montreal to the Stanley Cup that year. But MacNeil, who couldn't speak much French, wasn't well liked by his mostly francophone stars. Bowman was bilingual, and Pollock knew he was a hot young protégé who might take his team back to its dynasty days. He was right.

Bowman's eight years with the Canadiens resulted in five Stanley Cups, including four straight from 1975–76 through 1978–79. These were the great Canadiens of Guy Lafleur, Larry Robinson, Steve Shutt, and Ken Dryden.

The 1976–77 Habs are often called the best team of all time, one that went an incredible 60-8-12, an .825 winning percentage. The team had eight players with 20 or more goals, led by Shutt's 60. Dryden went 41-6-8, with 10 shutouts. There was probably no more intimidating team to play against. Teams would feel second class coming into the glorious Forum, with its elegant organ music; out-of-this world hot dogs on buttered, toasted buns; and well-heeled lower-bowl patrons. Check out pictures from those days of fans in the stands and you'll see men mostly in jacket and tie, with the women wearing fur and lots of jewelry.

Then there was Bowman, with his upturned chin. It seemed he and the Canadiens were only there to satisfy the schedule makers. They appeared to have a mock disdain for the opposition. Everybody knew there was no chance to beat Montreal, most of all the opposing team. Largely it was because of Bowman's fanatical preparation regimens and psychological mastery of his players.

As Dryden put it in his masterpiece *The Game*, Bowman "knows each of us too well; he leaves us no place to hide. He knows that we are strong, and are weak; that we can be selfish and lazy, that we can eat too much and drink too much, that we will always look for the easy way out, and when we find it, that we will use it. He knows that each of us comes with a stable of excuses, 'crutches' he calls them, ready to use whenever we need them. The team with the fewest crutches will win, Bowman believes."

Prior to winning his fifth Cup, Bowman knew Pollock would soon step down as Canadiens GM. Now in his mid-40s, Bowman wanted the security and added income the GM's office afforded.

"I wasn't making much money in Montreal," Bowman said. "In 1971, I made $30,000 as their coach. Every year we won the Cup, I got a $10,000 raise. When I was finished coaching in Montreal, I was making about $100,000."

Maybe more than money, though, Bowman wanted control of his team's player personnel. Throughout his career, it always got under Bowman's skin that some other guy upstairs might have more power than him over which players to have on the roster. Sure, the owner was one thing; he signed the checks and could tell Scotty what to do without chafing him too much. But GMs and others with fancy titles like director of player development were another story. Bowman knew nobody worked harder than he observing talent around the league—around the world, for that matter. He knew what kind of players he wanted, so why did he have to consult with some lazy GM about it? Why couldn't he just make the deal himself, save everybody a lot of trouble?

"Scotty Bowman knew more about every other team in the NHL than their own coaches," Fisher said. "He was on the phone 24/7. We would go in the other towns, and you'd get pissed off at what you'd read in their papers."

When Pollock was ready to step away from the Canadiens in 1978, Bowman figured he deserved the job. But he didn't get it. The Canadiens were sold around this time by the Bronfman family to Molson Breweries. A Molson executive named Irving Grundman, who had business ties with the Bronfmans (he was partners with the family on a new bowling alley), got the job. Fisher did the impossible, which was scoop Bowman of the news in the *Gazette*. Bowman was hurt.

"Scotty said, 'I can no longer accept the fact that Red Fisher knows more about this team than I do' at a press conference when he didn't get the job," Fisher said. "He was always such a conniving son of a bitch, always to make him look a little better, but also to make his team look better. In the end, Scotty always put the team's success ahead of everything, because that's how he got success."

Bowman, feeling slighted after all he'd done to restore the Canadiens to their former glory, put out feelers around the league. He made it clear, though, that he wanted more control of the personnel he might coach—perhaps wear the GM's hat, too. It wasn't long before the Buffalo Sabres, who had some great teams in the 1970s that couldn't quite make it all the way, offered Bowman his dream job: coach and GM. Bowman would finally run the whole show, and at a whopping salary of $200,000 a year.

Another reason Bowman left Montreal was his wife. Suella was thrilled to get out of Montreal. Born in Illinois, she never had the time to learn French, having five children in the eight years the couple spent in Montreal, and was happy to be back on American soil.

"He came in with so much hype, and rightfully so," said Jim Kelley, the Sabres beat reporter for the *Buffalo News*. "He was the coach of the legendary Canadiens, now in Buffalo. Everybody made bets about how many Stanley Cups the Sabres would win now that he was there."

The answer would be zero. Oh, they came close, losing in six games to eventual Cup champion New York Islanders in the Wales Conference finals his first year behind the bench, 1979–80. But something always seemed to go wrong at a critical time. His stay in Buffalo, until 1986–87, would mark the only time in Bowman's career he did not take a team to the Stanley Cup Finals. In the long, glorious display of his year-by-year coaching records, there is only one season in which the losses outnumber the victories, and it wasn't even a full season: 1986–87, his last, abbreviated year in Buffalo, at 3-7-2. Only one of the teams on which he coached a full season, the 1985–86 Sabres, ever missed the playoffs.

"We were too young in Buffalo," Bowman said. "We had to be careful with the budget, because in those days you couldn't buy your players, you had to grow your own. Team only came in the league in 1970. Still was growing. We couldn't have a farm team, because they felt if they had a farm team and they'd have good players, they couldn't keep them anyway. We lost a five-game series twice, in Quebec and Boston."

Bowman inserted himself into the coaching role whenever he felt things weren't right with the men he hired, which became something of an ongoing soap opera. After coaching the Sabres in 1979–80, Bowman moved up to the GM suite full-time and hired Roger Neilson to coach the team in 1980–81. Neilson led Buffalo to an Adams Division title. But a loss in the conference quarterfinals meant sayonara for Neilson. The next season, Bowman brought in his old friend Jimmy Roberts, but Bowman took over late in the year when things were going sour. Bowman would coach the next three seasons, only to hire Jim Schoenfeld to start the 1985–86 campaign. Bowman sacked him late in the year and again took over the job himself.

"I don't think Scotty the GM always helped Scotty the coach," Kelley said. "He could act impulsively about players. You'd hear stories about how, at the draft, the scouts would be all set to draft some kid and Scotty would come in at the last second and announce some other selection. They'd look at him like 'What was that?' and Scotty might go, 'Oh, I talked to my friend about this kid a few minutes ago.'"

Indeed, in the 1981 NHL draft, Bowman's Sabres chose the immortal Jiri Dudacek with the 17th overall pick, passing on such later picks as Chris Chelios, Mike Vernon, and John Vanbiesbrouck. Dudacek would never play a game for the Sabres, becoming entangled with his Czech team over his rights and developing a mysterious illness. While Buffalo's top picks in 1982 and 1983, Phil Housley and Tom Barrasso, would go on to excellent careers, from 1984 to 1986 Buffalo took the forgettable Mikael Andersson, Calle Johansson, and Shawn Anderson with their top picks—passing on Patrick Roy, Stephane Richer, Brett Hull, Luc Robitaille, Gary Suter, Joe Nieuwendyk, Brian Leetch, and Vincent Damphousse.

With the Sabres' fortunes plummeting and friction starting to develop with the Knox family, which owned the team, Bowman was fired shortly into the 1986–87 season. But by then, the Bowmans had fallen in love with the Buffalo area. Scotty looked for work elsewhere, but it was decided Suella and the kids would always maintain a home in Amherst, a suburb of Buffalo—mainly because of the excellent care found for the couple's son, David, who was born with hydrocephalus, a serious neurological disorder that left him mostly blind and mentally disabled. The Bowmans found top-notch care at an area infant home and at the New York State School for the Blind in Batavia.

"He's in a really good program where he is, and it's hard to find that," said Scotty's son Stan Bowman, who in 2005 was an executive in the Chicago Blackhawks organization. "He's been stable there since 1979 in Buffalo. I always wondered growing up what it would have been like to have him more normal. It's really sad, but it happened and we've dealt with it as good as we could have."

In Buffalo Stan Bowman came to know his father as a hockey savant, and a stickler for fine craftsmanship.

"In Buffalo he built a rink in the backyard for us," Stan recalled. "Every night when he would come home, he would always go out and he'd clear off the snow and flood the ice and kind of use that time to cool down after a tough loss. By the time he'd done all that, he'd come in and my mom would say, 'He's OK.' He could put it behind him. He would take a lot of pride in trying to make the ice really nice. He'd chip the ice away and make it nice for the kids the next day.

"I was exposed to hockey a lot. One of my favorite things for me to do as a kid was just to sit and listen to him talk to other coaches or other GMs. I would just sit there and listen to him for hours, talking about strategy, breaking down the night before. I was kind of a fly on the wall. He didn't so much talk to me about hockey, but he'd just let me come everywhere with him and absorb it all. When I got older and actually had an opinion on things, he would ask me after a game, 'What'd you think?' I think the thing that was pretty innovative about him—and it's actually a pretty basic thing—was that he listens to people. Even though he's the most successful coach, if I noticed something they were doing on the power play was bad or wrong, he would take it to heart and if it actually made sense he would incorporate it with his coaches. He's willing to listen to anybody with a good idea or unique idea. He wasn't one of those guys who had to come up with everything on his own."

* * *

After Buffalo, Bowman took a job as an analyst with *Hockey Night in Canada*, and gave what those who worked with him for three years said was his usual hard-working, professional effort. But everybody knew he itched to get back on the other side of the microphone, where the real action was. Problem was, the Buffalo stint stained his reputation; the Sabres not only didn't win a Cup, they regressed in Bowman's time. And everybody knew his preferred job was as GM, something that naturally gave current GMs pause.

So for a while Bowman was, in effect, blackballed from the league. It wasn't until the Patrick family came calling again that Bowman drew a check from an NHL club. In 1991 GM Craig Patrick hired Bowman as director of player development for the Pittsburgh Penguins.

The team was coached by "Badger" Bob Johnson, a warm, quiet man who was well liked by everybody. Initially, Bowman probably second-guessed his coaching decisions from time to time, but he came to greatly admire Johnson. Some of Bowman's first decisions would benefit the Penguins for years, such as the drafting of Jaromir Jagr and a heist of a trade with Hartford that brought Ron Francis and Ulf Samuelsson. The Penguins won their first Stanley Cup in 1991 with Johnson as coach. But by the following September, Johnson was in the late stages of terminal brain cancer. Johnson died on November 26, 1991. Patrick asked Bowman to step in as Johnson's replacement, which he did reluctantly.

"He was a great, great man," was all Bowman could say of Johnson, before becoming quiet.

The Penguins won the 1991–92 Stanley Cup with Bowman behind the bench. He showed the world he hadn't lost his touch as the game's best bench boss, and the job he did in the front office helped patch up some of his tattered executive reputation.

Along the way, Bowman hired a pro scout named Pierre Mc-
Guire, who later became an assistant on the bench. Bowman
got to know McGuire when he was hockey coach at St. Law-
rence University, where Bowman's daughter, Alicia, was a student.

"Scotty used to drive up for *Hockey Night* games on Thursday in Montreal, and he would stop in and watch practice, and
then he and I would go out to dinner," McGuire said. "We
always played Friday-Saturday, and we would talk on the phone
every day. From about the second or third day that I met him,
we would talk on the phone every day."

In Pittsburgh Bowman lived alone, as he would the rest of
his career. Suella stayed back in Amherst, tending to David and
the rest of the family.

When McGuire came to town as his new hire, Bowman
took him under his wing. That meant putting him up at his
apartment, where McGuire said, "It was hockey, 24/7."

"Our day was pretty simple," McGuire said. "I'd get to the
office early, he'd get there a little later. Barry Smith, Scotty, and
I would all hang out together all the time. We had a satellite
dish in the office and watched games there, then we'd go have
a late dinner and then we'd go to the room and watch more
hockey on SportsChannel America or ESPN. We watched
hockey all the time. There was no Internet back then, but we
would have all the scores. We'd be calling different radio stations for scores. If he didn't call, I would."

The two would develop a close friendship, not easy with
Bowman. McGuire got to see Bowman's soft, family-man side.
Despite the fact his family lived in the Buffalo area, Bowman
kept in constant touch. His phone bills were sometimes into the
hundreds of dollars.

"His son, David, was 18 years old, I believe, when he
learned to brush his teeth on his own. It's one of the first times
I really saw Scotty emotional. I was living with him and he

came into my room and said, 'David learned how to brush his teeth,'" McGuire said. "It was so matter of fact, but it was so heartfelt that it kind of showed a different perspective.

"Another time, we're playing in Pittsburgh, playing against Winnipeg on a Saturday afternoon. And we're leaving for Western Canada on a Sunday to start a long road trip. Scotty gets in his car, right after the game against Winnipeg, and drives to Buffalo. He gets there at probably 1 or 2 in the morning, has breakfast with his children, takes them to church, spends the day with them and drives to Toronto, gets on a plane and meets the team. He did that a lot. This guy was really committed to his family, and it rubs off on me. Lesson was, if you can get back on the first red-eye, do it."

Being a pal of Bowman's didn't mean getting special treatment on the job, though. McGuire would soon learn firsthand the confounding methods of Bowman, the boss.

"One time I made a [scouting] tape, and in front of the whole team he said, 'Who made this tape?' And he knew darn well I'd made this tape," McGuire recalled. "And he said, 'This is one of the worst pieces of tape I've ever seen.' It really wasn't, but his way was to get me focused, because we had a huge bunch of games coming up.

"Another time, I'm writing down the Rangers lineup, and he goes, 'What are you doing?' I said, 'I'm doing what I do before every game, I'm putting together the matchups: Francis versus Messier, etc.' He goes, 'How many days you been in this league?' I said, 'Two years.' He goes, 'I've been in 32, get out of here.' I was mad. I slammed the door and walked out to watch the warm-ups, I figured I was getting fired anyway. I walked back in, and I heard the vacuum cleaner, cleaning up all the broken glass. Bob Johnson had these beautiful pictures on the wall, and after I'd slammed the door, a bunch of the pictures had come down and the glass had broken. Scotty says to people loud enough for me to hear, 'That kid's got a bad temper, but he's going to be a good coach someday.' So, we're walking onto the ice, and in Pittsburgh from the home dressing room to the home bench is a long walk, and he's behind me and he says, 'I think you're focused for the game tonight, aren't you?' Little things like that.

"Scotty's biggest thing is excellence. He's so enamored with it. If he thought you had the ability to go to another level, and you weren't getting there, he would find a way to cajole you to get to that level. Now, maybe you didn't appreciate it and maybe it was very hard, and maybe it was overbearing sometimes, but I can tell you that it works. He's done it to me."

The 1992–93 Penguins were a powerhouse, the prohibitive Stanley Cup three-peat favorites. The team might have had the best top-six forward combination in NHL history, with Mario Lemieux, Jagr, Francis, Kevin Stevens, Rick Tocchet, and Joe Mullen. But the Penguins were upset in the second round by the Islanders.

Bowman's buddy McGuire moved on to the Hartford Whalers as an assistant and, later, head coach, but by 1994 was dismissed and soon landed in Ottawa as a pro scout. Prior to McGuire's arrival in Ottawa, the Senators offered Bowman the head-coaching job.

"They were telling him the job was his if he wanted it," McGuire said. "It was this kind of commitment, and this was the money he was going to get, this that and everything else, and at the end of the day Scotty was like, 'You know what, I'm not interested.' I think the offer was about $150,000 a year [less than he was making in Pittsburgh]."

Bowman would soon get a lot more than that, thanks to Detroit pizza magnate Mike Ilitch, who was looking for someone to guide what he thought was a young, up-and-coming Red Wings team. Bowman's old colleague from St. Louis, Jimmy Devellano, initially wanted to hire Islanders legend Al Arbour for the job, but turned to Bowman when Arbour declined. In the summer of 1993, Ilitch gave Bowman a two-year contract worth $800,000 a year. The son of a Montreal blacksmith had never seen so many zeroes in his life.

Bowman thought he might only coach the Red Wings a year or two, then maybe, if he played his cards right, move back into the GM's suite. At 60, he was starting to feel his age a bit. He had a bum knee, along with some pain in a hip joint. All those years of standing behind the bench could take a toll. Better to get a nice, comfy chair upstairs and let the coach and players take the fall if things went south.

But right away, Bowman knew he had a pretty good team on his hands. Steve Yzerman was still around, along with his intriguing mix of skilled Russian players.

The goaltending was a problem, which led to conference leader Detroit's ouster in the first round by eighth-place San Jose in the 1994 playoffs. Bowman set out to fix that with the acquisition of Vernon from Calgary.

Vernon heard all the stories about Bowman before coming, about how he'd be miserable playing for him. Right away, he was surprised at how untrue they seemed.

"I think he changed his game when he met Bob Johnson, that era in Pittsburgh. Changed his game quite a bit, from the intimidator to just letting them play hockey," Vernon said.

Not quite. There would be plenty of occasions in Detroit when the old Scotty would come back, in Technicolor, and the first people to feel it were those around him, those who worked in the Red Wings public relations office, for instance.

Mike Kuta, a former Gulf War marine reconnaissance specialist, was hired by the Wings to serve alongside public relations director John Hahn shortly into Bowman's tenure. It didn't take long for Kuta to get a second form of military education from Bowman—and to learn the best way to make him like you, like McGuire did, was to stand up to him.

"I remember one time he was sitting in the coach's room, before or after a practice. All the coaches are in there watching video," Kuta said. "I had a bunch of requests that I needed to go over with him. If he knew you needed something, he would kind of blow you off. I was standing in the doorway. He just kept cutting me off, going, 'One minute, one minute.' And then he looked at me and he goes, 'Go get me a coffee.' I was like, 'What?' I said it out loud, even though I didn't intend to, I said, 'Fuck off.' It just came out. The second I said it, I thought, 'Oh Christ, this is the end of my career. I just told Scotty Bowman to fuck off.' My whole future flashed in front of my eyes, I'm going to be in the unemployment line forever. And he laughed out loud. After that, he was nicer to me. It was almost like he tested people. Our relationship from then on was better."

Bowman's assistants were his former Pittsburgh colleague Barry Smith and former longtime NHL defenseman Dave Lewis. The three were a tremendous team—and something of a funny-looking one. In the middle of the three on the bench was Bowman, always with one hand in his pants pocket, the other often grabbing ice chips out of a cup to munch. Smith had whitish hair and intense eyes that were buglike in their proportion to his face. Lewis, the calm one, had a Charlie Chaplin mustache and sleepy-eyed look.

Smith was used to Bowman by then, but Lewis had to go through the usual Bowman boot camp.

"The very first practice we had in training camp, my first year with him, we had gone over the practice before in the locker room and he's putting the drills down," Lewis said. "We get on the ice and he said, 'What are we going to do now? What are we doing?' I'm thinking after, 'Is he testing me? About my recall?' Was he? I have no idea."

It was the same with most every player who played for him. Always keep them guessing. It was the Bowman way.

"There were times he was around my kids, and then he's like Mr. Grandfather," Darren McCarty said. "But then the next day, he'll walk right by you in the hallway and not say anything to you, and you're like, 'What's up with that?'"

Wings defenseman Aaron Ward couldn't take it under Bowman anymore early in his career, and stormed into his office to ask for a trade.

"So Scotty starts reading the league stat sheets from that day and he goes, "Oh, Pittsburgh is 29th on the power play, 23rd on the penalty kill," Ward said. "I mean, he never answered me at all, never addressed anything about a trade. Just started reading stats to me. I'm like, 'Where's the *Twilight Zone* music?'"

It was the same with every beat reporter who ever covered his teams.

"He was the Wizard of Oz, the guy behind the curtain pulling all the strings. Hardest guy to predict I've ever been around, bar none," said Chuck Carlton, who covered the Wings for the *Oakland (MI) Press*. "But Scotty made you a better reporter. You had to work harder. He would quiz you. He'd ask you who scored the goal from the other night, and if you got it wrong, interview over."

In the mid 1990s, when the Internet was just coming into being, Bowman became fascinated by its possibilities. Even though he had a satellite dish at home on which he faithfully watched hockey games all night long, keeping up to date on the road on off-nights was a problem.

If the hotel bar didn't have a dish, Bowman would grumble his way back to the room and watch the CNN Headline News sports ticker for scores. But that didn't tell you who scored, or if the goalie got pulled, or if a trade just happened.

But when the Internet came, Bowman took a laptop on the road with him and would listen to streaming hockey radio broadcasts on the NHL's Web site. This was in the early days, however, when high-speed access was impossible to get. So there would be Bowman in his hotel room late at night, straining to hear a San Jose or Anaheim game on stop-and-go dial-up technology.

"When the Internet first came out, he didn't know the Internet from the interstate," Carlton said. "But he demanded the Wings get him a state-of-the-art laptop. Pretty soon, he knew what time each paper's early editions came out online and he'd read every hockey story from every city."

"I'd get a lot of calls: 'How come I can't get my computer working?'" Stan Bowman said. "But once he got the hang of it, he read every single hockey story in every single paper in the country. For a guy who is 72, he's on the computer all day, reading stories on the Internet."

Bowman was not a screamer in the locker room. He was never much of a screamer, period, although he had his moments in St. Louis and Montreal. In his later years, you could tell how mad he was by how quiet he got.

"He'd just come in and kind of softly say, 'You know you guys, this isn't satisfactory. You guys have got to pull your fuckin' socks up, end of story,'" said Vernon, doing his best Bowman impression. "'Because you know what, I make changes, I don't care. You guys gotta decide you want to play this game.'"

Said Lewis, "Sometimes, between the three of us, we'd prepare for a game, do a game, and then Scotty would get upset with the players and he'd just quit coaching. He did that a lot, even in the playoffs. He'd stare at the rink where there was nothing going on."

Said Kuta, "Dave Lewis tells the story about in the Finals against Philly in '98, the play is down at one end, and Scotty was standing down at the other end, looking at the other end. He said, 'Louie, is that Gordie Howe?' Play is going on, Stanley

Cup Finals. Lewis said, 'I think so Scotty.' Scotty says, 'You think they could have gotten him better seats.' Sometimes I just wondered where his mind was. As far as hockey goes, he was just so far ahead all the time. I think he just got bored sometimes."

Bowman never got bored with statistical minutiae. It was why he was dubbed Rain Man in Pittsburgh, for his love of numbers.

"The guy would know every single stat of all time," Red Wings goalie Chris Osgood said. "If he were here today, he would know exactly what the Carolina Hurricanes' game plan was the night before, and what they would do tonight."

Bowman was an incurable hockey gossip, always wanting to know the smallest details of everybody's life in the game. If a player was in the midst of a divorce or recently got picked up for jaywalking, chances were good Scotty already knew.

"Maybe the most compulsive gossip I've ever met," said former *Free Press* writer Jason La Canfora.

It wasn't all hockey, all the time for Bowman. He did enjoy assembling elaborate Lionel train structures at home in the off-season, and by the early 1980s he began what would be an extensive sports memorabilia collection, much of it from another sport he loved to play and watch as a youth—baseball.

"It's got to be worth seven figures," McGuire said. "I remember he got Mickey Mantle's autograph on a plane once. He was real happy about that."

Bowman also developed close relationships with some of sports' other top coaches, most especially New York Yankees manager Joe Torre. He also maintains strong contacts with Sparky Anderson, Larry Brown, and Don Shula.

Bowman's other big passions were antique cars and golf. He loved to play 18 holes, but also kept score for the PGA at major tournaments. One of the highlights of his life was keeping score for Tiger Woods at the Masters Tournament one year, and for Jack Nicklaus in his final Masters.

In his later years, Bowman maintained a vacation home in Florida for the family. He also did promotional work for the erectile dysfunction medicine Levitra.

Bowman's final years as a head coach would see his brother, Jack, die of a heart attack, and his own heart scare in 1998. Some of the battles with the Avalanche, before and after he underwent angioplasty that year, no doubt weren't very good for his stress level. But they were great for the hockey world.

And there were still plenty ahead.

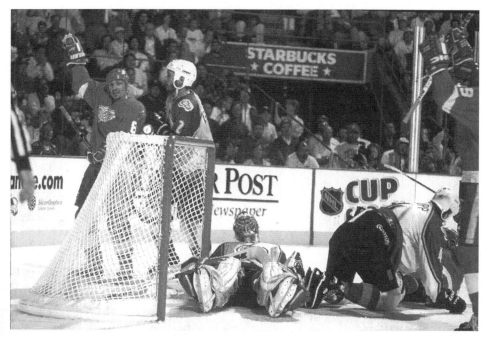

Patrick Roy is beaten on a shot during the 1996 Western Conference finals—and not looking too happy about it. *Photo by Tim De Frisco.*

Claude Lemieux accepts congratulations from Valeri Kamensky and Craig Wolanin. Lemieux could be an agitator to opponents, but also teammates, too, as Wolanin found out in the 1996 Western semifinals against Chicago. *Photo by Tim De Frisco.*

Bob Hartley, who coached the Avalanche to four
straight Western Conference finals his first four years
on the job, 1999–2002—an unprecedented feat for
an NHL coach. Hartley wasn't always liked by his
players, but he got results. *Photo by Tim De Frisco.*

Patrick Roy, flashing a smile following
Colorado's 1996 playoff defeat of Detroit. Only
a few months before, Roy was embarrassed out
of Montreal by the same Red Wings. *Photo by
Tim De Frisco.*

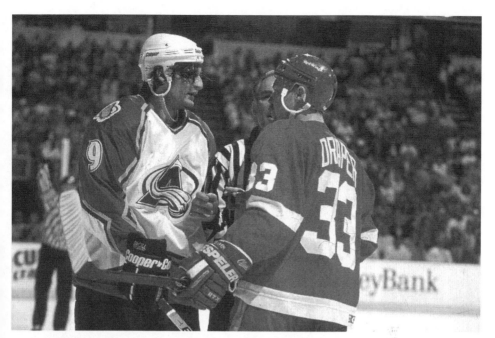

Colorado's Mike Ricci and Detroit's Kris Draper have words. Ricci had a motor mouth on the ice, and on team buses and airplanes. *Photo by Tim De Frisco.*

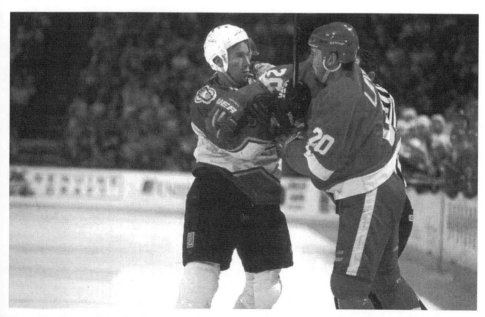

Peter Forsberg of the Avalanche tussles with Detroit's Martin Lapointe. Forsberg, sometimes to his coaches' dismay, often got into it with players bigger than him. Detroit was only too happy to trade Forsberg for Lapointe in matching penalties. *Photo by Tim De Frisco.*

Claude Lemieux waits to shake hands with Detroit players following the Avs' 1996 playoff triumph. Later, Detroit's Dino Ciccarelli would utter, "I can't believe I shook the guy's frickin' hand." *Photo by Tim De Frisco.*

Colorado defenseman Adam Foote, in happy playoff times against Detroit in 1996. Foote was a regular combatant in the rivalry, particularly against Detroit's Brendan Shanahan. *Photo by Tim De Frisco.*

Avalanche captain Joe Sakic skates with the puck. The classy native of Vancouver never got his nose bloodied in the rivalry, always concentrating on scoring goals instead. He and Peter Forsberg made for a deadly 1-2 punch at center for Colorado. *Photo by Tim De Frisco.*

Patrick Roy giving it to Dino Ciccarelli in front of the net. The two would clash often in the 1996 playoffs, with Roy jabbing his stick into Ciccarelli's groin area. *Photo by Tim De Frisco.*

Coach Marc Crawford with some loud words for his Avalanche players. Crawford's baby face and anchorman hairstyle belied a fierce temper, one he wouldn't hesitate to display against anybody, including Red Wings coach Scotty Bowman. *Photo by Tim De Frisco.*

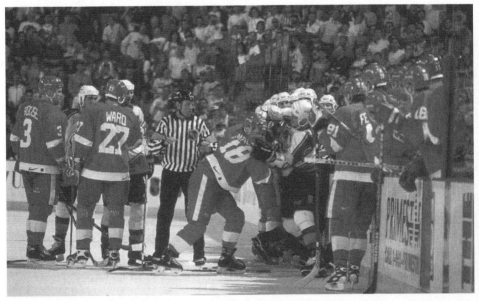

Another in the countless tussles between Red Wings and Avalanche players, this time with Detroit's Kirk Maltby in the middle of it. Maltby had a particular knack for getting under the skin of Avalanche players. *Photo by Tim De Frisco.*

Detroit's Igor Larionov faces off against Colorado's Adam Deadmarsh. In between all the blood, there was some of the greatest hockey ever played in NHL history between the teams. *Photo by Tim De Frisco.*

Darren McCarty of the Red Wings gets his and the team's revenge on Claude Lemieux, March 26, 1997. Lemieux would return to the game, only to watch McCarty score the game-winning goal in overtime. The game would turn around the fortunes of both teams, Detroit's for the better. *Photo by Mark Hicks, West Side Photographic.*

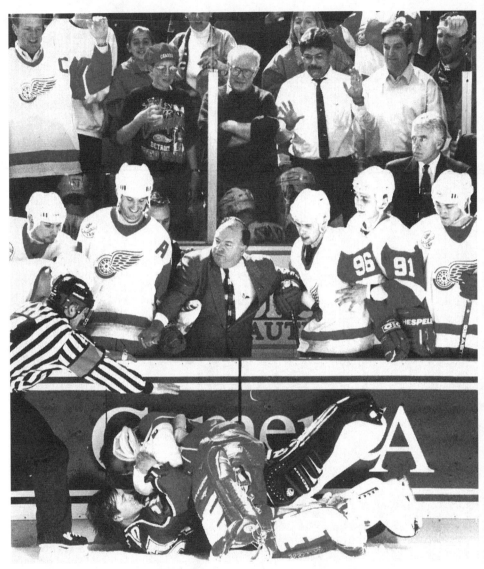

Patrick Roy, in his second fight with a Detroit goalie, this time Chris Osgood, in as many years, April 1, 1998. Roy's attempt at manufacturing the kind of emotion Detroit used the year before to win the Stanley Cup backfired. Detroit won the Cup again that year. On the Red Wings bench, at center, is legendary coach Scotty Bowman. *Photo by Mark Hicks, West Side Photographic.*

"There Ain't No Party . . ."

Prior to the 1997–98 season, Avalanche coach Marc Crawford sat down and had a talk with Claude Lemieux. At the top of the agenda were Crawford's instructions that the stuff with Darren McCarty and Kris Draper couldn't go on any longer. It clearly had come back to hurt the team, and Lemieux had to make it right.

"Bottom line is, I had to settle the issue," Lemieux said. "And, I couldn't do it at home, not sucker punching, not hitting from behind; I just had to go square with the guy that took me out."

The Avalanche's first game with Detroit that season was November 11, at the Joe. Lemieux had it circled as the night he would drop the gloves with McCarty and fight, face to face. Lemieux's manhood had continued to be questioned, not only from smart-aleck fans but also from teammates whispering behind his back. One unnamed teammate, in fact, used a profane word to describe Lemieux in an off-season *Denver Post* story, blaming him for the team's 1997 downfall. Lemieux fired back, telling the newspaper the anonymous teammate "can kiss my ass."

Despite his size, Lemieux was not a good fighter. Sure, he could throw a punch and generally handle himself in physical situations, but while he relished the psychological battles of hockey, fighting just wasn't his thing.

To prepare for fighting the tough, hardened McCarty, therefore, Lemieux sought the help of Colorado's top enforcer that season, a molasses-slow skater named Francois Leroux. Leroux, who stood nearly 6-foot-8, had for all practical purpose ended the career of star Pat Lafontaine the season before while with the Pittsburgh Penguins as a defenseman. Like Brent Severyn the year before, Leroux was repackaged into a tough-guy forward enforcer by Crawford.

In the month leading up to the Detroit game, Leroux served as the Angelo Dundee to Lemieux, telling him to always keep his hands up and lead with a left jab. Lemieux also consulted with Colorado's smaller enforcer, Jeff Odgers.

"Odgers was my roommate, and he didn't want me to fight McCarty," Lemieux said. "McCarty was in the peak of his career, obviously a pretty tough guy. But I wanted to get it over with. You don't get hurt that much in a fight anyway; maybe your nose gets broken."

In a season that would be the worst of Colorado's first nine in Denver, the night of November 11, 1997, was probably its highest point.

Backup goalie Craig Billington shut out Detroit 2-0, but it was what happened just three seconds into the contest that had everybody around the Avs feeling fired up. Before the opening faceoff, Lemieux sidled up to McCarty and said, "Let's go." McCarty said a few words back that he doesn't recall and when the puck dropped, the players stood square to each other and tossed away their gloves. Everybody in the building, including those of us on press row, stood up to watch the high drama in front of them.

Even Paul Devorski put aside some off-night amorous activity with his fiancée when—with the game on in the bedroom, of course—he saw Lemieux and McCarty squaring off out of the corner of his eye.

"We were just about in the middle of having some fun, eh?" Devorski recalled. "When they dropped the puck, I stopped and watched the fight. Boy, did I catch some shit for that."

Surprisingly, Lemieux handled himself well. He landed a couple of blows to McCarty's head, took a couple himself, but fought to what most everybody among the many hockey press members assembled that night called a draw—some even giving the nod to Lemieux. Everybody, that is, except the *Free Press*, which continued to see the world through red-tinted glasses.

"Claude Lemieux, the impetus for much of this hatred, attempted to stir it up again by switching wings with Jeff Odgers to line up against Darren McCarty on the opening face off. . . . this time Lemieux didn't cower into a protective shell as he did last March," wrote beat writer Jason La Canfora. "He caught McCarty in the chest with a punch, but soon McCarty freed himself of his jersey and had Lemieux's helmet and visor off, and after a long exchange in which Lemieux landed a few punches, he was finally dumped to the ice."

Lemieux was given a lot of macho slaps on the back by his teammates, and at that moment Avalanche fans had to wonder if perhaps the fight would serve to again turn around the fortunes of the teams, as a similar incident had the previous March 26.

But the game, indeed, was the season's high point for Colorado. The team never got any consistency going, and the many star players it sent to the 1998 Winter Olympics seemed to be too tired for the playoff run.

In a desperate, late-season attempt to insert some fire into his lackadaisical team, Patrick Roy again came to center ice at the Joe to fight a Red Wings goalie. In an April 1, 1998, game in which the Avs eventually lost, 2-0, Roy came to the red line during a stop in play with other scrums going on and motioned for Detroit's Chris Osgood to come out and throw down.

The startled, pint-sized Osgood knew he couldn't back down from such a challenge. It would give Roy and Avalanche fans ammunition to call him chicken. In hockey, as Lemieux had seen, that can't happen.

Up in the Avs' radio booth, Mike Haynes was practically frothing at the mouth.

"Roy is furious! He wants to help out his teammates. Now he's pointing to Osgood. Come on Osgood! Here they go, here we go! Oh yeah baby! It's Roy and Osgood at center ice!" went Haynes's call.

Like Mike Vernon in March, for Osgood this would be his first fight in the NHL.

"I had a couple fights in junior," Osgood said. "When I was skating out, the only thing I was thinking about was which arm I was going to throw at the start."

It turned out Osgood threw few punches in the fight. Roy got the majority of good shots in the first half of the bout, but began to tire quickly. That allowed Osgood to lower his head and bulldog his way into pushing Roy back toward the Red Wings bench. With Detroit players on the bench openly laughing at the proceedings, Osgood landed on top of Roy, drawing the last good roar from the crowd.

"Ozzie held his own!" became the rallying cry around the old building. Still, listening to Haynes, one would have thought Osgood needed an ambulance: "Roy gets in, holds on to Osgood. A left by Osgood, a right by Roy, he connects on another right, another right by Roy, another right by Roy, pulled Osgood's sweater off, a right by Roy connected, another right by Roy, another right, an uppercut by Roy, a right by Roy, a right by Roy, an uppercut, he's holding on, he's going crazy on Osgood at center ice. Yeah, you better believe it baby!"

Osgood, like Vernon, saw his stock go up with Wings fans.

It was almost a duplicate situation; after the fight, Osgood went from never having won the big ones to being a "fighter" in the blue-collar Detroit mold. He would parlay the night into a run that culminated with a Stanley Cup.

"I get asked to sign those fight pictures with Patrick more than any other, by far," Osgood said. "I was never so tired in my life after that fight, just like Vernie. I remember thinking I hoped I got kicked out of the game, too. I know what Patrick was trying to do in that situation. He was trying to fire his team up."

Roy's attempt at turning the emotional tables, though admirable, failed miserably. Colorado went on to lose its next four games, while the Red Wings went into the playoffs healthy and on a roll. Colorado flamed out in the first round of the playoffs, blowing a 3-1 series lead to Edmonton and losing Game 7 by a 4-0 score at McNichols.

Despite losing the division to Dallas, Detroit got a big boost from the late-season free-agent signing of one its own, Sergei Fedorov, who held out the first half of the year and might have all season had it not been for a six-year, $38 million offer sheet from Carolina Hurricanes owner and Michigan native Peter Karmanos—a bitter personal rival of Detroit owner Mike Ilitch. Karmanos probably handed the Red Wings the Stanley Cup in 1998, as the fresh, energized Fedorov came back after signing Detroit's matching offer and had a terrific playoffs, scoring 10 goals and 20 points in 22 games as Detroit swept Washington in the Finals. Fedorov arguably deserved the Conn Smythe Trophy, but Steve Yzerman won it instead with a 24-point, six-goal playoff performance.

A touching moment occurred on the ice of the MCI Center following Detroit's sweep of Washington. Vladimir Konstantinov, who was partially paralyzed and suffered brain damage following a limousine crash after a summer team golf outing the year before, was brought out in a wheelchair to celebrate with his former teammates. All season, the Red Wings kept Konstantinov's locker the way it had always been, as a reminder. "Win one for Vladdie" became the Red Wings' unofficial rallying cry, and the fact that Detroit was able to dominate the competition in the playoffs without one of their best players was a testament to the team's resilience and depth.

Fedorov and others gingerly pushed Konstantinov around the ice, with Konstantinov giving the thumbs-up to everyone.

Fedorov, an elegant skater with marvelous passing ability, was almost as well known then for being the boyfriend of Russian tennis vixen Anna Kournikova. Kournikova caused many an opposing player—and sports writer—to bump into walls from craning their necks back to get a glimpse of her, usually in tight black leather pants, waiting for Fedorov outside the Red Wings dressing room.

The Red Wings had their second Stanley Cup in a row, their eighth overall, and Bowman's seventh as a coach. The Avalanche seemed in tatters, first-round losers and no longer competitive with the Red Wings. Following the season, Crawford left the team under hazy circumstances.

Following Colorado's ouster, Pierre Lacroix and Crawford sat for a bizarre McNichols press conference in which Lacroix refused to say whether Crawford would be back, saying some time needed to pass for the "dust to settle."

The truth was, Crawford wanted to leave the team for a vacant coaching job with the Toronto Maple Leafs, but had one year left on his contract with the Avalanche. Lacroix would not let him out of it, and the two became entangled in a contentious battle that went all the way to the office of NHL commissioner Gary Bettman. Bettman ruled that Crawford was still Colorado's property. Crawford, no longer wanting anything to do with Lacroix, said he would sit out the year. He briefly worked as a color analyst for Canada's CBC television before the Vancouver Canucks offered him a vacant position. The Avs let Crawford out of his contract early, but not before getting a draft choice from the Canucks as compensation.

The loss of Crawford, not to mention Detroit's on-ice dominance two years in a row, figured to cool off the Red Wings–Avalanche rivalry a little. Detroit fans now mocked the Avs as a one-year wonder, a team of French-Canadian and European wimps who had gotten their butts literally and figuratively kicked two years in a row.

The following spring, in the playoffs, it seemed certain the streak of Detroit dominance would continue for a third year. But Lacroix and the Avalanche had a few surprises in store for Hockeytown.

1998–99: Never a Dull Moment

The 1998–99 Avalanche team and season was straight from the mind of a demented soap opera writer. It was absurdly comic at times, deeply tragic at others, and never dull. I covered it all for the *Post*, and I was a basket case most of the year myself. The night before training camp started, my wife told me she wanted a divorce. After trying to work it out for a few months, during much of which I was unable to sleep or eat much, I came home from the NHL All-Star Game in Tampa to find our apartment half empty and a note on the table. Welcome home!

To replace Marc Crawford, the Avs promoted Bob Hartley, the coach of the team's minor-league affiliate Hershey Bears. A native of Hawkesbury, a blue-collar Ontario town about halfway between Montreal and Ottawa that was known for its giant glass and windshield factory, Hartley was a failed junior goalie prospect who seemed destined for a life assembling windshields after his father died at a young age and he needed to support the family.

Hartley coached a local kids' team, however, and eventually worked his way into a job coaching the Laval Titans of the

Quebec Major Junior Hockey League. After winning a championship with Laval in 1993, Hartley was hired into the Avalanche organization, first with the now defunct Cornwall Aces of the American Hockey League. Hartley followed Cornwall's move to Hershey, Pennsylvania, where he led the Bears to the 1997 Calder Cup championship in the AHL.

Despite having no NHL coaching experience, Hartley got the job as Crawford's successor. After the first four games of the 1998–99 season, many were openly wondering if the Avs had made a big mistake.

Colorado started the season with four straight losses, and eked out a 5-5 tie in the fifth, against a bad Los Angeles team. The Avs still had Peter Forsberg, Joe Sakic, Patrick Roy, Adam Foote, Valeri Kamensky, and two good-looking rookie forwards named Milan Hejduk and Chris Drury. But they also still had Eric Lacroix, and his presence finally became too much of a distraction.

Fair or not, the younger Lacroix had become a scapegoat around parts of the dressing room for some of the team's troubles. During training camp and into the early season, more than one player took me aside and said I needed to write a story saying Lacroix needed to go. "We can't be a team as long as he's here," one player told me.

Eric Lacroix's new contract with the Avalanche was completed ahead of others with more tenure, including probably his two best friends on the team, Stephane Yelle and Rene Corbet. They had more contentious negotiations with the elder Lacroix, which bruised both their egos and impacted their friendship with Eric, who was caught in the middle. Privately, more than one player wondered if things that were said in the sanctity of the dressing room might occasionally filter from the son to the father. It seemed ludicrous that Eric Lacroix would ever "rat out" a teammate to his father; for one thing, he hated being asked questions about his dad being the GM, and he was always a well-liked teammate on his previous team, the Los Angeles Kings. But the appearance of a conflict was always there, and however good the intentions were, it probably was a big disservice to his son's career that Pierre Lacroix ever acquired him in the first place.

The Eric Lacroix situation seemed more serious than just idle grumbling; it clearly had become a real problem to many, making it fair game to write about. But with no players willing to go on the record, I couldn't write much as a beat reporter and I didn't want to write another "anonymous player" story like the previous one about Claude Lemieux.

So I handed the information I had to columnist Mark Kiszla. Columnists have much more leeway to write in situations in which people won't go on the record, and on October 27 he came out with a piece entitled "It's Time for a Total Eclipse of This Son."

"In the giddy days after his first sips from the Stanley Cup, Colorado general manager Pierre Lacroix smugly traded for his son," Kiszla wrote. "And the Avalanche has slowly slid downhill ever since that moment in 1996 when Eric Lacroix joined the team. Coincidence? Not entirely.

"Eric Lacroix was the Avalanche's first mistake by an NHL dynasty that never was. . . . Eric Lacroix is an unproductive player on a lifeless, spineless team that has become hockey's biggest embarrassment because Colorado management forgot to spend its money wisely. Now, the son must pay for the sins of the father. For the good of this team, his coach and himself, Eric Lacroix must go. . . . During the summer of 1997, the G.M. kept the wallet in his pocket as he watched proven leader Mike Keane get out of Denver. At the same time Colorado was unloading payroll, however, 'Father Pete' gave his son a generous allowance, handing out a three-year contract that will pay Eric Lacroix $700,000 this season. What message did that send?"

The morning the column appeared, I knew right away it would be a very long and loud day at the Avalanche offices—and it was more than that. Chaos ensued, with Lacroix demanding from Hartley who the malcontents were who were badmouthing his son. Lacroix left Kiszla a high-decibel voice-mail saying, among other things, "I will pummel you." Lacroix called *Denver Post* sports editor Neal Scarbrough and vowed to prevent Kiszla from working at the paper anymore. Hartley called a team meeting, standing in the middle of the room with a copy of Kiszla's column in his hand.

From several sources in the room that morning, the following picture emerges: Hartley demanded to know if the story was true, saying also that he didn't have any problem with Lacroix being on the team—which wasn't altogether true. Hartley said he wanted to know if anybody had any issues with Lacroix, who was waiting outside in the team's medical room and could hear the proceedings.

One veteran player stood up and, in effect, told Hartley, "That's a stupid question. Nobody on a team is going to tell the coach he has a problem with the GM's son, so you can go back and rat us out to the GM."

The meeting, supposed to last only a few minutes, stretched on for about an hour. Hartley at first accused rookie Hejduk of being one of the malcontents, which was ridiculous because he could barely speak any English at the time and had one of the nicest dispositions of any player on the team. Another veteran player stood up and told Hartley he was out of bounds talking to Hejduk like that, and was the first to say, in effect, that yes, there was a problem with Lacroix being on the team.

Hearing that, Eric Lacroix immediately recognized he could no longer be on the team. When the meeting broke up, he went to his father and told him he should trade him.

"For the best of the team, it was best that I leave," Eric Lacroix told the media.

Two days later, he was sent back to Los Angeles for a journeyman forward named Roman Vopat—who never played a game with the Avs—and a draft pick. After the trade was announced, Pierre Lacroix met the media and quickly dissolved into tears. In one sense, it showed his humanity, his wonderful love for his son. In another, it contradicted everything he had ever said about making personnel changes, about how they had to be done with "no emotion" and for the "good of the team." Clearly there was emotion involved here, which was the whole point to many teammates who had experienced the tougher side of Lacroix.

The Avalanche did not immediately play much better without Lacroix, which might have given his father a perverse sense of satisfaction. On January 9 the team's record was 17-19-4, and things only got crazier.

After a December 21 game in Anaheim, California, which Colorado won, 4-2, over the Mighty Ducks, Roy actually smashed up Hartley's visiting coach's office with his stick—all because he did not get personal credit for the win.

To give his tired team more of a breather before an upcoming power play late in the game, Hartley pulled Roy from the game in favor of Craig Billington. When a team changes a goalie, extra time is given for the substitute to warm up by stretching and taking a few shots. The change of goalies worked, as the rested Avs scored on the power play to take a 3-2 lead. But because Billington was in net when the winning goal was scored, he got credit for the victory—even though he never made a save.

Roy, who at the time was chasing Terry Sawchuk's all-time NHL record of 447 victories, was furious. With Hartley and assistants Bryan Trottier and Jacques Cloutier savoring the triumph and the masterstroke that helped get it, Roy stormed in, still in his full equipment, including stick. Like the goalie-mask-wearing Jason from *Friday the 13th*, Roy went on a wild slashing spree with his stick, smashing two televisions and a VCR, and yelled in French, "Don't ever fucking do that again."

Hartley turned white. What was he supposed to think of this? Here was a player upset after his team *won*—just because he didn't get the credit. What kind of a team guy is that? Hartley could have easily lashed back at Roy, maybe benched or fined him to set an example to the others that nobody was above the team.

Instead, Hartley played it cool, partly by necessity. He knew he didn't have much clout with the veterans because he "never played the game," and knew benching Roy might make him quit on him, like he did to Mario Tremblay. For Hartley, it turned out to be the right move, as Roy later apologized and gained more respect for his coach for not overreacting like he had.

"I think that throughout all this, I was kind of put on fast-forward," Hartley said. "My learning curve was put on fast-forward. There were incidents that don't happen every day. You had to react quickly and pretty good, because you're under the microscope. And I knew it.

"Patrick's blowup with me was the glue between Patrick and me. Something similar happened with me and Marty Lapointe, in Laval. We were close, but we got closer the next morning. What Roy did in Montreal was similar to what Marty did with me.

"Patrick answered his phone on the first ring the next morning, around 7 o' clock. He said he was about to head to the rink. I knew right there we were in good shape. Patrick said, 'I was stupid, shouldn't have done this.' Years later, we can laugh about it. At a golf tournament later, we laughed about it."

The affair in Anaheim was kept under wraps for two weeks by the team, until I finally heard about it and put it in the paper on January 4. It just so happened Roy's old team, Montreal, was in town that night, and he then became furious with me.

I was just trying to embarrass him with all the Montreal media in town, Roy said. He immediately went on a witch-hunt for the source of the leak. That the Canadiens were in town was pure coincidence, but Roy wouldn't hear it. Because I had a good working relationship with an agent named Paul Theofanous, who represented Valeri Kamensky, Sandis Ozolinsh, and Alexei Gusarov, Roy deduced that one of them was probably the leaker. It was soon narrowed down to just Kamensky, who was definitely not the culprit, but I wasn't going to say who it was to him or anybody else. Then some miscommunication between Roy and me falsely implicated Adam Foote as the leaker. A meeting between Roy, Foote, and me ensued in which, if looks could kill, I would have been dead from Foote's initial glare. The finger was pointed again at Kamensky, and another long, drawn-out meeting happened in which Roy, Theofanous, Kamensky, and I went round and around alone in the McNichols lunchroom, sitting in a circle on chairs. I told Roy that Kamensky was not the leaker, but that was all I would say, and that, hey, I'm sorry to have to write the story in the first place, but that's part of the job.

Roy finally seemed convinced that neither Theofanous nor one of his clients was the leaker, but a strain continued between Roy and Kamensky—with Kamensky rightfully upset at Roy—that lasted much of the season.

Lacroix traded away several players who he may or may not have suspected as having done his son wrong, either by bad-mouthing him or by not saying enough in his defense. One of them was Keith Jones, traded to Philadelphia for left wing Shjon Podein. Jones wasn't afraid to speak his mind to the media, and years later made a joke about Eric Lacroix's weight when working as a television analyst for an Avalanche game in which Lacroix served as the team's video coach. Late in the season, Corbet, Wade Belak, and a prospect named Robyn Regehr were traded by the Avalanche to Calgary for pint-sized superstar winger Theo Fleury and throw-in forward Chris Dingman.

Fleury was a dynamic scorer who stood just 5-foot-6 or so. He grew up in a troubled home where alcohol and prescription painkillers were prevalent, but in 1999 he hadn't yet let his past affect his career.

Fleury's addition gave Colorado a big injection of talent and enthusiasm, but it didn't seem enough to unseat Detroit as two-time Stanley Cup champs. New Red Wings general manager Ken Holland, a former goalie who played four career NHL games, stunned the hockey world by acquiring star defenseman Chris Chelios from Chicago at the 1999 trade deadline, along with former Avs malcontent Wendel Clark, goalie Bill Ranford, and veteran defenseman Ulf Samuelsson, in separate deals. Detroit already was the favorite in the Western Conference before the deals; with Chelios added to a team that included some of the biggest stars in the game, the Red Wings looked unbeatable.

When the 1999 playoffs began, the Avalanche drew the San Jose Sharks in the first round, a team that included former Red Wings goalie Mike Vernon. On the morning of April 20, the Avalanche had practice in preparation for Game 1 at home. On the way to the team's practice rink, in the suburban Colorado town of Centennial, I drove down Bowles Avenue in Littleton, a short-cut road off of which a high school named Columbine was just to the south. Columbine was a school I had been into a few times, back in my days covering prep sports.

I drove by the school at around 10 a.m. on the brilliantly sunny day. A little more than an hour later, the most deadly shooting in a school in US history took place. Two teenage Columbine students named Eric Harris and Dylan Klebold shot 13 people to death and injured 24 others before shooting themselves dead.

With the Avalanche on the ice going about their paces, word of the shootings quickly came in to everybody at the rink; nobody could believe it, least of all me. I had just driven by the place. (Later that day, after getting back to my apartment complex about three miles from the school, I saw a young man in a black trench coat standing by a car, smoking a cigarette with a weird look on his face, staring back at me. It wasn't until later that I learned that Harris and Klebold allegedly belonged to a group called the Trench Coat Mafia, and that authorities believed the two might have had accomplices.)

About the last thing on anybody's mind that day was the Avs-Sharks series, but as a reporter I had to find out what this horrible event meant for it. At first there was just talk of postponing the game a day or two. But the magnitude of the tragedy to the community made it clear to Lacroix and new owners Bill and Nancy Laurie that it would be at least several more days before anybody in Denver could even think of going to a hockey game.

Lacroix met in his office with Sharks personnel, including GM Dean Lombardi and chief operating officer Greg Jamison. After further consultation with the NHL, it was agreed the Avalanche would start the best-of-seven series with two games in San Jose, followed by Games 3, 4, and 5 at McNichols, Game 6 in San Jose, and Game 7 back in Denver.

Wearing patches on their uniforms to remember the victims of Columbine, the Avalanche won the first two games in Silicon Valley, but lost the next two at a somber McNichols, including Game 4 by a 7-3 score in which old friend Mike Ricci scored a hat trick. Vernon played well in both wins, but Sharks coach Darryl Sutter made the bewildering choice of starting backup Steve Shields in Game 5. Games 4 and 5 were on back-to-back nights, and Sutter felt the 36-year-old Vernon might need the rest. Through the first four games, Colorado mustered only 10 goals on Vernon, whose career playoff record against Roy to that point was 2-1.

For the Avs, Shields was a godsend, as they peppered him for six goals in an easy victory. Colorado closed out the series in overtime in Game 6, on a Hejduk goal.

"I played back-to-backs all year long," Vernon said. "I don't know why, all of a sudden, they thought I couldn't do it again, in the biggest game of the year for us."

Detroit, meanwhile, had a fun time with the Mighty Ducks of Anaheim in the first round, sweeping them four straight and allowing only six goals. That set up a second-round series against the Avalanche, with number-two seed Colorado having home-ice advantage.

After the first two games in Denver, the only question was: How many more games will it take for the Red Wings to close out the series? Detroit won the first game in overtime on a Kirk Maltby goal and shut Colorado out, 4-0, in the second.

Maltby was a player the Avalanche, particularly Roy, had little respect for. While the Detroit papers killed several forests bemoaning Lemieux's lack of intestinal fortitude and Forsberg's "diving," they ignored that they had one of the NHL's biggest whiners and flop artists on their own team, Maltby. Maltby wore a shield and never dropped the gloves—which at least Lemieux did once, with a tougher opponent.

Lemieux was hit into the glass from behind by Darren McCarty in the third period of Game 1, but so was Detroit's Brendan Shanahan by Forsberg. Shanahan had a large cut opened above his right eye, and Forsberg was kicked out of the game with a misconduct penalty. McCarty, like Forsberg, received a five-minute major for his hit on Lemieux, but once again escaped getting kicked out.

"McCarty's hit on Lemieux was twice as worse as Forsberg's hit on Shanahan," Colorado's Hartley told reporters.

"Detroit's Darren McCarty hit Colorado's Claude Lemieux midway through the third period with a shot from behind that was every bit as vicious as what Forsberg gave to Shanahan," Kiszla wrote in the *Post*. "The blow left Lemieux dazed and sprawled on the ice against the boards, as 16,061 fans raged against the violence. But the NHL keeps score in blood. Brain damage doesn't count. The rule book gives no discretion to a referee. He must eject a player who draws blood. The same ref could let a thug like McCarty come back to do more damage, because there wasn't any physical evidence of how badly Lemieux was hurt."

By the end of Game 2, Red Wings players were barely stifling laughter at the Avalanche. Detroit so thoroughly dominated the game that Hartley was reduced to sending out a goon line of Dale Hunter, Warren Rychel, and Jeff Odgers in the final minutes, to try to rough up the Wings. All that did was evoke scornful pity from the likes of McCarty and Maltby, and the Avs were booed off the McNichols ice—even by many of the moms in attendance on Mother's Day. The old building was slated to be demolished later that summer, and the *Post*'s Woody Paige thought it would be the last sporting event it would ever see.

"The Avalanche played poorly, passively, putridly, pedestrianly and . . . and . . . and . . . nincompooply in the finis to our 24 years of adventures at Denver's Microcosm Sports Arena," Paige wrote. "Kirsten Marie Flagstad, opera's famous Norwegian soprano 'fat lady,' should have been brought out to sing the swan song. Because it's over. Over for the Avalanche, over for Big Mac. And out. Turn out the light at Big Mac. The party that lasted 24 years is over."

In the *Free Press*, Jason La Canfora summed up Detroit's general attitude: bring on the Wings' next sacrificial lamb.

"The Red Wings outclassed Colorado, 4-0, Sunday afternoon in Game 2 of their second-round series, and clearly have been the NHL's premier team in this postseason," he wrote. "The Avalanche must win four of five games to advance. That doesn't seem likely. The Wings have won 11 straight playoff games dating to Game 6 of last season's Western Conference finals against Dallas, creeping up on the NHL record of 14 set by Pittsburgh early this decade.

"The Wings are 15-2-1 since acquiring four key players at the trade deadline, including forward Wendel Clark and goalie Bill Ranford. Colorado has proved no match. What the Avs lack in depth and execution is compounded by their lack of discipline—they lead the playoffs in penalties per game."

But things started to get a little weird all of a sudden for the Red Wings, starting with the flight back to Detroit. Despite allowing only two goals to that point in the series, and coming off a shutout, some teammates noticed Ranford didn't seem to feel right. He was playing in place of Chris Osgood, who had a sprained knee. A former Conn Smythe winner with Edmonton, Ranford was just 32 at the time. But for whatever reason, he allegedly confided some surprising news to Osgood, which Shanahan said was later relayed to him.

"He went to Ozzie and said, 'I'm done. I can't play anymore,'" Shanahan recalled. "Ranford, for whatever reason, didn't want to play anymore. He was spent."

Ranford denies he ever said such a thing, and Osgood doesn't remember what happened.

"No, I wasn't tired or anything," Ranford said. "That's a mystery to me."

When the Avalanche arrived at the Detroit airport, they were greeted by Northwest Airlines maintenance workers, some of whom held up brooms. "Sweep, sweep," a few chanted.

"That woke the guys up a little," said former Avs trainer Pat Karns. "That got them a little pissed off."

For Game 3, the Avs got the stylish Kamensky back in the lineup. Kamensky's forearm had been broken by a slash in a regular-season game by Maltby. For Maltby and the Wings, Kamensky would recover just a little too soon, as his presence made a big difference in Colorado's game.

Still, Detroit looked ready to put the series all but away in the first few minutes of Game 3, taking a 1-0 lead. Steve Yzerman looked ready to add to it with a shot past a committed Roy in close. But Yzerman's backhander hit the crossbar. Soon after, Detroit's Nicklas Lidstrom took an uncharacteristic double-minor high-sticking penalty on Fleury, giving Colorado a two-man advantage for nearly two minutes from a previous penalty. As Paige put it, "The lethal Lilliputian is 5-foot-6. If a defenseman cuts Fleury, he should be penalized for 'low-sticking.'"

Lemieux scored to tie it. Four more unanswered Colorado goals ensued, the last one a wrist shot from near the blue line by low-scoring defenseman Aaron Miller, and Ranford was pulled early in the second period for third-stringer Norm Maracle. Colorado held on for a 5-3 win, cutting the series deficit in half. Roy made 44 saves, and according to Kiszla, had the eye of the tiger again: "If you want the truth, look into a man's eyes. If the Detroit Red Wings dare, they will stare into the steel blue eyes of Colorado goalie Patrick Roy and see truth so real it's frightening. After the Avalanche's 5-3 victory Tuesday in the NHL playoffs, the hunger was back in Roy's eyes with a vengeance. Detroit might be the defending league champ. But, in this best-of-seven series, the Wings are now the hunted. The Wings should be very afraid."

Wrote Paige, "Feeling right at home on the road—once again—and proving Dorothy wrong Tuesday night in Schlockeytown (trademark pending), the Avalanche flogged the Detroit Dread Wings 5-3."

Lemieux still thought the series was over after the victory—over for the Red Wings.

"I'd been around Patrick a long time, and I knew he was going to win that series for us after that," he said. "He wanted to win that series as much as the one in '96. He was motivated, and I always knew we'd win if he was confident and motivated to beat someone."

Game 4 was a rout, a 6-2 Avalanche victory. Ranford again was awful and chased early, and would not play the rest of the series. A team that was laughed out of Denver by the Red Wings went into Motown and danced like the Temptations on their ice.

"I don't think you want to buy a car built in Detroit on Friday. The assembly-line wrench jockeys are not very happy workers this morning," Paige wrote. "Many of those local knowledgeable, sophisticated, suave and debonair hockey fans were clinging to the fence outside Joe Louis Arena late Thursday night, spewing beer and venom at the Avalanche players boarding their bus. 'Hey, you . . . (a string of words Lenny Bruce wouldn't have used even in private),' the candidates for doctorate degrees in English literature shouted. It was as if the Avalanche had driven new Toyotas around the ice Thursday evening. Rather, the Avalanche drove the Detroit Chicken Wings deep into the ice for the second time this week.

"Schlockeytown, Choke City, Gagville and The Big Three—Ford, General Motors and Scotty Bowman—won't put up with that nonsense. . . . 'Home ice doesn't seem to matter,' said Scotty 'The Brain' Bowman. His brilliant deduction came shortly after one of the knowledgeable, sophisticated Detroit media types asked him: 'Did you expect your team to play like that tonight?' Gee, why didn't I come up with that question? I did want to follow up with: 'Other than the score, Mrs. Lincoln, what did you think of the game?'"

The Avalanche finally started to get better play from Forsberg against the Red Wings in Games 3 and 4. Too often in the past against Detroit, the gifted Swede was thrown off his game with retaliation penalties, either after taking big hits or trash talking. Teammates Foote and Roy were always telling him to keep his cool, to ignore it. But early in his career, Forsberg often felt pressure to prove he wasn't the typical "Chicken Swede," who couldn't handle the rough stuff of North American hockey. Many times, however, he would overcompensate with returned hits and get himself in trouble.

Hartley, too, started to coach better. He devised something of a neutral-zone trap after Game 2 that got to Detroit's puck-carrying defensemen more quickly, forcing a few more turnovers. Hartley helped turn around Colorado's regular season by putting Forsberg at left wing on a line with Sakic, and went back to the combination for much of Game 3. And he started to make the great Scotty Bowman realize he wasn't any pushover in the mind-game department.

"Before they put in the hurry-up faceoff, he was probably the one coach of all time that I ever coached that knew how to stall," Bowman said. "Bob played a pretty short bench, and he had all the tricks. He was a big match-up guy, and he'd send guys out on the ice all the time to get this or that done. He had all the tricks."

Like Crawford, Hartley knew a good sound bite could sometimes deflect attention away from his players, and maybe get in the minds of opponents. Hartley had a quick wit, and his jokes, spoken in a heavy French-Canadian accent, sometimes were hilarious. Before one of the games in the series in Denver, Hartley dressed the team's new enforcer, Scott Parker, during warm-ups. Parker got into a macho staring match with Detroit's Lapointe and McCarty, nearly leading to an incident. Afterward, Hartley said Parker was just "admiring some of his heroes" on the Red Wings, like Yzerman and Shanahan.

Hartley began nearly every sentence with, "Like, ah," as in, "Like, ah, we know we need to generate many more scoring chances against that team over there." Hartley was nearly manic in his demeanor, always in motion, always with somewhere to get to or some other thing to do. Only after games would he slow down somewhat, but even then he was always thinking and talking hockey. Like his boss, Lacroix, Hartley was a teetotaler, but not a prude. He liked a good, bawdy joke or story, and profanity was his preferred language on the ice.

Like Bowman, he was a taskmaster. Unlike Bowman, Hartley often got right up into his players' faces, or unleashed loud rip jobs on the team between periods. Some players called him "Bobby Hartless." He was tough on younger players, especially rookies who shuttled back and forth from the minor-league team in Hershey. Occasionally at practices, players said, Hartley would turn up his nose and yell, "I smell chocolate," when giving it to one of them for a screw-up. The fact that he never played in the NHL grated on those he criticized. But Bowman never did, either.

The Red Wings knew they were in trouble entering Game 5. It was clear to Bowman that Ranford couldn't be trusted anymore. And Maracle hadn't played very well, either, which left only Osgood to consider for the rubber game at McNichols. Osgood still was bothered by the knee, but Bowman thought he might be able to steal a win if the Wings packed it in enough defensively, and maybe caught Roy on an off day. Roy never played very well at home in afternoon games for some reason, so what the heck?

Detroit did pack it in around Osgood, playing a good defensive game. The trouble was, that didn't leave much for the other end of the ice, and Colorado won the game, 3-0. The defining moment came when the light-scoring Odgers beat Osgood with a slap shot from beyond the blue line for a 1-0 lead. Osgood had trouble with the occasional long shot even when healthy; with the bum knee, he could only hobble around in net. Roy had one of the easier shutouts of his career, and Colorado was only one win away from dethroning the two-time Stanley Cup champs.

How did this happen so fast? Weren't the Red Wings taking pity on the Avalanche just a few days before in Denver? Wasn't Bowman a master of finishing teams off when he had them down? Wasn't Hartley just a neophyte lightweight next to him?

"The thing that I kind of focused on was not to get involved with trying to beat Scotty Bowman, but just try to beat the Red Wings," Hartley said. "I kind of said to myself, 'I cannot play into his hands.' I have to really coach my game and think that I don't coach against Scotty Bowman. It's just another game. I didn't really put my focus against Scotty."

It wasn't easy, though, for a man who grew up idolizing the Canadiens, who thought Bowman was a god behind the Habs' bench.

"I met Scotty the first time in person at Laval. They had drafted Marty Lapointe, and Marty was my captain," Hartley said. "Scotty attended one of our games, and to my surprise, he showed up very early and he showed up at my office. He wanted to get some views on Lapointe, and I can tell you even today, that's probably one of the biggest highlights of my career. Why I love and respect Scotty so much is because, when I was 10, 12, 13 years old, I was probably the biggest Montreal Canadiens fan around."

Detroit tried to pull out all the stops for Game 6, with the "Ain't No Party Like a Detroit Party" song, and Karen Newman's national anthem, and lots of octopus in the stands—but nothing could overcome Detroit's suddenly fatal goaltending issue.

The Avalanche won Game 6, 5-2. Colorado jumped to a 4-0 lead on Osgood, still limping, and weathered a brief Detroit rally. To La Canfora, Detroit's mini-rally was nothing short of the defense of the Alamo in its gallantry.

"These Red Wings would not go down quietly. They would not bow to a four-goal deficit. They would not give up the Stanley Cup without a fight. Their rampage came quickly. It was fast and furious," La Canfora wrote in the *Free Press*. "It had the Avs wondering what happened; where this ruthless attack came from, how safe their 4-0 lead really was. Goalie Patrick Roy was nursing 98 minutes of scoreless hockey when the first goal came. Yzerman (who else?) started it by feeding Nick Lidstrom on the power play, and the defenseman found a seam high on Roy, making it 4-1 with 2:36 left in the second period. The Wings were torrid now. Joe Louis Arena was absolutely deafening.

"Todd Gill pummeled a rolling puck from the blue line, finally there was traffic in front, and Darren McCarty snapped a 28-game funk by deflecting the puck in. Roy never saw it. After stopping 134 of 139 shots, he gave up two straight goals. It was 4-2 after two periods. Fresh blood coursed through 20,000 hearts. It looked and felt like a new beginning."

Forsberg stopped Detroit's "ruthless attack" with a brilliant breakaway goal late in the game, with Igor Larionov nearly draped over his back.

"Ding, dong, the Dynasty is Dead," wrote Paige. "The Red Wings, Stanley Cup champions the past two seasons, were favored to prevail again after loading up with four veterans on trade deadline day. But, with the Avs' fourth consecutive triumph—including three in Detroit (and a 6-0 overall record away from Denver in the playoffs), the Avalanche has eliminated the Red Wings. It must be doubly difficult for the Red Wingnuts to see their team thumped by the unsophisticated Avalanche and also to have to go on living in Detroit. Plus, it should be remembered that the Avalanche has whipped the Red Wings in two of the three playoff series they've ever played, and the winner in the previous two hugged the NHL's Holy Grail."

After two straight years of having their manhood crammed

down their throats by Detroit, Avalanche players finally could walk with a swagger again out of the Joe. For players such as Lemieux and Roy, whose blood had been spilled on the same ice two years before, the feeling was one of sweet closure. For the Red Wings, the loss was and still is hard to comprehend for some.

"There were people saying we might go 16-0 in the playoffs," Shanahan said. "The funny thing is, the team in '99 might have been our best team. We were real strong. But in the first 10 minutes of the last four games, it was like 3-0. Guys were coming down the wall and taking slap shots and scoring. It was fast. For a team that was 6-0 in the playoffs, it was the fastest four games I've ever had the displeasure of playing."

Said associate coach Dave Lewis: "I don't know if it had something to do with the amount of energy it takes. I just think that the energy level to win another Stanley Cup wasn't there."

Countered Shanahan, "I disagree we ran out of gas. We didn't run out of gas. Our No. 1 goalie was hurt, and our No. 2 goalie got hurt. It might have looked like we ran out of gas, but when you know your top two goalies are hurt and the other team is scoring two or three soft goals early, it takes the wind out of your sails."

The Avalanche looked like a solid bet to go on and win the Cup, especially after winning Game 1 of the following series on the road in Dallas. But Colorado lost Hejduk, the NHL's leading rookie scorer, for the remainder of the playoffs to a shoulder injury on a hit from defenseman Richard Matvichuk. Later in the series, Matvichuk drove Forsberg into the boards, causing a separated shoulder. Colorado's offense was further weakened from a bad series from captain Sakic, whose mind was distracted by an illness that briefly hospitalized his wife, Debbie. Then there were the issues surrounding Fleury.

Raised by parents with drug and alcohol addictions, Fleury inherited the same afflictions. Around the time he was traded to Colorado, those close to him said, he began having problems with heavier drugs than just a few beers.

Fleury missed Game 5 of the Western finals against Dallas. The team listed Fleury out with "flu symptoms." Multiple sources around the team said Fleury's absence had more to do with consumption of other questionable substances the night before. But nobody has ever gone on the record about it, and Fleury dodged questions about what really happened in following seasons, even after entering the NHL's substance-abuse program.

The Avs won Game 5 to take a 3-2 series lead. Fleury came back for Games 6 and 7, but Dallas goalie Ed Belfour slammed the door shut and Colorado helped him by missing three or four open nets in the first period of Game 6 at home. Dallas won Game 7 easily—helped by two goals from Mike Keane—and went on to win the Stanley Cup. Lemieux thought the team's chemistry actually was hurt when Fleury was allowed to play the final two games.

"We won Game 5 without him, and he comes back and it changed our lineup too much and how we played," Lemieux said. "He spent a lot of time on the power play, things like that. To me, the problem was one of coaching decisions in that case. Theo is a great guy and I'm not trying to throw him under the bus and say he's the reason we lost, but I think it hurt our game, him coming back like that."

In the late stages of Game 7, the Reunion Arena crowd chanted, "Eddie's better," a jab at Roy as much as praise for Belfour. In the series, that was true. But there was no goalie in NHL history who was as good as the native of Quebec City over such a long period of time. And few players, if any, ever wanted to win hockey games more than Patrick Jacques Roy.

Saint Patrick's Fire

Where Patrick Roy got his manic passion to succeed was always something of a mystery.

Born on October 6, 1965, the same day as another Quebec hockey legend, Mario Lemieux, Roy did not grow up in the kind of impoverished home that might breed zeal for a better life. His father, Michel, was an executive with the provincial auto insurance board and a part-time jazz musician who would later put out his own albums. His mother, Barbara, was a successful real estate salesperson. She had a fiery Irish temper, one that would be passed along to her son.

Roy had a younger brother, Stephane, and sister, Alexandra. Stephane was a talented skater, considered a probable NHL talent at an early age. Patrick was more interested in swimming in his earliest athletic endeavors. His mother was a champion synchronized swimmer as a youth, and drove him to and from meets, where he usually placed in the top three.

For Christmas one year when Patrick was six or seven, he received a hockey goalie mask and catching glove. The masks then were the white kind made famous by *Friday the 13th*, form fitting on the face with small slits for the eyes and mouth. Patrick loved the way he looked in the mask—tough, a little scary, and mysterious.

But there was little hint he would ever go on to become the greatest goalie in NHL history. While he did start playing hockey as a boy, at first he was a forward like his brother.

"One day, our goaltender got hit in the leg with the puck. He started crying and didn't want to play goalie anymore," Roy said. "I said, 'I want to be the goalie.' Our coach said I was too small. The next year, I played hockey in an outdoor hockey league. I loved wearing goalie pads. Even though they were heavy, I thought they were cool."

Before long, Patrick and Stephane battled each other day and night in a skinny hallway upstairs, whacking a tennis ball around with nicked-up sticks. Each brother wore goalie pads made of pillows cinched around their legs with belts.

Patrick soon became enamored with all things hockey. That included a love for hockey cards, which in Canada were manufactured by O-Pee-Chee, a spin-off of legendary American card maker Topps.

Young Patrick spent virtually all his money on the cards, then arranging various teams on his bed as the "GM." (As an adult, Roy amassed what is believed the largest hockey card collection in the world, with well over 100,000).

As an eight-year-old boy, Patrick, along with his mother and father, walked into the office of Bob Chevalier, director of youth hockey in nearby Sainte Foy.

"I want to play hockey," Chevalier remembered Roy saying. "When can I start?"

"I thought, 'Quite a bit of confidence in this kid,'" Chevalier said.

Confidence is something Roy never lacked—outwardly. But the cocksure, snap-of-the-neck, snatch-of-the-glove persona he developed as a pro hid a deep insecurity that was there his whole career. It was something of a coping mechanism he developed, a never-let-them-see-you-sweat attitude, whereas there were half-moons under his armpits always. The sweat produced from a fear of failure.

The nagging feeling that he would be exposed as a fraud probably started at age 15, when he was cut from his AA midget team. Or maybe during his first year of junior hockey with the QMJHL's Granby Bisons, where his goals-against average was an astronomical 6.26.

His father remembers his son's being cut from the AA midget team as a major turning point in his life. He could have quit hockey altogether, maybe tried to be a lawyer, a career path that was in the back of his head. Everybody knew he was good in arguments with his siblings, either for the best seat in the car or the last piece of French toast on Sunday mornings.

But Michel Roy's oldest child wasn't going to quit over just one rejection. Instead he developed a lifelong fire to prove people wrong when they told him he couldn't do something. Doubting Patrick Roy was always the worst possible thing a competitor could do. Time and again, Roy would "show them" after a personal slight, real or perceived.

Still, Patrick was never supposed to be the star hockey player in the Roy family. Stephane, two years younger but bigger and stronger than his skinny brother, was the one the scouts drooled over. Agents were all over Stephane, hoping to get his signature on a contract to be his representative. One was a young Pierre Lacroix, who left a career as a successful hockey business liaison for Carling-O'Keefe Breweries to start his own player agency he named JanDec—to show his commitment to working for his clients "January through December."

Lacroix visited the Roy home in pursuit of Stephane. Michel Roy was delighted in Lacroix's interest, but over hot coffee and pastries told him he had another good young prospect he should sign—Patrick. At the end of the night, the elder Roy told Lacroix he could sign Stephane on one condition: that he also take Patrick as a client. Lacroix reluctantly agreed, thinking privately the addition of this unheard-of goalie prospect was a price of doing business.

Patrick grew up a big fan of the Quebec Nordiques, which entered the old World Hockey Association in 1972 and joined the NHL in 1979. His favorite player was a blond-haired goalie named Daniel Bouchard. His mother had a friend who knew Bouchard; she asked if the friend could get Bouchard to sign a stick for his son, which he did. Patrick would sleep with the stick for the next few nights.

After he was cut from the AA midget team, Roy had a good season at the CC level in Sainte Foy and was given a shot at the AAA level the next year for a team coached by Jean-Lois Letourneau. Roy's mother drove him to the team's four practices a week, along with the two games.

Roy's legendary temper would inititally surface on Letourneau's team. In the 1981 AAA playoffs, Roy was suspended for two games after arguing with a referee. Still, Roy returned to lead his team to the league championship and a berth in the AAA Air Canada Cup. Following that success, Roy was drafted by the expansion Bisons and left home for Granby. There would be many long, downcast phone calls in his first season, 1982–83, as he posted a sky-high GAA and finished with a 13-35-1 record.

Granby had a positively awful team in front of Roy. The defense was perhaps the worst in QMJHL history. Roy regularly saw more than 40 or 50 shots a game. This, it turned out, might have been one of the best things that ever happened to him. All that rubber coming at him toughened Roy, making him shockproof in the face of future withering assaults.

Granby was the favorite opponent on every team's schedule; not only did Claude Lemieux enjoy padding his scoring stats against Roy, Mario Lemieux's mighty Laval Voisins often scored in double digits against the Bisons.

But after surviving the season well enough that Granby wanted him back the next season, 1983–84, Roy improved noticeably. He lowered his GAA to 4.44 and posted a 29-29-1 record. The many NHL scouts that habited the dingy QMJHL arenas noticed Roy's development, particularly those from the Canadiens. With Ken Dryden having long since retired, the Canadiens were still suffering from an unfilled void in goal. In the 1984 NHL draft, the first two goalies taken were Craig Billington and Daryl Reaugh. Montreal liked Roy enough to take him as the third goalie, with the 51st pick overall. It would go down as one of the most astute selections in NHL history.

When Roy joined the fabled Canadiens, he was given the number 32. Roy had worn number 30 in junior, but always thought the number 3 was his luckiest number. So he brazenly asked Montreal's trainer, Eddy Palchak, if he could wear number 33. "OK kid," Palchak said, "whatever."

Roy was sent back to Granby following his first training camp with Montreal in 1984, where his numbers ballooned again, to 16-25-1 and a 5.55 GAA. The Canadiens called Roy up from Granby late in the season, to give him a taste of the big time. On February 23, the Canadiens were in Winnipeg, Manitoba, for a game with the Jets. At the Winnipeg Arena, under a massive overhanging portrait of Queen Elizabeth, Roy was told by Canadiens coach Jacques Lemaire to play the third period of a game that was 4-4 after the first two.

Montreal's top two goalies were Steve Penney and Doug Soetaert, but Lemaire was about out of patience with both. As it turned out, Lemaire probably could have put an orange pylon in net for the third period, as the Canadiens tightened up the defense, thinking all hell might break loose with the skinny rookie in net. Roy faced only two Jets shots in the period, stopping both in a 6-4 Montreal victory.

Despite the win, Roy was immediately sent to Montreal's top AHL farm club, Sherbrooke, where he played one regular-season game after starter Greg Moffett had trouble with his equipment. Roy allowed four goals on 27 shots, but was impressive nonetheless in Sherbrooke's victory, and management decided to make him the starter in the playoffs. He went 10-3 with a 2.89 GAA, and was the MVP of the postseason as the team won the Calder Cup.

But all Roy could think about was his one NHL victory, and how much he wanted to add more. He would—five hundred fifty more, to be exact.

The 1985–86 Canadiens were seen as an older team, with too many question marks to be seriously considered for the Stanley Cup.

Stars such as Bob Gainey, Larry Robinson, and Mario Tremblay were past their prime, and there were too many unproven youngsters such as Chris Chelios, Stephane Richer, Claude Lemieux, and Patrick Roy.

Roy's playoff performance with Sherbrooke and 1985 training camp showing convinced the Canadiens to take him on full-time, although they still kept Penney and Soetaert around.

As a rookie, Roy roomed on the road with Tremblay, the man who would drive him out of Montreal 10 years later. At home, Roy lived in the basement of Canadiens veteran forward Lucien DeBlois. He subsisted mostly on a diet of hamburgers and French fries, which in Montreal were most often served in tall, skinny boxes with the company's name, "Casseau," written in red italics. For the first few years of his career and beyond, Roy would be known as Casseau to his original Canadiens teammates.

"He ate so many French fries, it was unbelievable he was still so skinny," DeBlois said. "He lived with us for about his first two years with the team, even after we won the Cup. I didn't give him a lot of advice, because he was so focused and serious about his job. But one time, when he was just starting to play more his first year, he got off the ice the same time as some of the older veterans at practice. I told him he was too young and unproven to be doing that yet. I told him he should still be the first one on the ice, and last one off. And I think that stuck with him, because he was the last one off after that."

Like his brother, Stephane Roy would be drafted 51st over-all, in 1985 by the Minnesota North Stars. But his NHL career would last only 12 games, all in the 1987–88 season; Stephane didn't work hard enough, North Stars management felt, and he and coach Glen Sonmor didn't get along. The rest of his hockey career would be spent at various minor-league outposts.

Patrick Roy posted a 23-18-3 record as a rookie with Montreal. A big debate about who should be the Canadiens' playoff goalie ensued in the hyperintense Montreal media. Many felt the veteran Soetaert should be the starter, but new Canadiens coach Jean Perron decided to go with Roy. It was a decision that won the Stanley Cup.

Roy was otherworldly in the 1986 playoffs. He went 15-5 with an incredible 1.92 GAA. He was never better than in over-time of Game 3 of the Prince of Wales Conference finals against the Rangers. New York outshot Montreal 13-1 in OT, including several glorious chances. But Roy stopped them all, and the Canadiens won on the one shot—by Claude Lemieux.

"I remember he called me after that game, and he was really excited, more than I'd ever seen him about anything," Roy's father told the *Denver Post*. "I was a little concerned about that. I thought it was dangerous to get too high about one game. So, I told him, 'Celebrate in your hotel room if you want to, but there are a lot of challenges ahead.' I think that made him stop and think. I think he controlled his emotions a lot more after that. The real time to celebrate isn't until after winning the last game of the season."

After the Canadiens beat Calgary for the 1986 Cup, Roy was an easy choice as the Conn Smythe winner. It was a remarkable turn of events; Roy had gone from a kid not good enough to make a local midget team a few years before to the MVP of the playoffs for the most storied hockey franchise of all time.

"It happened so fast in those playoffs," Roy recalls. "We just caught fire as a team, and I felt like I could make every save. It's hard to explain. It was a great feeling."

Suddenly Roy was a star. Kids throughout the province started wearing his number 33, and copying his funny mannerisms, such as the frequent snapping of his neck in games. Many wondered if Roy had Tourette's syndrome; in fact, Roy's head bobbing was a nervous tic, but not caused by Tourette's syndrome. He did not exhibit such mannerisms off the ice. But on it, his extreme intensity manifested in the tic. Roy sometimes talked to his goalposts, saying stuff like, "Thanks, buddy," after pucks clanged off them. Like many goalies, Roy fussed over his crease like a little old lady tending her garden, always landscaping the ice and checking for rough spots.

Kids also started copying Roy's goaltending style, called the butterfly. Although he didn't invent the butterfly technique, Roy perfected it. A style whose purpose was to induce the shooter to shoot for the spot between the pads and then close it shut, like a butterfly's wings, Roy bred a succession of butterfly goalies from Quebec who idolized him, including Martin Brodeur and Jean-Sebastien Giguere.

A couple of years into his Montreal career, Roy met a strikingly beautiful, athletic woman named Michele Piuze at a softball game. Roy was smitten, and the two were soon married. The couple would produce three children: Jonathan, Frederick, and Jana.

Roy's next few years in Montreal included some great regular seasons, including a 33-5-6 mark in 1988–89. He didn't play as much as he wanted, though. From 1986 through 1989 he shared the goaltending duties with Brian Hayward, who, like Ken Dryden, played college hockey at Cornell.

Hayward's saves percentage and GAA were lower than Roy's in 1986–87, and some friction developed, with Roy perhaps feeling a bit threatened.

"I think Pat was always a little bit frustrated at me playing so much in 1986–87," Hayward said. "I remember he and I discussing it, and him saying, 'I can't just play, if we have four games in a week, I can't play two of them. I need to play three or four.' And I would just kind of say, 'Well, then you go out and outplay me, because I'm going to go out and try and outplay you.' That's just the way it was. Very competitive."

But the Canadiens didn't win another Stanley Cup until 1993. Roy again was the Conn Smythe winner, thanks to his brilliance in overtime—10 times.

Roy's first weeks as a member of the Avalanche were not easy. The outgoing smile he displayed in the Avs dressing room the night of December 6, where a makeshift press conference was held along with Keane, hid insecurities.

Although Roy demanded a trade out of Montreal, his ego was bruised by how fast it happened. Wouldn't the Canadiens put up more of a fight to keep him? After all, he was *Patrick Roy*. Lots of people were saying he was on the downside. Were they right? Roy didn't know the city of Denver from John Denver, had never been there in his life. Was this team really any good? Would his family, all of whom spoke mostly just French, hate it there?

Roy wore a plain white mask his first game as an Av, December 7, at home against Edmonton. He lost, 5-3, but it didn't seem to matter to the McNichols crowd. Roy's number 33 sweater became an instant best-seller, and the team's growing fan base couldn't believe Saint Patrick was one of their own.

Neither could his new teammates, many of whom hated Roy from their days as bitter Canadiens rivals in Quebec.

"No question, we didn't like him when he was in Montreal," Joe Sakic said. "And then, here he was, with us! It didn't seem real at first. I mean, he was such a big star in Montreal and everywhere."

Roy lost his next home start, December 18 against Vancouver, and was beside himself afterward. None of the four goals against him were much his fault, but Roy pounded on a wall in the dressing room, saying over and over, "If I had just moved one second faster" on the winning goal. Teammate Troy Murray looked at Roy as if he were on drugs, as Roy was probably the team's best player that night. But right then, he started to show his teammates the fire he had to win. Before Roy, losses were accepted more easily by an Avalanche team that had never advanced to a Stanley Cup Final. Now, a midseason loss to the Canucks was a cataclysm.

Despite several months in Denver, Montreal was still somewhat on Roy's mind as the playoffs started. Before Game 1 of a first-round series with the Canucks, the video screen above the McNichols ice was playing live action from Montreal's first-round series. During his warm-ups, Roy couldn't help looking up at the screen, watching how his successor, Jocelyn Thibault, was faring. Roy kept tabs on Montreal's games more than he admitted initially. A hockey nut at all hours, one of the first things Roy did upon arrival in Denver was shell out $15,000 for a huge television and all the NHL satellite programming he could buy; on off-nights, whenever the Canadiens were on, Roy often watched from beginning to end.

After the Avs lost Game 1 to Vancouver, Roy called his father, telling him he was having trouble concentrating on his own team. He was always peeking at the scoreboard, he admitted, checking the score of the Habs game. Michel Roy told his son to forget about it. The past was past.

Things immediately improved. He led Colorado to wins in four of the next five games to close out Vancouver, then bested Ed Belfour in an epic series with the Blackhawks. Then came redemption against Detroit, and, finally, a brilliant Cup Finals in which he set a record in Game 4 with 63 saves in a 1-0, triple-overtime thriller.

After the game inside a steamy Miami Arena, with his third Cup in the books, Roy was hugged by PGA golfer Craig Stadler, who had a home in Denver and was a big hockey fan. "You fuckin' brick wall, you!" Stadler told Roy.

✳ ✳ ✳

Roy's temper did not only surface in fights with Red Wings goalies. There were two well-publicized incidents in Colorado that landed him in trouble with the law, one involving his wife.

Earlier, though, in 1997, he got into a physical altercation with a 6-foot-10, 295-pound man named Kevin Morris at a famous hotel in Colorado Springs, the Broadmoor. The Avs were having a team function for a weekend there when Roy and teammates such as Claude Lemieux and Adam Foote relaxed in a disco late one night, having a few drinks and laughs.

Music was playing, but Roy wanted it a little louder. He asked Morris, working as a part-time disc jockey, to turn it up a little. Morris said he couldn't. Roy asked why not. Because it was the rules, Morris said. Before long, Roy had his hands on Morris's throat, inflicting scratches but not much more.

Morris pressed assault charges, and the case was settled out of court.

In October 2000, early in the regular season in which Roy would win his fourth Cup and an unprecedented third Conn Smythe Trophy in three different decades, he was involved in an ugly incident in which his wife dialed 911 from their suburban Denver home. Not long after Roy had a Denver street named in his honor for breaking Terry Sawchuk's all-time victory record of 447, he went out to dinner at a local steakhouse with his wife and teammate Ray Bourque and his wife, Christiane.

Details remain murky, but what is clear is that the Roys had a fight on the way home from dinner that spilled over inside. The argument, some said, had to do with Roy's parents being in town the week before. It was well known that Michel Roy and Barbara Miller did not get along since their divorce years before, and their simultaneous visit to honor their son may have produced some icy feelings among everybody involved.

What also is not in dispute is that during the argument with his wife, Roy ripped two doors off their hinges in the master bedroom. Obviously scared, Michele dialed 911, but hung up before talking to anyone. She may have just been trying to scare her husband, and that might have been the end of it. But what she didn't realize is that any 911 call from a residence is traced and automatically followed up by a visit from the police—even if the call isn't answered by an operator.

Seeing the doors off their hinges, police charged Roy with criminal mischief in connection with an act of domestic violence. His annoyed-looking mug shot would be published in the Denver media, and before long it became a three-ring circus. After being charged, Roy came into the Avalanche dressing room at the team's practice headquarters and nervously delivered a prepared statement. Roy had some reason to be nervous, as a conviction could have meant his deportation. In the United States, Roy was considered a "nonimmigrant" under a P-1 work visa, commonly given to athletes and entertainers. As a nonimmigrant, if convicted of such a crime, Roy could have been deported under US law. But things never got that far. The charges were eventually dismissed, partly helped by Michele Roy's insistence that the whole incident was a misunderstanding, that she was in another room when the doors were ripped off, and that they were a loving couple. (Five years later, after Roy retired, the couple divorced.)

Roy, of course, was not always a hothead. Most of the time, he was actually very calm and cordial with everybody, reporters included. He liked kids, and was very gentlemanly around older people and women.

He liked to hang around with golfers, especially PGA pro Fred Couples, who was on hand to see Roy break Sawchuk's record in Washington. Roy would play 18 holes as often as he could, but his temper sometimes came out on the course.

"I kicked his ass every time," Lemieux said with a laugh. "I saw him break a few clubs over his knee in my day. But he worked almost as hard at his golf game as he did his goaltending techniques."

Roy and Lemieux played all the time on the road. The two would wager $500 to $1,000 on a round.

Roy had a few other celebrity friends, including tennis star Monica Seles, who was a guest once at his Montreal home.

Roy, like many pro athletes, whiled away the time on airplane rides playing cards with the boys. It was sometimes hold 'em poker, but most often hearts and a variation called "schnarples."

Roy was a nervous flier, however. Whenever turbulence hit, he would fold up his cards and walk to the front of the plane to sit quietly and ride it out, sweating and breathing heavily.

He was also extremely claustrophobic. He hated elevators most of all, fearing they would become stuck. Whenever possible, Roy would request a room on a lower floor of a hotel, and he often walked the stairs. One time on a team flight, Roy had to use one of the plane's tiny bathrooms. That combined his fear of flying with his claustrophobia, and he had something of a panic attack inside.

"We were trying to get him out, pulling at the door and banging on it, but he couldn't or wouldn't come out for a long time," Lemieux said.

Roy also did not like scary movies. He would leave the room whenever a movie got too intense, inducing laughs from his longtime roommate, Adam Foote. His favorite shows were harmless mysteries, such as *Murder, She Wrote* and *Silk Stalkings*.

"He absolutely loved *Murder, She Wrote* and Angela Lansbury," trainer Pat Karns said. "He would have me tape the show sometimes and bring them to him on the road."

Roy was not much of a reader, but he liked Agatha Christie and became absorbed in Sawchuk's life while reading his biography as he closed in on his record. As for music, Roy was partial to Supertramp, with maybe a little Rod Stewart and Celine Dion thrown in.

Otherwise, it was all about hockey. He had an amazing memory for past games, everything from who refereed that night to who scored all the goals for both teams.

"It would blow your mind," Lemieux said. "He'd say to me, 'Hey remember that game with St. Louis two years ago, when so and so scored against us. We gotta watch that guy tonight.' And I'd be like, 'Uh, no, I don't remember.' He never forgot a thing on the ice. It's probably partly why he was so great, because he knew everybody's moves and what they would do beforehand."

Roy was not much of a trash talker on the ice. He knew he intimidated many opponents already, and wanted to remain as mysterious as possible. Sometimes, though, he would showboat on a glove save, holding it high for all to see like a piece of bagged game. In the 1993 Stanley Cup Finals, Roy also famously winked at Los Angeles forward Tomas Sandstrom after robbing him with a save. Roy's unspoken message to Sandstrom seemed to be, "Not tonight, big fella."

Most of all, Roy thrived on trash talk *against* him. Roy looked for anything he could use as "Go ahead, make my day" motivation. What, you think I'm washed up—as perhaps the Red Wings and others did following his infamous last game in Montreal? I'll show you. You think I'm not good enough for the Canadian World Cup team—as Edmonton and Team Canada GM Glen Sather didn't in 1996? I'll show you. You think you've found my weakness—as his boyhood hero, Bouchard, publicly stated as Quebec's goalie coach after the Nordiques took a 2-0 series lead in the 1993 playoffs? I'll show you.

Roy beat the Wings and won the Stanley Cup in 1996, went 9-1-1 against Edmonton from 1996 to 1997 after Sather's slight, and allowed nine goals in Montreal's four straight victories over Quebec in 1993.

In Roy's first game against Montreal following the trade, November 9, 1996, he flipped the puck at Tremblay walking off the ice following Colorado's 5-2 victory. It was a move Roy later regretted, but at the time he was still so angry at Tremblay that he couldn't help it. In Roy's first game in Montreal following the trade, March 5, 1997, he and Keane posted a $10,000 bounty that would go toward a team party if the Avs won. They did, 7-3, lighting up Thibault like a Christmas tree in the first period, chasing him from the game.

"That was a great night for him, I know," Lemieux said. "There was no way we weren't going to win that game for him."

As long as Lemieux played with Roy, though, he and most former teammates felt they never got to know him well. Like many great players, Roy kept an emotional distance from teammates. Perhaps he felt they just couldn't relate to his level as a player. Or perhaps because he was a goalie, he felt he couldn't get close to anyone, as a guy might be a teammate one day and an enemy shooting pucks at him the next.

"He was always a bit of a loner," said former Canadiens teammate Mike McPhee. "In six or seven years, I never really got to know him. For a while, though, I started to develop a passion for hockey cards, and so did Patrick and Stephane Lebeau. Together, we'd all three go to different card shops in different cities sometimes. But other than that, rarely did I ever go out to dinner with him or hang out much."

Round 4—No Contest

The 1999–2000 Red Wings were a lot like the Avalanche of the year before. There was a lot of drama on and off the ice, but unlike the Avs the Wings seemed to get worse as the season wore on.

Sure, the team had a fine 48-22-10-2 record, but the Wings were too easy to score goals against for Scotty Bowman's taste. Chris Osgood and veteran Ken Wregget split the goaltending duties, both of whom struggled at times. There was a lot of age at defense, with veterans Larry Murphy and Chris Chelios logging major minutes—probably too many.

The Avalanche, too, struggled at times that season. Along the way, Claude Lemieux was traded. A major player in the Red Wings–Avalanche rivalry went back to New Jersey on November 3, 1999, when he was traded to the Devils for Brian Rolston.

Lemieux wasn't stunned; in fact, he requested Pierre Lacroix trade him after realizing the Avs weren't going to give him the kind of contract extension he wanted. But the deal was something of a surprise to many Avalanche and Red Wings fans. They knew now the rivalry would never be quite the same.

The Avalanche carried only a 30-27-10 record into a March 7, 2000, game in Calgary. The night before, however, the team—and the entire hockey world—was rocked when Colorado announced the acquisition of legendary Boston Bruins defenseman Ray Bourque. Along with 600-goal scorer Dave Andreychuk, Bourque joined the Avs after nearly 21 seasons in Boston. All it took to get him was third-liner Rolston, two marginal prospects named Martin Grenier and Samuel Pahlsson, and a first-round pick in the 2000 draft—who turned out to be a forgotten player named Martin Samuelsson.

"Ahhhhhggg," is the guttural sound Bowman made years later, remembering the trade. "They didn't have to pay through the nose for Bourque, that's for sure."

Bourque's presence would further shift the balance of power between Colorado and Detroit toward the Avs for the next two years. It might go down as perhaps the greatest steal of a deal in NHL history, probably more so than Lacroix's heist of Patrick Roy and Mike Keane from Montreal.

When Bourque walked into the Avs dressing room for the first time, at Calgary's Saddledome, it was as if he was the Messiah (a term Phoenix forward Jeremy Roenick would derisively use against him in the playoffs a couple months later). Avs players, even veterans such as Adam Foote, sat slack-jawed when Bourque arrived. As with Roy, it didn't seem real. How, everybody wondered, had Lacroix been able to do it again? Nobody suspected Colorado would be the destination for Bourque, who publicly stated he would prefer to be traded to an Eastern team to be closer to his family. Bourque thought he was going to the Philadelphia Flyers, and so did Philadelphia GM Bob Clarke, who thought he had a deal with Bruins GM Harry Sinden.

But as Lacroix often did, he got another GM—in this case Sinden—to agree to call him when he had his supposed last, best offer from another team. When Sinden called and told Lacroix of Philly's offer, he talked him into believing his was better. Pahlsson was going to be a player, Sinden was told, and so was Rolston. And don't forget about that first-round pick! It turned out Sinden was sold a bill of goods.

The Avalanche scored eight goals in Bourque's first game and went 12-2-1 in the final 15 games with him. Bourque's superb outlet passes freed up Colorado's speedy and skilled forwards from some of their defensive chores, resulting in numerous odd-man rushes.

Bourque's dedication to the game and fitness rubbed off on everybody, even Roy, who sometimes viewed exercise as a crashing bore. Bourque had what have to be the biggest thighs in hockey history. They were massive, virtual Sequoia trees masquerading as legs. He was built, as Roy said, "like a bear."

Bourque had never won a Stanley Cup in all his years in Boston, and wanted one last shot before he retired, something he knew wouldn't happen with the mediocre Bruins. By the time the playoffs rolled around, Colorado started to become everyone's choice to win it all. "Win One for Ray" became the sentimental story line for the Avs, their fans, and even those from Boston.

The Red Wings had their usual easy time with a first-round playoff opponent from Southern California, this time sweeping the Los Angeles Kings. The Avalanche had some minor trouble with the Phoenix Coyotes, but still whipped them in five games. As fate would have it, for the second year in a row one of the Western Conference semifinal match-ups featured the Red Wings versus the Avalanche.

Even though Detroit had a better regular-season record than Colorado, the Avalanche had home-ice advantage for the series because they won their division, gaining an automatic top-three seeding. Detroit lost the division to St. Louis, drawing the fourth seed.

It was an advantage from which the Avs quickly profited. Colorado won the first two games rather easily, by scores of 2-

0 and 3-1. The Red Wings, the highest-scoring team in the NHL that season, couldn't do anything against Colorado's suddenly powerful defense, led by Bourque and Foote. If Detroit managed to get past them, there again was Roy, as tough in the playoffs as ever.

The Red Wings played like the Avs of the 1997 playoffs, taking too many stupid penalties. In Game 2, Detroit had 13 separate penalties, 34 minutes overall. The Avalanche was the disciplined team now, the Red Wings a frustrated, retaliatory bunch.

"The Detroit Red Wings' new playoff website should be www.dumb@ss.com," wrote the ever gracious Woody Paige in the *Post*. "The Wings have played the first two games of the series with the Avalanche, to be kind, like a mutant, mutton-headed mule team.

"Duh . . . troit!

"The Wings' locker-room passion is crossword puzzles. What's a four-letter word that starts with 'd' and ends in 'b' and means dimwitted, boys? Could they have a vowel, Vanna? Curly-Larry-and-Motown thought that Coloradans had recently toppled from the turnip truck? Have the Avs been smarter so far, Kirk Maltby? 'Maybe little bit.' And Einstein was maybe a little bit smarter than Shemp. . . . Coach Scotty Bowman dismissed an evaluation that his team hasn't been the sharpest tool in the shed. 'Not really. Maybe a couple of (Steve) Duchesne's weren't' so brilliant. The eight-time Stanley Cup championship coach prefers to blame the officiating. He certainly can't blame a short-sheeted bench, a lousy locker room or Claude Lemieux this year.

"The good news for the Red Wings is that the team that lost the first two games in the 1999 series came back with four consecutive victories. The bad news is that the Avalanche was that team—and it won three games at The Joe."

Detroit wasn't helped by the fact that captain Steve Yzerman failed to get a goal in the entire playoffs. The Cranbrook, British Columbia, native had a fine regular season, too, with 35 goals and 79 points in 78 games.

Throughout his long career with Detroit, Yzerman occasionally had the bad playoff run—one of the few knocks against him. He also had the occasionally excellent playoffs, too—as his Conn Smythe in 1998 proved. But, while he was well above a point-a-game scorer in his regular-season career, Yzerman wasn't in the playoffs. He could get himself into slumps, and when he did, Detroit always seemed to sag with him.

Still, Yzerman will go down as one of the all-time great NHL players—and one of the most mysterious. He was certainly that way to Red Wings beat writers, who often rolled their eyes in exasperation when trying to get insight into his personality or off-ice life. Many times a Detroit reporter would leave the Wings dressing room cursing Yzerman's name, usually because he stayed too long in the off-limits part of the room, past their deadlines.

But Red Wings fans loved their Stevie Y. Apart from Gordie Howe, Yzerman will probably go down as the most beloved hockey player in Detroit history, maybe surpassing even Howe. Women swooned over his dark, rugged looks. The men loved his tough exterior and Motown work ethic.

Yzerman was a great teammate, those who played with him the longest said. He didn't care about his statistics, only those of the team. In many ways, his Avalanche mirror image was Joe Sakic. Both wore number 19, both were born in British Columbia, both were longtime captains of one franchise and both started their careers on horrid teams before winning multiple Stanley Cups.

Of the two, Yzerman was a bit darker, more aloof. Sakic

was teased sometimes by reporters as "Quoteless Joe" for his frequent vanilla comments, but actually he was a very sharp-witted person who loved to cut teammates and everyone else in the locker room down to size.

Like Yzerman, Sakic was occasionally dogged earlier in his career with the tag that he wasn't a playoff player. That all changed with a brilliant 1996 playoffs in which he won the Conn Smythe, scoring a league-high 18 goals, 6 of them game winners.

Sakic came from a hard-working Croatian family; his father, Marijan, was a carpenter whose hands were tough as sandpaper. Joe left home early to play junior hockey in freezing cold Swift Current, Saskatchewan, where he found great success and horrible tragedy. On a dark, snowy day—December 30, 1986—Sakic and his Swift Current Broncos teammates were in a bus bound for a Western Hockey League match against the rival Regina Pats. On the slippery Trans-Canada Highway, the bus hit a patch of black ice and careened past a railway overpass before flipping on its side. Sakic, 17 at the time, was sitting at the front of the bus with teammate Sheldon Kennedy. The bus driver went through the windshield and was injured. Sakic and Kennedy emerged dazed, with some cut glass in their clothing, but otherwise unhurt. Four players in the back—Trent Kresse, Scott Kruger, Brent Ruff, and Chris Mantyka—weren't as lucky. All were killed, two from being trapped under the bus.

Sakic was shaken by the tragedy, but developed a thicker hide to life's mysterious ways. Very little ever perturbed or shocked the Vancouver native after that, especially hockey's comparably trivial ups and downs on the ice.

Yzerman was similar, but wore his emotions outwardly a bit more, especially when things weren't going well on the ice. He always seemed to have a bit of a scowl, his eyebrows pinched together. Yet Yzerman could surprise those around him with acts of kindness, even the lowest on the totem pole.

"In the '99 playoff series, Jamie Macoun, Joey Kocur, who were not playing, and me, we went to the Diamond Cabaret [a gentleman's club]. Lunch turned into dinner and we closed the place down," said Wings' PR man Mike Kuta. "We get a per diem on the road. I didn't want to be a freeloader, so I'm throwing in for the beer fund with the boys. But I go through all my money, like $200–$300. I'm done, and we have like three more nights in Denver.

"Well, word starts getting around that I blew all my money. Later on, we're getting on the bus, going to the rink for the game. About halfway in the back of the bus, Yzerman's sitting there and he's doing his crossword puzzle. He was always doing them, all day long. I happen to be sitting right behind him. Stevie doesn't look up from his crossword puzzle and he goes, 'Hey Recon, I heard you blew all your money last night.' My nickname was 'Recon,' because of my military service. I'm thinking to myself, 'Oh no, Yzerman knows.' I figure, 'Oh no, I'm going to get this lecture, whatever.' John Hahn was sitting across the aisle from Stevie, and he's my boss and I don't want him to know this, and I've got my head down and I'm just thinking, 'Stevie, please shut up about this.' Next thing I know, he reaches back and he's got his hands closed. He handed me something, and I look and it's four one-hundred-dollar bills. John sees him handing me the money and says, 'You giving him a loan?' And Stevie said, 'No, he's out there representing the team, that's his allowance for the rest of the week.' He never said another word about it. I said, 'Thanks Stevie.'"

Yzerman was a tremendously smart player who could do just about anything. He had great patience with the puck, a hard slap shot, and excellent passing ability. Winning Stanley Cups helped turn his naturally withdrawn nature in media accounts from "moody" and "irritable" to "stoic" and "quiet leader."

"We always called Stevie the 'social conscience' of the team. He was always very serious. I always thought that maybe he was just unhappy. I would joke around and say Yzerman was the most miserable millionaire I've ever met in my life," Kuta said. "This guy had the world by the balls, and yet he never cracked a smile. But I think maybe my first couple years I just didn't get Stevie. He had a very dry sense of humor. But he just wanted to show up at the rink, do his job and go home. He would always kind of break Mac's and Draper's balls for being available all the time, always talking. They would always help me out. Stevie could be difficult after games, and we would get in arguments about it."

When Yzerman was in the rare mood to talk to reporters, he gave surprisingly insightful, meaningful answers. He would probably make a good coach someday, as Yzerman could break a game down as well as anybody, remembering every little detail of what happened and when a game turned.

"Stevie was always pretty quiet in the dressing room, but he was definitely one of those guys that when he had something to say, you could hear a pin drop in the room," Darren McCarty said. "You just had so much respect for him, and maybe a little bit of fear, too. In some ways, he was a little like Scotty. I mean, nobody was like Scotty, but Stevie really learned a lot from Scotty, I think."

Sakic almost always had one mood—steady-going. Not too high, not too low. If you saw Sakic in the dressing room after a game and didn't know who won, it would be impossible to tell by looking at him. Maybe after a season-ending loss you could, or a Stanley Cup championship, but otherwise he was always right down the middle. And very classy. Sakic did all kinds of things that never made the papers, like donating thousands of dollars to the homeless or bankrolling youth teams across the state. Sakic went from earning $2 million a year to an average of $7 million in the summer of 1997, but the money changed him not one ounce. Through the many years he played, not a single teammate or opponent ever had a bad word to say about Colorado's captain.

"One of the best teammates I ever had," said Keane. "He worked so hard on and off the ice all the time, but he did it so quietly, too. He never showed off about anything. A great guy."

Sakic made his living darting in and out of holes, beating goalies with quick little wrist shots off the wrong leg. He was particularly good on shots coming down the right side, to a goalie's right, leaning into wristers that could be pinpoint in their precision. He and Peter Forsberg were a deadly one-two punch at center; teams had to pick their poison over which line to throw their checking units against. It rarely worked.

"I always worried more about Sakic. He had such a quick release with his shot," Mike Vernon said. "And don't kid yourself, Forsberg was a handful too, trust me. But that Sakic just seemed to always get himself into the open space. I really admired him for his shot; just a tremendous shot."

Sakic's only brush with controversy in Colorado came when he signed a three-year, $21 million restricted free agent offer sheet with the Rangers in 1997. The Avalanche's ownership group, Ascent Entertainment, was in a precarious financial situation at the time, with company revenues lagging from its hotel pay-per-view business and the Pepsi Center mired in red tape.

The deal included a staggering $15 million up-front signing bonus, intended by the rich Rangers to blow the Avs out of the water. The Avs had a week to match the offer or accept five first-round draft picks, and in the interim Sakic was quoted as saying he would love to play in New York with his boyhood idol, Wayne Gretzky. That rubbed some fans the wrong way, so there were some mixed feelings when Ascent struck up a quickie partnership with Liberty Media Group that included a 4 percent portion of the Pepsi Center, just to raise the money to keep Sakic.

When Ascent announced the signing of Sakic and the partnership with Liberty, CEO Charlie Lyons sent Rangers management a framed photograph of former New York governor Nelson Rockefeller giving the finger to protesters at a political convention. Lyons, who had worked in Rockefeller's office as a youngster, said the photo was just a joke, but bad feelings between the Avalanche and Rangers lasted for years—with New York foolishly overpaying for some of Colorado's future free agent castaways, including Keane, Theo Fleury, Valeri Kamensky, Sylvain Lefebvre, and Greg de Vries.

The Avalanche closed out the Red Wings by winning two of the next three games, including a thrilling overtime victory in Game 4 in Detroit.

With comedian Billy Crystal sitting behind the Avalanche bench (he was in town shooting his acclaimed Roger Maris–Mickey Mantle biopic, *61**), the Avs took a 3-1 series lead on Chris Drury's OT goal past Osgood.

Detroit was only 4:27 from tying the series when the veteran Andreychuk scored his most important goal as a member of the Avs. Osgood failed to wrap up a rebound of a Milan Hejduk shot that hit the post, allowing Andreychuk a chance to jab at the puck with his enormously long stick. Midway through the first OT, Forsberg set up Drury for an easy backhand winner, on a 2-on-1 breakout.

The game featured some of the old nasty stuff; McCarty nailed Foote into the boards with a big hit from behind—one very similar to the Lemieux hit on Kris Draper. Foote emerged unhurt, but spent much of his time afterward trying to pay McCarty back.

Bourque did not play in the game or the rest of the series, twisting a knee in Game 3. But he gave a pep talk between the first and second periods that teammates credited for giving a good boost.

Colorado won Game 5, 4-2; Forsberg was brilliant. He scored the winning goal on a rare slap shot off the rush, and hammered Detroit's Sergei Fedorov with a huge open-ice hit.

Earlier in the day, Bob Hartley did his best Henny Youngman impression with a string of one-liners, including one directed at Bowman. At the time, a nasty computer virus with an e-mail taglined "I love you" was invading the country's computers. Open the attachment to the e-mail, and your hard drive was destroyed.

"This morning, I was up and I looked at my computer screen and it says . . . 'I love you.' I swear, I thought it was from Scotty," Hartley said. "I thought it was Scotty trying to send me a little message. I was disappointed when it wasn't."

By now, Avalanche fans had long mastered the chant "Red Wings Suck." By game's end it was heard over and over at the new Pepsi Center. But it was now the Avalanche and the Denver media's turn to feel somewhat sorry for the Red Wings.

"Despite what the 18,007 at The Can chant, the Red Wings do not s**k," Paige wrote. "Detroit has a great team and a proud tradition. Denver has a greater team and a grand new tradition."

Hartley became the first coach in NHL history to beat Bowman in back-to-back best-of-seven playoff series. The Avalanche now had beaten Detroit in three out of four playoff series since 1996.

"Against the Wings that year, I thought that basically we were flawless," Hartley said. "The four wins, the entire duration, even the game they beat us we were still pretty good. We were skating well, got good games from everyone."

Said Detroit's Brendan Shanahan: "They just outplayed us. I think in any playoffs, you need breaks and health, and as much as I think the health of our goalies in '99 played a part, in 2000 they were just better."

Bowman predicted the Avs would go on to win the Cup, as did just about everybody. But it didn't happen. The Avs dominated the Dallas Stars for much of their Western finals series, but were frustrated beyond belief again by Ed Belfour. Roy had one of the few poor playoff series of his career, one in which his play clearly was a factor in a negative way. The Avs had a 2-1 series lead, with Game 4 at home, but blew the game and lost in another seventh game at the dreaded Reunion Arena.

"The best team lost," a furious Lacroix said after the series.

For the Avs, it was the Cup that got away, the one big sore spot in the team's history.

"We should have won that year," Roy said. "In Game 7 [a 3-2 loss], I never had more strange goals go in on me than that one."

"Mac"

After Game 5 of the 2000 series, Darren McCarty had a look of what seemed beleaguered relief. It was a look suggesting he knew the Wings' glory days were over, but it was much deeper than that.

McCarty's father, Craig, had died the year before, on November 24, from multiple myeloma, an incurable cancer of the bone marrow and blood.

For Darren, it was the hardest few months of his life. When Craig McCarty was diagnosed with the disease in 1995, his son was dealing with his own battle with alcoholism. Just as he had about kicked alcohol, his father was gone.

The roots of Darren McCarty's drinking problem might have originated from a tough first few years of life. Born on April 1, 1972, in Burnaby, British Columbia, Darren McCarty's name at birth was Darren Francottie—a fact never publicly disclosed until now.

His biological father, Doug Francottie, abandoned the family shortly after his birth. He had his own problem with booze, and McCarty would not see him again for about 30 years. Until he was 7, Darren and his mother, Roberta, lived at the house of his grandfather, Bob Pritchard, or "Jigs"—the name McCarty had tattooed on his shoulder. When he was seven, Darren had a new family.

Craig McCarty met and fell in love with Roberta, eventually marrying her and adopting Darren. Craig ran a heating and cooling business in Leamington, Ontario, just across the Detroit River and where he brought his new family to live. Life as a Leamington youngster would be good for Darren, full of sports and family outings and lots of friends.

Darren's first love was baseball—he was a catcher—and he would be good enough to draw interest from several major-league teams as a teenager. A future in hockey seemed out of the question, however; he was a clumsy skater, too slow to keep up with the play. His hands were OK, but probably not fast enough for the big time. But he was good with his hands when it came to landing them, hard, against an opponent's face.

Life under Craig McCarty's roof wasn't all one big party, either. He worked hard at his business to provide enough food and clothing for Darren and his sister, Melissa. He demanded Darren work just as hard at his schoolwork, and for Craig when he hired him on as summer help.

Darren hated his father's line of work. The two clashed often about it. Darren dreamed of life as a pro athlete; Craig felt it was all a foolish pipe dream. At 16, when Darren was cut from an under-17 Ontario hockey team, Craig tried to gently tell him to forget about his hockey dream, to focus on a real education and more realistic goals.

"And that's when I kind of had a fire lit under me," McCarty recalled. "I wanted to be an NHL player more than ever at that point. I kind of quit baseball and decided to devote myself 110 percent to hockey, and to get better any way possible. I think, truly, I made it to the NHL because of the thought of working at a job like my dad's. Why get up at 7 every morning for that?"

Darren took a job at McDonald's when he was 16, working until 1:30 in the morning, eating all the burgers and fries his bosses would let him have. He loved it at Mickey D's, but Craig worried nonstop. Here was his son, almost a man now, working at McDonald's and dreaming of a career in the highest hockey league in the world. Hadn't he seen himself skate? When was he going to wake up and smell the coffee? Better to learn a trade and prepare for an honest, decent life—like he'd done. But Craig McCarty knew hockey dreams died hard for Canadian boys. As a youth, he had been a pretty good hockey player himself and dreamed of the big time. It took a long time to get over it when it didn't happen, and he was determined to see a better life for Darren than the one he had.

But Darren wouldn't be dissuaded. He begged his parents to send him to an expensive hockey camp in August of 1988, and there he met Brian Drumm, the coach of a Junior B team in Peterborough, Ontario. Drumm liked McCarty's feisty attitude and overall leadership skills. He was convinced he could improve McCarty's skating and skill level, and offered him a roster spot with his team the following fall.

Craig and Roberta reluctantly agreed to let Darren leave for Peterborough, a five-hour drive from Leamington. Darren actually lived in Drumm's house after unsuccessfully trying to find another billet family. Darren took a little razzing at first for being the coach's "brown nose," but not for long. If there was one thing all of Darren McCarty's teammates would always say about him, it was that nobody was quicker than he to stand up for them. McCarty would get in a lot of fights with the Peterborough B's, racking up 135 penalty minutes in 34 games.

And Drumm showed that McCarty would not get any favorable treatment just because he ate at the family dinner table. If McCarty missed a curfew—which he did—he was suspended for the following game, no questions asked.

Craig and Roberta bought a small cottage on a lake near

Peterborough—a stretch on his salary—to be closer to Darren. It turned out to be a wonderful purchase, as the family spent winter weekends skating on the frozen pond and summers fishing its sun-speckled waters.

McCarty showed improvement under Drumm. His skating slowly got better, and scouts started to notice his toughness along the boards and in front of the net. It didn't hurt that many of his fights were over in a couple of seconds, as McCarty had a hard right-hand punch that quickly floored opponents. He could also take a hard punch and emerge laughing all the way to the penalty box.

His favorite team growing up was the Red Wings, and he idolized their tough guy, Bob Probert. To McCarty, Probie was the ultimate hockey player, one who could beat you with his stick or his fists. Unfortunately, McCarty would share some of Probert's off-ice fondness for the bottle.

McCarty had a good enough first season with Junior B Peterborough to be drafted in the fourth round of the 1989 Ontario Hockey League draft by the Junior A Belleville Bulls.

It was with the Bulls that McCarty was introduced to the temptation that is alcohol. Playing with players sometimes three years older, first-year Junior A players naturally can get swept into a life of partying. Once the game is over, you're a star in your Podunk small junior town; bar owners want you in their place—it's good for business. Women—or puck bunnies—are always around in the Junior A towns, willing to buy the players a drink and save a place in a warm bed in exchange for a potentially comfortable NHL future. It is a bargain many young junior players accept, and McCarty was no exception.

He met a pretty girl named Cheryl his first year with Belleville, and it wasn't long before he was spending most nights with her. Her family practically became his new billet hosts, and life was good.

But McCarty did start a drinking lifestyle that would follow him his first years in the NHL and would always be a potential hazard. What else was there to do in Belleville, Ontario, on a weekday off-night for a kid playing hockey, with no real educational responsibilities? Have a couple of pops at the bar, on the house, and let the fun begin. For McCarty, it was a welcome change from Craig McCarty's strict household.

Still, McCarty did not let the drinking interfere with his devotion to hockey. His skating kept getting better, thanks in part to the instruction of a noted Connecticut-based speed-skating coach named Laura Stamm. McCarty visited Stamm during the summers, and developed a skating style that was lower to the ice, making him less susceptible to being knocked off his feet.

Being able to stand his ground in front of the net, where the majority of goals are scored in the rough-and-tumble junior ranks, meant more scoring chances for McCarty. After scoring only 12 goals his first season with the Bulls, he improved to 30 goals in 60 games in 1990–91, and a league-leading 55 the following season. Combined with his 72 assists in 1991–92, McCarty was not only a top OHL scorer, he already had the reputation as perhaps the league's toughest fighter, pound for pound.

Those kinds of attributes made NHL scouts take notice—an unbelievable concept a couple of years before. A Red Wings scout named Mike Adessa visited Darren and his father, and was impressed enough to pass along his recommendation to Detroit management.

With their second pick, 46th overall, the Red Wings chose McCarty in the 1992 draft at the Montreal Forum. What a thrill it was for the kid who supposedly wasn't good enough to play beyond the Junior C level. What a thrill, too, for Craig McCarty, who kept shaking his head in disbelief at his son's perseverance and good fortune. There would be no following in his footsteps in the heating and cooling business; instead, a life in the big time of hockey, with millions of dollars and adulation lay just ahead.

Scotty Bowman always liked players like Darren McCarty: guys who made it to the NHL the hard way—with no silver spoon, or stick, in their mouths. Bowman hated the prima donna players who didn't work hard enough. It was why he couldn't stand Paul Coffey anymore after the 1995–96 season.

From the start, Bowman knew he had a tough, dependable player in McCarty. Sure, his skating wasn't much, but he had a nose for the puck and wouldn't take crap from anybody.

"You could tell he was an eager kid," Bowman said. "He had some good toughness, a good fighter. And his hands weren't too bad. He was a little raw, but we thought we could develop him into a pretty good player, which he became."

After a year with the Adirondack Red Wings, Detroit's top farm club, in upstate New York, McCarty made the Red Wings full-time in 1993–94. From the outset, he established himself as a middleweight enforcer, willing to take on anybody.

The Red Wings of 1993–94 under Bowman posted the most points in the Western Conference, but lost in the first round of the playoffs to eighth-seed San Jose. McCarty had nine goals and 26 points in 67 games, with a career-high 181 penalty minutes. He also had two goals and four points in seven playoff games. All in all, not bad.

"Your first year in the NHL, you never forget any of it," McCarty said. "It was amazing to wear a Red Wings uniform."

The drinking got worse, however. Nights after a game, he popped a few beers, but things started to get worse when he discovered a taste for tequila. Anyone who has had more than a couple shots of tequila knows how potent it is, and what kind of hangovers it can leave. For McCarty, practices weren't just to get better as a player, they served to work off the bender from the night before. Kris Draper was his roommate in Adirondack, where there were many nights of drinking.

Fortunately, McCarty was not a mean drunk who did self-destructive things. He was a "beers for everybody on the house" kind of drinker. Fun. Lots of laughs. Good times. There weren't a lot of barroom brawls or any drunk-driving convictions. Plus, his Red Wings teammates and training staff monitored the situation, giving him rides when he needed them and keeping everything from Bowman—not an easy task.

"We'd go out and drink beer and have fun and do our thing," Draper told the *Detroit News* in 1999. "But when it was time to go home, we'd go home. And we'd be able to get up the next morning and go to practice. That was something Darren could never figure out.

"I would always say, 'Let's just do beer.' And he could do beer for a little while, but then he always had to put it in overdrive. Then it'd be shots and . . . well, Darren never had closure at night. Once he started going, he wouldn't stop drinking until he couldn't drink anymore. It was kind of scary."

McCarty told the *News*: "I had (Paul Coffey) and Stevie (Yzerman) harping on me for two years, saying, 'Hey, slow down.' But it'd be in one ear and out the other. I'd tell them what they wanted to hear. That's how it works: you tell yourself one thing and tell everyone else something different just to get by. . . . You're lying to yourself mostly."

A lockout in 1994–95 resulted in just a 48-game regular season, of which McCarty played only 31. Detroit's loss in the Finals to New Jersey was a blow to the city, which thought it would have its first Cup winner since 1955. McCarty again played well in the playoffs, though, and started to get more playing time in 1995–96. He scored 15 goals, and by the play-offs he, Draper, and newly acquired Kirk Maltby formed the successful Grind Line. As third-line checking units went, the Grind Line was the best in the league. McCarty and Maltby were in-your-face protagonists who could score a little. Draper had blazing speed, and though his scoring touch wasn't great, it would improve over the years.

After the 1995–96 season, though, McCarty knew the drinking was out of control. The fact his father was recently diagnosed with multiple myeloma didn't help matters at all. Neither did the pressures of being a new father himself; on May 20, 1996, his first child, Griffin, came into the world. At 24, he was a father, a husband, and a man with a drinking problem. He knew it was time for help.

"That's the hard part, admitting it at first," McCarty said. "Once I was able to do that, it became something I could deal with."

At Red Wings training camp in 1996, McCarty went public with his drinking problem. He received support from the team's fans and, more important, its management. At the same time, Craig McCarty was undergoing painful chemotherapy. In an emotional phone call between the two, on July 8, 1996, they made a pact to help each other through their diseases.

Both knew Craig's was the more formidable foe. Multiple myeloma is a terminal condition, but Craig gave it a tougher battle than any hit or punch Darren ever dished out. Through agonizing radiation treatments and sky-high hospital bills, he showed a strength that had a lasting effect on Darren. If his father could take the nastiest thing his rebellious body could dish out, and do it with courage and dignity, he certainly could whip alcohol. And he did, entering a period of extended sobriety that would bring some of the happiest personal and professional times of his life.

And one of the worst: on November 24, 1999, Craig McCarty passed away peacefully. He lived longer than any of the medical experts thought he would, and got to see his son raise two Stanley Cups.

In 1997 Darren established the McCarty Cancer Foundation, which to date has raised more than $4 million.

※　※　※

In 2003 McCarty reentered treatment for alcoholism. The label "recovering alcoholic" is used for a reason: it's a disease always just one sip away, always gladly willing to reenter a victim's life.

Not long after, he and Cheryl divorced. McCarty remarried and said he has a "great" relationship with his ex-wife and their four children. McCarty's interest in rock music manifested in his forming a professional band, Grinder, in which he is the lead singer. Smoky bars may or may not be the best place to stay away from the temptations of booze, but McCarty's addiction to being onstage—whether one made of ice or wood—probably never will go away.

In 2002 McCarty finally reconnected with his biological father, in Edmonton. It took 30 years for McCarty to begin to forgive Doug Francottie.

"I had to do it on my time," he said. "We've built a friendship since then. It was neat recently; I came out of the locker room in Edmonton and there was my real dad, mom, and sister all in one place. I'd never seen that."

In 2005 McCarty was cut loose by the Red Wings. A victim of the new NHL salary cap—and a player whose value to the Wings had lessened as the league got suddenly less physical—McCarty was fortunate to find a suitor in the defending Western Conference champion Calgary Flames.

In April 2006 McCarty declared Chapter 7 bankruptcy. Listing debts of $6.2 million and assets of $1.9 million, McCarty was forced to publicly address his problems, which he called "embarrassing."

The lockout of 2004–2005 hurt McCarty's finances, as did the divorce from his first wife. When the Red Wings bought out the final year of McCarty's contract in 2005, he had to give

75 percent of it—nearly $405,000—to Cheryl. McCarty also listed casinos in Detroit and Los Angeles as debtors, to the tune of $185,000. McCarty lost the money playing poker, which became his game of choice in the wake of a boom in its popularity on television in the United States.

But good fortune has always seemed to find McCarty somehow, after whatever tough times he has faced.

"My life is kind of a miracle, when you look at it," he said. "I'm just a very lucky person to have experienced everything I have. I mean, to play in the NHL to begin with, then play for the team you loved as a kid, then to win Stanley Cups with that team—and to have a great family and friends. I mean, I still can't believe it."

Media Wars

When the Avalanche moved to Denver in 1995, the city was in the final stages of one of the most colorful and nastiest newspaper wars of its kind.

Believe me when I tell you there was real hatred between us at the *Denver Post* and "the other paper," the *Rocky Mountain News*. There were some notable press box fights between reporters from the two papers over the years, including one in which baseball reporter Mike Klis of the *Post* literally jumped on the back of the *News*'s Tracy Ringolsby at Coors Field. Mike Monroe, who covered the Denver Nuggets of the NBA for many years at the *Post*, did not speak to his *News* counterpart, Dave Krieger, for the last few years at their beat. Even sitting side-by-side on press row, they never said one word to each other, so great was their disdain for one another.

I guess I was lucky covering the Avalanche. Rick Sadowski of the *News* was a veteran who had covered the Los Angeles Kings for the LA *Daily News* for many years when I got the Avs beat as a rookie, but he was and is a very nice guy. We've actually hung out a few times on the road (Shhh! Don't tell the boss), all the while having a running joke about getting "scooped" by the day's events. ("Say, did you *hear* what Sakic said today?!!" was a typical refrain.)

There was and always will be a natural wariness between beat reporters from different newspapers—if newspapers survive much longer, that is. Even though Sadowski and I are friends, he wants to scoop me on a story as much as I do with him, and we wouldn't hesitate to do it. The absolute best feeling in the world for a reporter is to see a big, juicy scoop on the front page of your paper, then check the other one and see . . . nothing. Then, watching them scramble to catch up in the next day's paper.

The rivalry between the sports columnists at the *Post* and *News* in the mid-1990s was doubly vicious. At the *Post*, Woody Paige and Mark Kiszla were a combination of acid sarcasm, brutal second-guessing, wicked humor, and, at times, shameless opportunism. At the *News*, Bob Kravitz was the paper's lead columnist, and he always chafed at the money and attention Paige received. Norm Clarke, who found greater fame as a society columnist in Las Vegas, was the *News*'s sports notes columnist at the time and he and Paige hated each other. The two had a noted confrontation at a hotel pool in the early 1990s, with Clarke—who was blind in one eye and wore a patch—challenging Paige to a fight and calling him "fat boy."

Kravitz, a former club team hockey goalie in college, was an excellent writer who knew his stuff when it came to hockey. But it seemed no matter what he wrote, Paige or Kiszla got more attention. It burned Kravitz to no end, but he went on to become the big shot in one-newspaper-town Indianapolis, writing for the *Star*.

Paige was a case study unto himself. Today he is much better known for his work on ESPN than he ever was at the *Denver Post*. He will forever be known to a generation of sports fans for his witty and ranting style on some of ESPN's various roundtable shows, but the Paige I'll always remember is a true, hard-core newspaper man.

I knew that was true when driving with him in a rental car from Calgary to Edmonton and back one year in the playoffs. I drove the roughly three-hour trip, and Paige had a copy of the day's *Calgary Sun*, a lowbrow tabloid that was part of a Canadian chain that featured a daily photo of a scantily clad "Sunshine Girl." For nearly the entire trip, Paige read the paper from cover to cover—I mean, every word of it, very intently. Finally, he carefully folded the paper, set it gently down on the backseat, and took a nap the last 75 or so kilometers.

Paige couldn't resist the big money and bright lights of television fame when he finally left the *Post*, and probably every one of us would have done the same. But I guarantee you the first thing Paige does every morning in New York is pick up a newspaper and read it. Once you get ink in your veins, it never goes away. There's something about the written word that will always have it all over TV; when the paper comes out, the words are there in black and white, forever. On TV, unless the VCR is running, it's gone instantly.

Paige, with his slight Tennessee twang, could tell some great stories on the road—especially in the earlier days when he had a few drinks in him, something he gave up several years ago. A lot of them were about editing screw-ups of his columns— which writers always bicker about when together over a few beers. One of his best stories involved a writer—for what paper I can't remember—who, in a panic, called his editor and told him to "change all my Army's to Navy's" in a game story.

Kiszla, a wiry man with dark eyes and a mood that sometimes matched, came from the school of sports columnists that thought there was never a wrong time to stick the poison pen into a subject. Some of his columns were brutal in their attacks on players or teams that underachieved for whatever reason.

But nobody, not even a team's own beat reporters, worked

harder than Kiszla when covering an event. Kiszla would go to almost any length to get the story, whether it meant waking people at midnight on the phone or staking them out well into the night in the parking lot. He took great delight in scooping the beat reporters on a story, which happened often. To his credit, Kiszla always made it a point to show up the next day at a team's practice or game following a rip-job, in case somebody wanted to come back at him.

As bad as the hatred was between the Denver newspapers, a funny thing always seemed to happen whenever the Avalanche and Red Wings met; it almost became a case of "the enemy of my enemy is my friend" in that it suddenly became "Denver media versus Detroit media."

In the 1997 series between Colorado and Detroit, things became heated between Keith Gave and Jason La Canfora of the *Free Press* and me, to the point where we were nose to nose with each other.

Following Game 3 of the series, with the Wings up 2-1, Gave included a line in his column about how Avs coach Marc Crawford was preaching to the converted, "even to some Denver reporters who kneel to kiss his ring each day."

The absolute worst thing you can call any self-respecting sports writer is a homer. The sacred rule of the profession is "No Cheering in the Press Box." Violate it, and you bring everlasting shame on yourself and employer—and plenty have done so over the years. One thing sportswriters hear all the time is, "Hey, you must have been happy/sad when your team won/lost the game/series." And the answer, to a professional, must always be, "No, I couldn't care one way or the other."

By the 1997 series, I was into my second year covering a team that won a Stanley Cup its first year and was back in the conference finals the second. And yet I had already been threatened by Avs management a couple of times with banishment from the locker room for alleged negative coverage. And having grown up near Boston, where the papers could be absolutely vicious, and rooting for a onetime cursed team I loved to hate, the Red Sox, I naturally developed a sarcastic writing style and general outlook on life.

So upon reading that line by Gave, I fumed. Kissing Crawford's ring? Apart from being ridiculous, what was the overall point—that Crawford should be ripped apart for his defending championship team being down 2-1 in a best-of-seven series?

The line made us in the Denver media even madder, considering an incident several people, including myself, thought happened during Game 2. When Detroit's Steve Yzerman scored to wrap up the game for the Wings, a few of us could have sworn *Free Press* beat reporter La Canfora let out some kind of loud noise in the press room—suspiciously like a cheer.

The little potshots toward Denver and its media seemed to continue following Gave's line, to the point where I'd had enough and—stupidly—decided to fire back, in print. During Game 5, the 6-0 Avs rout, I was compiling notes for the early edition of the paper. Needing more material to fill it all up, I decided to write a snide little note detailing La Canfora's alleged cheer, and how he "broke the cardinal rule" of sportswriting. I never mentioned La Canfora's name, just the paper.

Immediately after sending in the notes, I felt stupid. The public doesn't care about that, and it was petty. So I called to have it taken out. The problem was, the first edition had already gone to press. No problem, I thought, it'll come out for the final edition, which is the only one people read in Denver anyway. Nobody except some farmers in Wyoming will read the snide note.

Wrong. Back in those days, early editions of the paper were the only ones available at Denver International Airport. The next morning, Gave, La Canfora, and company picked up their early edition copies of my paper at DIA and saw the item.

When my *Post* colleague Terry Frei and I got to Joe Louis

Arena later that day for practice, we were met by a red-faced, screaming Gave. He was ready to rumble, and a few days before, I might have eagerly obliged him. But the truth was, I felt embarrassed at having written the item, and was very conciliatory toward him and La Canfora. The incident blew over after a while, to the point where we could all have a laugh about it. And I should make it clear that I have no definitive memory or proof that La Canfora ever cheered in the first place. He's a good reporter and person, and went on to greater things at the *Washington Post* as the beat writer for the Redskins.

But the episode was a good example of the emotions that sometimes crept into the press box during the Wings-Avs rivalry. I'll admit, it was the only time in my sportswriting career where I did, in fact, feel myself mysteriously pulling for the Avs at times. It wasn't because I wanted the Avalanche to win the game the way an actual fan does. It was more like, "Ha, take that, Gave! Take that, pompous Detroit media!" You felt like the other side was a bunch of homers, so you wanted to see them have to write about how their heroes blew it. It was all macho caveman bullshit—but kind of fun, too.

It's a good thing Frei was there, because he is always the voice of reason in situations like that. He gave me a pretty good—and needed—lecture about staying away from any of the back-and-forth stuff with opposing media. And he's right; it should always be about the players and the games, and that's it. When he worked for years as a columnist for the *Daily Oregonian* in Portland, he saw some pretty bad media cheerleading, including a time when a news staffer assigned to cover a Trailblazers game in the NBA Finals jumped out of her seat and exulted when the Blazers scored. She got a swift lecture from the veteran sportswriters to sit down and shut up. It can be difficult sometimes not to subconsciously root for good things for the team you cover. First of all, you're human and you develop relationships with the players you cover. I mean, it's unavoidable. You see a player on the road, in a hotel lobby, and you ask how the wife and kids are or how the food is up the street and a little bond develops. But as journalists, you're taught to keep a certain emotional distance from the players, to stop any favoritism that might creep into your copy. The problem is that it's hard to write inside, colorful stories about the players—the kind readers like best—if you don't get to know them a little.

The truth is, all sportswriters secretly become homers after a while—toward themselves. We root for whatever will make our already pampered lives that much easier. If our team's winning means we get to go to a more exotic locale for the next playoff round, it's "Go team, go." If our team losing means we get to start our summer vacation early and see our spouses and kids again, it's "Go other team, go."

One Last Great Hurrah

The Avalanche of 2000–01 was a powerhouse, probably one of the 10 greatest teams in NHL history.

You had forward lines with names such Peter Forsberg, Joe Sakic, Milan Hejduk, Chris Drury, and Alex Tanguay. On defense, you had the great Ray Bourque alongside Adam Foote, in front of the greatest goalie of them all, Patrick Roy.

Then, late in the season, the Avs added another blue-chip player, Rob Blake, in a trade with the Kings that sent the popular Adam Deadmarsh to Los Angeles. The trade did not go over well at first with some Avs players, especially Forsberg, but there is no question it made Colorado better.

When Pierre Lacroix landed Blake, a shudder went through the Red Wings offices.

"We took a run at Blake, but they signed him instead. We couldn't quite get it done," Jimmy Devellano said. "We knew that would probably put them over the top."

It did. The Avalanche finally won their second Cup, five years after the first and a couple of heartbreaking close calls. Colorado waltzed through the regular season, winning 52 games, but had a hard time with Los Angeles in the second round. It was a 1-1 game entering the third period of Game 7 at the Pepsi Center, but the Avs finally broke through against goalie Felix Potvin for a 5-1 win. Forsberg, however, would be lost for the rest of the playoffs when he suffered a ruptured spleen. Eating a late dinner at the players' favorite postgame hangout, the Denver Chophouse and Brewery, Forsberg felt a sharp pain in his abdomen that landed him on an operating table. A total of 1.7 liters of blood had burst from the spleen's rupture, and if Forsberg hadn't gotten medical help within hours—highly probable if he'd been on an airplane or at his former Colorado mountain home, which he'd recently sold—he easily could have died. Forsberg's injuries always seemed to come at the worst time, and this one seemed like a deathblow to "Mission 16W"—the slogan the Avs used in hopes of getting Bourque his first Cup.

The Avs were so strong, however, they won the Cup without the world's best all-around player. They easily beat St. Louis in the conference finals, and knocked off defending Cup champion New Jersey in seven games—with Game 7 capping the brilliant 22-year career of Bourque in high style.

The Red Wings had a very good 2000−01, winning 49 games, their most since the 62 of 1995−96. But not only did the Blake trade help put Colorado over the top, it helped knock the Wings out of the first round.

Old nemesis Deadmarsh eliminated Detroit for the Kings with an overtime goal on Chris Osgood in Game 6 at the Staples Center, the Wings' first opening-round elimination in seven years. Steve Yzerman missed most of the series with a broken leg, and Brendan Shanahan suffered a broken toe in Game 1, missing the next three games.

Following the loss, the *Free Press* ran a large headline— "Past Their Prime?"—above a picture of Red Wings players leaving the ice.

The Avalanche had claimed superiority over the Wings for

three straight years now, this time with a Stanley Cup ring on top. The rivalry scorecard now read: Avalanche three playoff series victories, Red Wings one, with each team having two Stanley Cups.

Wings management spent the summer scheming for ways to get back on top, with the general consensus being that they needed an upgrade in goal above all. But how? Teams just didn't give top-flight goalies away, not unless they blew up at their coach and demanded a trade.

Or, as was the case with the cash-poor Buffalo Sabres of 2001, a team that needed to dump salary. Or both, as was the case when the Sabres realized they couldn't afford the $9 million option year on the contract of superstar goalie Dominik Hasek for 2001–02, and Hasek, frustrated at management's failure to deliver on its promise to provide "the tools to finish the job" after the Sabres' Cup run in 1999, demanded a trade to a legitimate contender.

Wings GM Ken Holland got a courtesy call from an old junior friend, Buffalo GM Darcy Regier, wondering if Detroit had an interest in Hasek. It was beyond Holland's wildest dreams that he had a shot at the lanky rubber-band-man Hasek, who took the Sabres to the Finals in 1999 and had six Vezinas and two Hart Trophies in his closet.

Holland, knowing the growing impatience of his spoiled Hockeytown fans, threw himself into trying to consummate a deal to land Hasek. He also held serious trade talks to bring either Eric Lindros or Jeremy Roenick to the team.

Holland, Devellano, Scotty Bowman, and owner Mike Ilitch had grown tired of the "Lacroix Does It Again!" type of headline, how the Avalanche fleeced the hockey world to land the latest superstar player. Sure, the Wings had made some good deals of their own over the years, but nothing that matched the acquisitions of Roy, Bourque, or Blake.

It was time for the Red Wings to make the hockey world's

jaw drop, and it happened in the wee hours of July 1. Like Colorado's acquisition of Roy six years before, it proved a steal when the Wings got Hasek for the relatively small price of Slava Kozlov, a first-round pick in the 2002 draft, and future considerations, which turned out to be another draft pick.

The Hasek acquisition gave the Red Wings a goalie on par with Roy for the first time in the rivalry—even though Mike Vernon is a multiple Cup winner and possible Hall of Famer. Hasek had the intangible of mystique that Vernon didn't, a goalie who could get into an opponent's head before the game even began.

Hasek broke almost every rule of proper goaltending technique, often flopping wildly to make saves, with his head staring up at the ceiling. Off the ice, he had many idiosyncrasies, including an obsession with clipping his nails to just the right length and frequent periods when he wouldn't talk to anyone.

Whatever his methods, the bottom line was he kept the puck out of the net. He had extremely fast reflexes, maybe the quickest in NHL history. Like Roy and New Jersey standout Martin Brodeur, Hasek wanted to handle every puck that went behind the net—often to the point where he was roughed up by checking forwards.

When Hasek came to the Red Wings, he already was one up on Roy in a big-time competition; in 1998 he led the Czech Republic to the gold medal in Nagano, Japan. One of the victories on the way was a thrilling shootout victory over Roy and Team Canada, a game in which Roy was beaten on a goal by Robert Reichel. The loss stung Roy, who wanted to prove on the world stage he was the best, especially when compared to Hasek. A gold medal is the only major hockey prize Roy never won.

Holland wasn't satisfied with getting Hasek, however. He felt the Red Wings could use a little more offensive firepower, even though future Hall of Famers such as Yzerman, Shanahan, and Nicklas Lidstrom were still around.

So he looked around the free-agent market and saw the names of two 500-plus-goal-scorers—Brett Hull and Luc Robitaille. Of the two, Hull was already an established Avalanche killer. He scored one big goal after another against Roy for Dallas in the Western finals of 1999 and 2000, the one player that probably put the Stars over the top against the Avs.

When the definitive history of the NHL is written, it should probably say that Hull had the most accurate shot of anybody. Hull could hit the hair on a gnat's behind with his fearsome slap shot. He needed only a fraction of a second to get his hard, pinpoint release on net, the kind of shooter that could only give Roy trouble on a regular basis. Along with Hull, Cam Neely probably gave Roy more fits than anybody in his career— although Owen Nolan scored more goals against him than any other player.

Robitaille, although slow on skates, had a knack for always being in the right place around the net. The puck always seemed to find his stick in a prime scoring position.

Holland signed both scorers to free-agent deals, giving Detroit four forwards—Shanahan, Yzerman, Hull, and Robitaille—who would exceed the 500-goal mark. The Grind Line was still intact, a good-looking rookie named Pavel Datsyuk emerged, and now Hasek was backing everybody up.

But the Avalanche weren't too worried. On the same night Hasek was traded to Detroit, Colorado re-signed Roy, Sakic, and Blake to multiyear contracts and had the comfort of knowing Forsberg had recovered nicely from his ruptured spleen and would return for the 2001–02 season.

Despite the retirement of Bourque and the Wings' new signings, the Avs still considered themselves superior to Detroit. The Wings were too old, they thought. Too many players past their prime and out of championship hunger.

The newly crowned Avalanche reconvened in Sweden for training camp, for a week of what was supposed to be European fun with a couple of exhibition games against Swedish and Finnish teams thrown in. It turned out to be one of the worst weeks ever.

On September 11, 2001, the Avs were supposed to be guests of honor at the American Embassy in Stockholm. The Avalanche's trip was sponsored by the NHL and American Airlines, with many of the league's New York City–based employees along for the ride. After a morning practice that day, Avs players returned to their hotel adjacent to the Globen Arena for lunch.

The hotel didn't offer much in the way of television: just a couple of Swedish channels, and CNN's European channel. Those who had CNN on were startled by a news flash from New York at around 2 p.m. local time: black smoke was shown pouring out of one of the World Trade Center buildings. A jet airplane apparently had slammed into it. It was a gruesome image, but one that seemed at first to be just a tragic accident.

About 30 minutes later, the other tower was hit by another plane. Obviously, these were not accidents. Then came word of the Pentagon being struck, and frantic reports of other possible targets, including the White House and the Capitol building.

The United States was under attack, and for the Americans in Stockholm, it was a helpless, sick feeling. The rest of the day was a blur—all preceding thoughts and plans instantly rendered forgotten, trivial.

When the towers fell to the ground, shrieks could be heard throughout the hotel. Nobody could believe their eyes, watching their tiny little Swedish TV sets. For the many NHL employees who had just left their New York City residences a couple of days before, disbelief was followed by panic.

Everybody, even those not from New York, tried to phone loved ones. Was anybody on a flight they weren't aware of? Was anybody actually in New York, on a vacation or on business? For the New Yorkers, however, it was a searing time. Many couldn't get through to family or friends. The lines were all down or too jammed.

All anybody could do for the rest of the day was look at CNN or try to log on to the Internet. For most of the Avalanche players and staff, this meant going to the hotel lobby, where a couple of free Internet kiosks were set up. Usually, only one of them worked. That meant long, impatient waits and those who were logged on found many news sites were overloaded.

It was the most lonely, foreign feeling for the Americans, in another country when their own was under attack. Everybody wanted to just go home right then and there, including the players. But with all flights to and from the United States grounded, nobody could go anywhere—not even on Avalanche owner Stan Kroenke's chartered jet.

The day was made worse when two of the victims of the hijackings were shown to have NHL ties. Garnet "Ace" Bailey and Mark Bavis, both scouts with the Los Angeles Kings, were aboard United Airlines Flight 175, which crashed into the second tower. Several Avalanche players knew both men.

That night, pretty much everybody either had a few drinks at the bar to try and numb themselves or retired to their rooms for a long night of CNN watching.

For the rest of the week, the Globen Hotel became a dreary domicile, a place nobody wanted to be anymore. And then, on Friday, a second shock hit the Avalanche: Forsberg announced he was taking a leave of absence from hockey.

After a couple of days skating with the team, Forsberg's ankles were killing him. His spleen problems were all fixed, but his ankles were swollen and painful. He announced to a shocked hometown and Denver media presence that he would stay in

Sweden for at least a few months, to get surgery on the ankles and let his body heal altogether from a tough last few years.

Now the defending champs were without Bourque and Forsberg. Several players weren't too pleased with Forsberg's decision, most notably Roy. Although nobody said it publicly, the feeling among a few veteran players was that Forsberg was "quitting" on the team, putting his own needs first and leaving the team in an awkward spot so close to the season. Was he really hurt *that* bad, they wondered? There was plenty of gossip, too, that Forsberg's protective parents became frightened by the events of September 11 and wanted him to stay home, not get on any more airplanes for a while. There were other rumors that Forsberg's always complicated love life might have been a factor, that there might have been a girlfriend back in Denver he didn't want to see for a good, long while.

Those were probably all hogwash, as there was no question Forsberg had serious issues with his ankles and only a few months before nearly met his maker from the ruptured spleen.

Amazingly, the Avalanche became the only North American pro sports team to play a game of any kind in the several days following September 11. On September 15 the Avalanche played Brynas of the Swedish Elite League in front of a sold-out crowd at Globen Arena, winning the game on a hat trick by Alex Tanguay. It was a game none of the players wanted to play, but with not much else to do and flights still grounded, they reluctantly agreed.

The next day, the team got permission to fly its chartered jet back to Denver. Kroenke and the Avalanche graciously allowed the rest of the NHL staff and media to come with them. Sweden seemed like a beautiful country and all, but everybody was glad to get the hell out of there.

The Red Wings, indeed, looked like an unbeatable team in the 2001–02 regular season. Hasek posted an unbelievable 41-15-8

record, and Shanahan, Hull, Robitaille, and Sergei Fedorov all scored 30 or more goals. Yzerman, increasingly injury prone in his later years, missed 30 games with various ailments but still was close to a point-a-game player when in the lineup.

The smooth Swede Lidstrom was rock-solid defensively as always, and Detroit got a good season from the aging Chris Chelios. Avalanche players derisively called Chelios "Fonzie" because of his penchant for yelling "Heyyyy" at the referees. Chelios always responded with a verbal comeback of his own—or a slash to the back of the leg.

Still, the Avalanche showed that even without Forsberg or Bourque, they would be a tough team to knock off. Roy had one of his best seasons, sharing the Jennings Trophy, given to the goalies of the team that allowed the fewest regular-season goals, with backup David Aebischer. Roy had had better records before than his 32-23-8 mark, but he led the league with nine shutouts and his 1.94 GAA was a career best.

The season had its usual share of further drama, too, as Forsberg's attempted comeback in January was curtailed by the unbelievable news that he would need more surgery on one of his ankles by Avalanche team doctor Andrew Parker when Forsberg returned to Denver. Forsberg's return was greeted like the Second Coming by Avs fans, but a routine medical exam turned up more damage to a tendon. It looked as if Forsberg's season was over for good, but he vowed to make it back for the playoffs.

Late in the season, on March 23, the Avs hosted the Red Wings for a Saturday matinee at the Pepsi Center. The Red Wings prevailed, 2-0, with Shanahan becoming the third player in the previous five years—Yzerman and Joe Mullen were the others—to score career goal number 500 against Roy.

In the third period, Roy nearly got into his third fight with as many Red Wings goalies. During a melee by the Avalanche net, in which Roy was furious about being run into by Kirk

Maltby and took some swings at him, Hasek left his crease and skated all the way down the ice. Proving he was a glover, not a fighter, Hasek slipped on Roy's stick and sprawled to the ice before he could lay a hand on Roy. Roy tried to go at Hasek, throwing down his gloves and mask, but linesmen broke it up.

"Nothing much happened, but I think it would have been more interesting if the ref had not been there," Roy said afterward.

Up in the Avalanche radio booth, Mike Haynes couldn't resist sticking it to Hasek.

"What are you, chicken, Hasek?" Haynes bellowed.

After the game, tempers overflowed again, this time between Red Wings PR man Mike Kuta and me. In the NHL, teams are supposed to open their dressing rooms to reporters 10 minutes after a game ends, and the Wings still had theirs closed by about the 15-minute mark.

As chapter chairman of the Colorado hockey writers association at the time, I informed Kuta about the 10-minute rule and wondered what the delay was about. After about 20 minutes, the room finally opened and I went up to Kuta again to ask about the delay. Obviously his reply, which I can't quite remember, wasn't satisfactory to me, because I erupted in a rage.

I loosed a few F-bombs on him. He returned fire and at one point grabbed me by the collar. That's when Detroit GM Holland got into the fray, along with Wings front office assistant Joe Kocur—in his time one of the NHL's premier heavyweight fighters. They began telling me to leave in a most profane way, and before I knew it I was going nose to nose with all three of them. Thankfully, temporary sanity prevailed upon my brain, and I got out of there before much more was done or said.

I've always had a bad temper. It stems from being one of those kids who was badly picked on in high school, as I was an amazingly skinny 6-foot-5, 140 pounds as a senior on the Mascoma Valley (NH) Regional basketball team. The harassment was brutal at times, with plenty of pushes from behind and the mocking nickname of "Twig." But it was good in the sense it made me want to "get back" at all of them, which I did by concentrating on my studies and upping my weight to about 220 pounds by my sophomore year in college from lifting weights six days a week and consuming nearly 10,000 calories a day. I'd eat three all-you-can-eat meals at the college dining hall, then go back to my dorm room and down huge, thick protein shakes on top of them—followed by a late-night "snack" of a sub sandwich and quart of chocolate milk. Even years later, any kind of confrontation with anybody always seemed to click a switch in my head that he was that kid from high school that I now had to get back at. Thankfully, a little therapy and common sense has mostly eliminated such foolish behavior on my part!

(After my screaming match with him, I learned that Kuta, a very decent guy, was a former marine. I'm certainly glad I didn't get into a physical confrontation with him or one of the best fighters in hockey history.)

The Red Wings entered the 2002 playoffs as the President's Trophy winners, still considered a jinx by many hockey people. That had been the case with Detroit in 1995 and 1996, after all, and the Avs in 1997.

The Avs tied an NHL record with their eighth straight division title by winning the mediocre Northwest, and gained a number-two seeding behind Detroit. Then, for the first game of the playoffs, Forsberg suddenly appeared.

After missing the entire regular season, "Foppa" returned to an enormous standing ovation at the Pepsi Center for Game 1 of a first-round series with the Kings. From his first shift through the rest of the playoffs, Forsberg astonished the hockey world with his play. He would lead the league in postseason scoring despite not playing in the Finals—despite not having played a real game for nearly a year. Everybody knew about Forsberg's talent, but his show in the playoffs dumbfounded even the most jaded hockey people.

For the second year in a row, the Avalanche were extended to seven tough games by the Kings before prevailing. The Red Wings, too, were given a major scare in the first round by Vancouver. The Canucks won the first two games in Detroit, but collapsed after Canucks goalie Dan Cloutier allowed a goal from nearly center ice by Lidstrom in Game 3 that turned a tight game in Detroit's favor.

The Wings obviously were a bit uptight from the season-long pressure of being Stanley Cup favorites, even Bowman. Prior to a game in Vancouver, Bowman shoved *Detroit Free Press* Wings beat writer Nick Cotsonika over a dispute regarding media access to a part of the visiting dressing room. Bowman wound up being fined $10,000 by the league, and the Red Wings organization another $25,000 for violating media requirements.

The Avalanche took on San Jose in the second round, and probably should have lost the series. But the Sharks blew a 3-2 lead, losing at home in Game 6 and getting shut out 1-0 in Game 7 by Roy, on a goal by Forsberg. In the opening minutes of Game 7, the Sharks' Teemu Selanne missed a wide-open net from about a foot out, symbolizing the rest of the game for San Jose.

In Game 6, an earthquake measuring 5.2 on the Richter scale hit the San Jose area. The whole building shook. The arena press box—nothing more than a suspended drawbridge, really—swayed back and forth, causing more than a few writers to grip their seats in terror. The Sharks had their own worlds rocked when Forsberg scored in overtime to win it.

The series with the Sharks was the fourth in the previous five playoff series that the Avs won in seven games, something that was starting to take a physical and mental toll. The Red Wings had an easier time with St. Louis in the second round, and Kris Draper remembers wanting the Avalanche to win the series with San Jose, because of the fatigue factor.

"We knew they might be a tired team in some ways," Draper said. "And I think, in the back of our minds, we wanted to beat the defending champions if we were going to go all the way. I mean, you don't *want* to face Roy and Sakic and Forsberg in a playoff series, but I think we were ready for the challenge."

Avs coach Bob Hartley was about out of motivational speeches after the Sharks series. But here were the Red Wings again. Not much needed to be said. Yet Hartley feared his team was at a disadvantage entering the series.

"Those first two series really took a lot of juice out of us," Hartley said. "We made it tough on ourselves that year. The year before, we beat Vancouver in four and St. Louis in five, and that gave us more rest."

For the first time since the 1996 series, the Red Wings had home-ice advantage for the 2002 Western Conference finals. Everybody knew this would be the real Stanley Cup Finals, as nobody from the Eastern Conference had a prayer against the Wings or Avs. Most of the hockey world turned its eyes toward Detroit for Game 1. It was a dream matchup for ESPN, which of course started any Avs-Wings broadcast with a bloody highlight reel from battles past.

Prior to Game 1, Hartley and Avalanche television play-by-play man John Kelly—a former broadcaster for Detroit's minor-league team in Adirondack—went to a Detroit athletic club for another of their many racquetball battles. The Hartley-Kelly games had about as much trash talking and hitting as the Wings-Avs rivalry, with the winner lording it over the loser for days.

When the two got to the club, the manager recognized

Hartley. A few minutes later, he and Kelly were walking back to the team hotel.

"The manager politely told us we couldn't play, that the rivalry was just too much," Hartley said. "We previously had played there, but the attendant refused us to play. 'This rivalry is so intense right now,' he said, 'that I don't think our members will appreciate this.' Walking back to the hotel, two or three blocks, cars drove by us and said stuff, yelling at us, like, 'We're going to beat you,' etc. That never happened to me anywhere else."

At least this time, there weren't any mysterious 3 a.m. fire alarms at the Avs' Detroit hotel the night before Game 1. But a Detroit television station tastelessly broadcast the Avalanche's hotel whereabouts and all but invited Red Wings fans to show up and harass them. For a television station, this wasn't a surprise. I've already written a little in this book about homerism among print reporters, but nobody holds a candle to the often moronic local TV people. The same people that give you a top story that, yes, it snowed in Denver or Detroit in January bring out the pom-poms and all but do cartwheels in the locker rooms after their local team wins a playoff game. Microphones in hand, with their camera people an inch from a player's face, they gush all over the winning player, asking hard-hitting "questions" such as, "Hey, that was quite a show out there tonight" or "How big was this win?" These are people that don't come to a single regular-season game all year, but, by God, there they are in the Finals, mangling names and embarrassing themselves with provincial puff-piece "journalism." Detroit's TV people were worse than Denver's in this regard, as there were a few solid pros among Denver's sports TV personalities, Gary Miller, Ron Zappolo, and Tony Zarrella among them. There was absolutely no length to which Detroit's TV guys wouldn't go in their "Go Wings, Go" nightly telecasts. On more than one occasion, I saw a Detroit TV guy or gal throw their fist in the air following a Wings goal or win.

Despite getting a good night's sleep, the Avs looked tired in Game 1. The team had one day in Denver after the San Jose series before going to Detroit, and the Wings took it to them, 5-3.

The unlikely offensive star was Darren McCarty, who scored a natural hat trick against Roy, the last three goals of the game. The player who always wore the black hat to Avalanche fans was showered with multicolored headgear after his final goal.

The Avs could have easily snuck out a victory, as they led late in the second period, 2-1, and had a great chance for more when Forsberg and Blake broke in on a 2-on-1 against Hasek. But Blake muffed the shot, and it wasn't long before Avs-killer Hull tied it up.

A 2-2 game entering the third period turned into the Mc-Carty show. McCarty scored only five goals in 62 regular-season games, and had even seen his agitator role somewhat usurped by a short, loud-mouthed winger named Sean Avery.

But he scored what proved the game winner at 1:18 of the third, on a long wrist shot from the blue line in which Foote screened Roy.

"It was bad luck," Roy said of the goal after the game.

That was a line Roy used countless times over the years. Most goals against him, at least judging by his comments, were "lucky" for the shooter. It was an example of Roy's supreme confidence—a confidence others called arrogance.

That the Wings were lucky, too, was evidenced by Woody Paige's column in the next day's *Denver Post*.

"Naturally, the Avalanche would have preferred to steal the opener of the Western Conference finals before 20,058 auto-makers and pizza delivery boys. But the Avalanche had only two days off while the Red Wings were on an extended vacation," Paige wrote. "Detroit, with the slimy squid raining on the ice, had better win in its own building because those old guys—11 of the Wings were born in the turbulent 1960s—will tire in the third period in the altitude in Denver. They'll need to be kept between games in a humidor."

Mark Kiszla, on the other hand, lacerated the Avalanche.

"Eight, count 'em, eight legitimate Hall of Famers lace up their skates in the Detroit locker room, and the Avs let some toothless goon named Darren McCarty beat them with the first hat trick of his NHL life? That ain't right," Kiszla wrote in the *Post*. "The Avs let McCarty—who hasn't scored such a lucky knockout against Colorado since Claude Lemieux made like a turtle during a 1997 fight—embarrass them? That's unconscionable."

The game had plenty of rough stuff, including a huge hit by Blake on McCarty that kept him down for a couple of minutes, and lots of jousting, with sticks and mouths, between Forsberg and Chelios.

Roy had a career record of 9-0 following playoff losses in which he allowed five or more goals, so the Avs went into Game 2 confident of victory. And that's what they got, 4-3 in overtime, on a goal by Chris Drury.

Two members of the baseball Colorado Rockies, Canadian native Larry Walker and Mike Hampton, took in the game. Kiszla tried to get a word with both, and succeeded with Walker. But Hampton, suffering through a terrible season on the mound and inebriated, yelled, "Beat it, get out of here, you faggot," at Kiszla and challenged him to a fight in the parking lot. Kiszla, whose ink comes in barrels, got the last word in, writing that it would be "as close to the playoffs" as Hampton would ever get.

If anybody not named Forsberg was a pick to get the winner in OT for the Avalanche, the safe bet was always Drury. A soft-spoken, intense player from Trumbull, Connecticut, Drury was the winning pitcher for Trumbull in the 1988 Little League World Series. He then won a national hockey championship with the Boston University Terriers, and was a big contributor to Colorado's Cup team of 2001.

Drury loved the most pressurized moments of a game. His low center of gravity and smallish size allowed him to dart in and out of high-traffic areas around the net.

Game 3, back at the Pepsi Center, was a one-sided show. The Red Wings were terrific, outshooting Colorado 42-21. And yet it took a Fredrik Olausson goal in overtime to beat Roy and the Avs, a long shot in which Roy was screened by his own defenseman Martin Skoula.

Roy was getting perturbed at his team, and it showed in a postgame interview session. He gave mostly one-word answers, which was one more word than he would give if he didn't like a question. If a reporter asked something Roy found offensive or would make for too much controversy with an answer, he would simply stand there and say nothing, causing a nice, long, awkward moment for the reporter.

In Game 4 the Avs again played poorly through two periods. Roy, Mike Keane, and Foote stood up in the dressing room before the third and shared some strong words. "Let's get our asses in gear" was the basic theme.

Colorado pulled out a 3-2 win, with Drury again getting the game winner. The Red Wings were upset they let the game slip away, with Bowman not overly pleased with Shanahan and Yzerman, who were a combined minus-4. Yzerman had a good excuse, though; he was hurt, playing basically on one leg, with a bad knee that would later need surgery. It was a tremendous testament to his toughness that he played at all.

Now it was back to Detroit, a best-of-three series. Red Wings fever was in full pitch in Motown, with the "Spirit of

Detroit"—a Greek god–like statue designed by Marshall Fredericks in 1958—wearing a giant Wings jersey.

The Avalanche limped into Detroit, lucky to be tied 2-2. Injuries were piling up, with Keane suffering from a broken rib, and Tanguay unable to play because of a sprained ankle. Forsberg's ankles needed constant care and Blake was dinged up with a bad leg. Still, Detroit had its share of aches and pains. One look at Yzerman was proof of that.

Game 5 would be a classic, perhaps the best game played between the teams in the long rivalry.

It again went to overtime, with Forsberg, alone with the puck, bearing down on Hasek. When Forsberg slipped the puck past Hasek for a 2-1 victory, the building turned into the Joe Louis Public Library. It got so quiet so quickly, people at the top of the arena could hear some of the things the jubilant Avalanche players yelled as they mobbed Forsberg.

"I'll never forget how quiet it got," said Detroit's Shanahan, who could have won the game in the last minute of regulation but hit the post on a tap-in, with Roy down and out of position. "I had the game-winner on my stick. It was just a devastating loss. You would have thought it was the end."

Many Red Wings fans broke down and cried in their seats after Forsberg's goal. The goal was a total fluke, as the winning play developed only after Drury swung and missed on a one-timer attempt following a crossing pass by rookie Brian Willsie. When Drury fanned on the shot, the Wings' defense was thrown off stride, which is what allowed Forsberg to grab the sliding puck and continue down the middle toward Hasek. Willsie might have been offside on the winning play after taking a long lead pass from Darius Kasparaitis. Bowman thought so, criticizing the officiating in his usual roundabout way afterward.

Luck seemed to be on the Avs' side, while the Wings seemed destined for their fourth playoff loss in five meetings with Colorado. Maybe Detroit was an overpaid, aging team after all.

Winning two in a row against Roy looked out of the question. Now the Avs were going back home, where even if they lost, they'd get another chance in a Game 7—and Colorado had won four straight Game 7s.

"There's no joy in Hockeytown; the mighty Red Wings have struck out again. From Monday night to Tuesday mourning," Paige wrote in the *Post*. "For the second time in a week in Hockeytown (copyrighted) and in the third game of the past four, The Greatest Team in the Whole Wide World and the Entire History of the Sport (copyright pending) has lost in overtime to The Little Club from Colorado That Could. The Spleendid Swede (trademark) scored the winning goal (patented) on Monday night."

Wrote Kiszla, "Colorado wins. Detroit whines. With the puck bouncing in the net, goalie Dominik Hasek flopping like a flounder on the ice and Avalanche hero Peter Forsberg celebrating a 2-1 overtime victory, all the Red Wings could do was play the crying game. 'You can't cry about it,' grumbled Detroit coach Scotty Bowman, who then whined shamelessly. Tears do not become him. They stain his Hall of Fame reputation. Rather than accept responsibility for a Detroit team that has more stars than substance, 'Boo Hoo' Bowman insulted the Avalanche's stunning Game 5 triumph in the Western Conference finals by trying to blame it on a bad call by linesman Brian Murphy."

Everybody in Detroit seemed to wear a frown the next morning. The Avalanche was going to beat their team again, and this one would hurt the most. This was the Hall of Fame team, built to win *now*. But here were those spoiled little Avalanche players and their fans again, ruining the party.

"And so it boils down to this: tonight. Nothing else. One game. One more chapter to be written in this storied series," wrote Mitch Albom in the *Free Press* on the day of Game 6. "Until that ink dries, finger-pointing will be easy. In some cases, even therapeutic. Fans need to blame something, because the outcome is so frustratingly out of their control.

"So they can blame the goaltending. They can say that Dominik Hasek has been excellent, but not as phenomenal as Patrick Roy. They can blame the goal-scorers—like Shanahan and Brett Hull and Luc Robitaille—who have not fired a shot past Roy when it mattered.

"They can blame the defense, for allowing Colorado too many rushes through the neutral zone. They can even blame the coaching, for failing to shadow the Avs' players who hurt the Wings the most. But ask yourself this: If Shanahan had scored that goal in Game 5, and Detroit was up, 3-2, instead of down, would they still be saying the same things?"

Detroit could take some solace by the fact the Avalanche had a recent history of blowing the sixth game of a series. Their losses to Dallas and Los Angeles (twice) in sixth games of play-off series extended them to a seventh game.

But Wings fans also knew Colorado hadn't really let Detroit off the hook before. The Avs had always shown the ability to close a series out on their team.

In the hours before Game 6, at the Pepsi Center, there was plenty of deep thinking around the Wings dressing room. Players and coaches knew there probably would be severe recriminations from management if they lost to Colorado again. Upper management itself might not be immune.

"That was a long 36 hours, after Game 5," Detroit associate coach Dave Lewis recalled. "I remember the preparation process. I remember watching Dominik go out on the ice, and then Larionov and Lidstrom, thinking, 'I wonder if this is Dom's and Igor's last game ever as a Red Wing?' I carried that down the hallway onto the ice. It's funny what goes on in your mind."

Bowman was nervous, too, for many reasons. He knew this

could be his last game ever as a coach. It was getting to be time, he knew. Time to spend more time visiting his kids and grandchildren. Time to give Suella more of the time he knew she deserved. His heart felt better than ever after the angioplasty, and his knee was good. Time to get out while the health was still there, enjoy some relaxing years for a change.

But what a way to go out this would be. Another loss to Colorado, a third straight to Hartley. No coach had ever beaten him three times in the playoffs. Bowman would end his career with a big "but"—"Scotty Bowman, the NHL's all-time winningest coach, wanted to go out on top, *but* the Colorado Avalanche had other ideas . . ." the stories would say. Helluva way to be remembered, Bowman thought. Maybe some smart alecks would say he was the coach who couldn't win with eight Hall of Famers on the roster.

When Game 6 began, one team indeed looked nervous, but it wasn't the Red Wings. The Avalanche reverted to their propensity to squander prosperity. Avs players showed none of the passion and urgency of the previous game. They again seemed to leave it all up to Roy, and for nearly one full period, he almost carried them.

But with 39 seconds left, one of the most memorable plays in the rivalry happened. For the Avalanche and Roy, it would infamously be known as the Statue of Liberty play. Yzerman put a shot on Roy from in close that the proud goalie wanted to show the world he had stopped. Thinking the puck was in his glove, Roy lifted his left hand high. The puck, however, was still on the ice—right there, a few inches from the goal line, for Shanahan to tap it in. He didn't miss the bunny this time. Detroit had a 1-0 lead, and Roy had an angry skate to the dressing room.

"I thought I had the puck. I made a great save on Yzerman, and I thought I had it in my glove," Roy said afterward.

The second period was an embarrassment for the Avalanche. Not only did McCarty score another goal on Roy, the Avs tried to catch what they thought was an illegal stick of Hasek's. Acting on a tip from one of his players, Hartley asked referee Kerry Fraser to measure the blade of Hasek's stick, thinking it exceeded the three-and-a-half-inch maximum. The Avs were on a power play when Hasek's stick was brought to the scorer's table. A penalty on Hasek, and the Avs would have a two-man advantage for more than a minute. Here was their chance to get back in the game. That was how Roy's Canadiens got back in the 1993 Stanley Cup Finals, after all, when LA's Marty McSorley was busted for an illegal stick in the final minutes of Game 2.

Instead, Fraser found nothing illegal about the stick. He handed it back to Hasek and assessed a two-minute penalty on the Avs. There went the power play, and, for all intents and purposes, there went the game.

"I will never [tell] on the player that told me to call it on Hasek's stick. Even before the series started, we had a player that was convinced his stick was illegal," Hartley said. "I'm not going to throw that player under the bus. We were down 2-0, and knowing [that] the medical condition [of] probably half of my team was bad, I would have made the same call. You can say whatever you want, not good sportsmanship or whatever; it's not about making enemies, it was about winning a hockey game."

Hasek finished with a 24-save shutout. The Red Wings had staved off elimination, gone into the belly of the beast, and snuck one out. Like Detroit rocker Bob Seger's hit song, the Red Wings couldn't wait to "get out of Denver baby, go go."

Now it was back to the Joe for the first Game 7 ever between the teams. Hope was restored in Motown. Time to grab a few octopi from the freezer, put on the Winged Wheel jerseys and crank up Kid Rock one more time.

For Wings fans, it truly was a party that didn't stop.

The end of the epic Detroit-Colorado rivalry should have been a quadruple-overtime thriller, if any sense of history had been followed. It should have come down to just a few players from each side remaining on the bench, the others gone from attrition. There should have been trash talk and face washes and brutal body checks and blood on the ice. It was none of that.

Instead, it was one team, the Avalanche, that went out with a whimper. On a warm Friday night, May 31, the Red Wings beat Colorado 7-0—a night forever to be known in Denver as the Motown Meltdown.

Detroit scored goals on three of its first five shots. The first, a gorgeous tip by Tomas Holmstrom, came at 1:57 of the first period. A goal by Fedorov followed at 3:17, then another, by Robitaille, and another by Steve Duchesne. After being beaten by Duchesne, Roy looked up at the Joe Louis ceiling from his back, probably wondering how it could all end like this.

But the truth was, nobody on the Avalanche felt very good about its chances in Game 7. Forsberg was playing with a broken pinkie, suffered in Game 6; Blake could barely skate with a badly pulled groin; Keane gamely played with the broken rib; Tanguay couldn't do anything on his ankle; and superpest Dan Hinote was out after breaking a leg in Game 5.

Hartley knew there was only one way his team could win Game 7: if Roy could steal it. But he'd played one Game 7 too many.

"The gas tank was simply too low," Hartley said. "Before Game 7, I remember telling Jacques Cloutier, 'Patrick will have to steal this game.' It was one of those games. I'm a former goalie who never played in the NHL, but I know there are games when the puck is getting away from you. Game 7, I remember my thinking was that we had to score early. We had to take control of the game, because I knew we couldn't play with a short bench for 60 minutes. I knew we didn't have the soldiers for 60 minutes. Their hearts and minds were in it, but their bodies couldn't keep up."

If somebody off the street walked into the Wings dressing room after the first period and didn't know the score, they would have thought Detroit was the team down 4-0.

"I mean, nobody said a word," McCarty recalled. "Nobody wanted to jinx it. Nobody could believe what had happened out there. It didn't seem real."

Said Draper, "We thought we needed to keep scoring more goals! We had the attitude that the game wasn't even close to over, that they'd make a big run at us in the second period and we had to be ready. But Mac is right, it was really quiet in there. We couldn't believe it."

Roy came out for the second period and Detroit pumped home two more goals. At the 13:22 mark, after an Olausson power-play goal, Hartley did what Mario Tremblay should have done seven years before at the Montreal Forum against the Red Wings: he pulled Roy after he allowed six goals on 16 shots.

"Now that's an avalanche. It rolled in off the Detroit River, it wore a red-and-white sweater, it skated as if its socks were on fire, and it scored one, two, three, four goals in the time it normally takes fans to find their seats," Albom wrote. "Then it scored five, six and seven. It didn't merely rise to the occasion, it pole-vaulted, getting relentless offense, smothering defense, shutout goaltending and more jump than a 1956 Elvis Presley concert. It was wild, voracious, a feeding frenzy in which everyone seemed to get to the trough. And at the final horn, for a brief but gloriously indulgent moment, everyone got to celebrate. The Detroit Red Wings just sent home the defending NHL champions in this city's most anticipated sporting event in a decade.

"And in doing so, they made one of the greatest goalies in hockey history look like just another man in a mask. Patrick

Roy, on the bench, too whipped to even smirk correctly? Now that's an avalanche."

Roy took an enormous razzing from the delirious Red Wings crowd, and nobody would have faulted him if he decided to watch the rest of the game from the dressing room. But, a warrior to the end, Roy showed his grace by sitting on the bench the rest of the game, stoically taking the abuse.

When the final horn sounded, Wings fans erupted in joy. The tears of a few nights before had been long forgotten. The Wings were going back to the Stanley Cup Finals, against a Carolina Hurricanes team everybody knew had no chance.

As loud music and champagne flowed in the Red Wings dressing room, Colorado's sullen soldiers unwrapped tape and appendages for the final time, lamenting another Western final that got away.

"I think they just wanted it a little more than us," Keane said. "We played hard, but that little extra was missing."

Wrote Paige, "The Red Wings' philosophy in the series was to keep coming with fresher, experienced troops and more powerful firepower. It worked. Detroit is boss. There was a similar result at the Alamo in 1836. A band of 189 game warriors held off more than 2,000 soldiers in a 13-day siege before the walls of the chapel/fort were breached. The siege in the Western Conference finals lasted 14 days in May before the wall, the defense and Roy collapsed. Roy could only plead, in French, 'M'aidez.' Help me. Mayday. But there was no help or hope."

As the night wore on, McCarty remembers standing in the hallway, watching Avalanche players walk to their bus. The joy of victory, surprisingly, was replaced for a few moments by sadness—sadness that the rivalry was likely at an end.

In reality, it was. Roy would play only one more year, his last game coming in the playoffs against not the Wings, but the Minnesota Wild. Forsberg left the Avs for Philadelphia in 2005, Foote to the Columbus Blue Jackets the same year.

McCarty left the Red Wings for Calgary in 2005, and Hasek retired, then came out of retirement and ended up in Ottawa.

Bowman retired after Detroit beat the Hurricanes in five games, leaving with a record ninth Stanley Cup as a coach. Lewis succeeded him before being replaced by Mike Babcock after two years. Hartley was fired early in the 2002–03 season before landing in Atlanta.

McCarty remembers thinking hockey would probably never get this good again. The hatred he'd always felt for the Avalanche was now drowned out by respect.

"I knew the feelings they were having at that moment, because they'd done it to us before," McCarty said. "We all had fought each other so hard, and you had the feeling it was finally over. And you realize how much respect you have for the other side, and what it was all about."

When Confederate general Robert E. Lee signed papers of surrender at Appomattox, effectively ending the Civil War on April 9, 1865, Union General Ulysses S. Grant tipped his hat to Lee as a sign of respect.

Wearing a Western Conference Championship cap as the Avs walked to the bus, McCarty called out to one of his biggest combatants over the years, Foote.

"Great series," McCarty said.

And then he tipped his cap.

Postscript

Claude Lemieux was about at the end of the line in 2002–03. Age and a few injuries had finally caught up to him. His final NHL season was in Dallas, and it was on the ice at the new American Airlines center that Lemieux approached Darren McCarty during a stop in play in a game between the Stars and Red Wings.

"I told him I hoped he was OK," Lemieux said.

McCarty had a relapse of his drinking problem in 2003. Having had his share of off-ice problems and personal pain, Lemieux told McCarty to hang in there, that things would work out in the end.

The hatchet, officially, was buried.

"I appreciated what he said," McCarty said. "It was a nice thing to do."

Sadly, no such reconciliation has yet taken place between Lemieux and Kris Draper. During the NHL lockout of 2004–05, Lemieux and Draper were both invited to a charity hockey game in Edmonton sponsored by Oilers star Ryan Smyth.

Lemieux accepted. When Draper heard Lemieux was coming, he declined.

Asked what he thought would happen if he and Lemieux were in the same elevator together by chance, Draper said:

"I've never seen him away from the rink. I've never been in that situation. Chances of us running into each other are slim. If he has something to say to me, I would absolutely look him in the eye and have something to say to him. I would have to hear him first. I can't answer until I hear something from him."

Lemieux, who today runs a minor-league hockey team in Phoenix, didn't sound eager to pick up the phone.

"It's something that happened. I've gotten over it, I've paid in several respects for what happened, but I'm not going to keep reliving it and apologizing for it," he said. "It happened in the heat of a game. Those things happen all the time in hockey. It started quite a rivalry, maybe the best in hockey ever. We all took some bumps and bruises in the rivalry. That's what made it what it was."

BIBLIOGRAPHY

The following books, newspaper articles, Web sites, and magazine articles were helpful in the writing of this book. The newspapers described in the text are thanked again. The Internet Hockey Database (www.hockeydb.com) is a treasure trove of information, as is the NHL's official site (www.nhl.com), the National Hockey League Players' Association site (www.nhlpa.com), and Hockey Draft Central (www.hockeydraftcentral.com).

Chapter 2

Joe Falls, "Those Magnificent Men in Red," *Detroit News*, n.d.

Chapter 4

Detroit's population decline discussed in the January 16, 2005, edition of the *Hindu* (India's national newspaper).

Michigan high school hockey participation totals taken from the Michigan High School Athletic Association Web site (www .mhsaa.com).

1967 Detroit riot information taken from www.67riots.rutgers.edu/ introduction.html.

Claude Lemieux, "What's that 'C' for, 'selfish'?" taken from Chris Stevenson, "Claude Lemieux's Mystery Alphabet," SLAM! Sports, May 17, 2000, slam.canoe.ca/2000NHLPlayoffsColumnists/may 17_stevenson.html.

Chapter 9

Some background on Scotty Bowman's family and upbringing came from Vince Evans, "Scotty Bowman—History On and Off the Ice," *Living Prime Time*, July 2002.

Ken Dryden, *The Game: A Thoughtful and Provocative Look at a Life in Hockey* (New York: Times Books, 1983).

Douglas Hunter, *Scotty Bowman: A Life in Hockey* (Toronto: Viking, 1998).

Bob Plager with Tom Wheatley, *Tales from the Blues Bench: A Collection of the Greatest St. Louis Blues Stories Ever Told* (Champaign, IL: Sports Publishing, 2003).

Chapter 12

Some information about Patrick Roy's childhood came from an article by Jerry Crasnick titled "King of the Mountain: Goalie Patrick Roy of the Colorado Avalanche Tells Why He Rules in Big Games," *Sports Illustrated for Kids*, May 1, 1997.

Chapter 14

Craig McCarty, *Rinkside: A Family's Story of Courage & Inspiration* (Chicago: Benchmark, 1998).

John Niyo, "McCarty Keeps Demons in Check," *Detroit News*, February 28, 1999.

Chapter 16

Nicholas J. Cotsonika, *Hockey Gods: The Inside Story of the Red Wings' Hall of Fame Team* (Chicago: Triumph, 2002).

INDEX

2001–2002 season, 216–36; background of, 23–28; versus Canadiens, 30–31; and Draper incident, 67–76; name, 24. *See also* meetings of Avalanche and Red Wings; rivalry

Devellano, Jimmy, 36, 68, 132, 211

Devlin, Neil, 20

Devorski, Paul, 84, 87, 91, 108, 140–41

de Vries, Greg, 191

Dingman, Chris, 153

Dion, Celine, 90

Draper, Kris: and 1997 Western Conference finals, 100, 106, 110, 113; and 2001–2002 season, 223, 234; injury to, 1–10, 67, 74–75, 237–38; and Lemieux, 52–54; and McCarty, 200; and payback, 86

Draper, Mary Lynn, 53

Drumm, Brian, 196–97

Drury, Chris, 147, 191, 226–27

Dryden, Ken, 123–24, 174

Drygas, Erik, 99

Duchesne, Steve, 22, 185, 233

Dudacek, Jiri, 127

Eastern Conference playoffs: 1995, 13

Farber, Michael, 64

Fedorov, Sergei, 31, 41, 74, 112, 143–44, 192; and 2001–2002 season, 219, 233

Fetisov, Viacheslav, 27, 41, 48, 63

Fillion, Maurice, 22

Fiset, Stephane, 27, 34, 103

Fisher, Red, 29, 32, 121, 125

Fletcher, Cliff, 40

Fleury, Theo, 89, 153, 164–65, 191

Foligno, Mike, 109–10

Foote, Adam, 22, 39, 48, 179, 235–36; and 1997 Western Conference finals, 107; and 1999–

2000 season, 185, 191; and 2001–2002 season, 227; and Draper incident, 7, 73; and Forsberg, 159–60; and payback, 83–84, 88

Forsberg, Peter, 22, 212, 215, 217–18, 235; and 1996 season, 48, 51; and 1996–1997 season, 71, 74; and 1997 Western Conference finals, 100, 103, 106, 112–13; and 1998–1999 season, 155, 159–60, 163–64; and 1999–2000 season, 191–92; and 2001–2002 season, 221–22, 225–26, 228, 233; character of, 82, 101–3; and payback, 82–83; and Sakic, 190

Francis, Ron, 129, 132

Francottie, Doug, 194, 202

Frank J. Selke Trophy, 41

Fraser, Kerry, 232

Fredericks, Marshall, 228

Frei, Terry, 81, 208–9

French language, 34, 40, 123

Freyer, Steve, 13–14

Fuhr, Grant, 42

Gainey, Bob, 171

Gallagher, Tony, 53

Gave, Keith, 81, 106, 207–9

Giguere, Jean-Sebastien, 173

Gilbert, Peter, 16

Gill, Todd, 163

Glitter, Gary, 17

goaltending techniques, 173, 214

Goodfellow, Ebbie, 24

"Gordie Howe hat trick," 24

Granby Bisons, 60, 168–69

Grenier, Martin, 183

Gretzky, Wayne, 42

Grind Line, 200–201, 215

Grundman, Irving, 125

Gusarov, Alexei, 27, 71–72, 83

Habitants. *See* Montreal Canadiens

Hackett, Jeff, 45